To Graham Downing
with Compliments —
Don Wall 6.97.

THE F FORCE

COLLATED BY

DON WALL

Cover by Clem Seale

By the same Author

Singapore and Beyond 1985

Sandakan – The Last March 1988
Revised Second Edition 1989
Revised Third Edition 1992

Abandoned ? 1990

Heroes at Sea 1991

Published by D. Wall
98 Darley Street West
Mona Vale. NSW 2103

ISBN O 646 16047 8

ACKNOWLEDGEMENTS

I desire to thank the many people who have made this account possible within such a short time. Particularly those who made available diaries in their care – Alex Dandie who not only assisted in the compilation of the Honour Roll but arranged many contacts including Betty Stone who kindly provided Eric's diary from April to October 1943; Glen Weiss for use of his twin brother Harry's diary up to the time of his death. Mrs. Gwen McIlwaine for permission to use extracts of Ron Johnston's diary. John Castle for use of his father's records.

To Ron Eaton who during that period was Joint Adjutant of the largest A.I.F. Camp and whose diary was used as the basis of the official record of 'F' Force.

Special thanks to Dr. W.J.E. Phillips, Dr. Roy Mills, Dr. Lloyd Cahill and Dr. Peter Hendry for their contribution.

Gordon Nicholl who served as a senior Medical Orderly with Major Bruce Hunt and Captain Frank Cahill and whose diary is invaluable.

Ken Marshall, hero of Cholera Hill who was one of the first to step forward to nurse the victims of the dark days of the outbreak of cholera; his mates Wally Southwick and Bill Jobe (served as Rerdon).

George Blaikie for his professional guidance.

The Director of the Australian War Memorial, particularly Ron Gilchrist, Marie Wood and Mark Jamieson.

John Hunt for access to his father's records.

Bob Kelsey for permission to use extracts of "Portrait of a Man", and to George Beecham, Ed Bennett, Ken Gray, Bob Wilson, Angus McDougal, Sid Musgrove, Doug Blanchard, Jim Ling.

Tadao Saji, Colonel Banno's civilian Interpreter up to the time of his return to Singapore in August 1943 for valuable insight to Force H.Q.

Warren Kennedy of P.S. Graphics; Glen Davison of Alken Press for meeting publication schedule.

To my many friends who took my phone calls to clarify some detail – my thanks.

DON WALL

AUTHOR'S NOTE

In May 1993, I commenced writing this account of 'F' Force which comprised 3,600 Australians and 3,400 British Prisoners of War who marched 300 kilometres into the hell of the Thailand jungle as part of the Construction Force of the Burma-Thailand Railway – we arrived there in May 1943 -

In November 1943 they came out of the jungle on the railway they helped build – they left 2000 British and over 1000 Australians dead.

I have spent eight months re-living and compiling this account and here are a few faces of those who kept diaries to record the hell of that period -

Ron Eaton

Eric Stone

Harry Weiss

Ken Marshall

Gordon Nicholl

Don Wall

PROLOGUE

Following the Japanese conquest of South East Asia in 1942 the Japanese Imperial H.Q. paused to review their strategy for the next major thrust.

General Yamashita, the Japanese Commander-hero, who captured Singapore in 70 days, wanted to proceed with an invasion of Australia. This proposal was rejected in favour of an invasion of India which did not require the long lines of sea communication and supply problems. However the plan involved constructing a railway from Thailand to Burma, thereby connecting the main railway from Singapore to Manchuria.

Years earlier, the British surveyed a route for a railway from the main Singapore-Bangkok railway commencing at Banpong to Thanbuyzat in Burma – this route followed the northern bank of the Kwai Noi River. Now the Japanese decided as part of the major offensive into India from Burma, the rail link would have to be completed by August 1943.

In 1942 the Japanese Government determined a policy towards Allied Prisoners of War which was "NO WORK NO FOOD", and immediately implemented a program of using POW labour to construct a number of airfields to protect the newly acquired region; they were first sent to southern Burma to build airfields along the Kra Isthmus.

Allied prisoners, comprising American, Dutch, British and Australians, commenced work on airfields in the Philippines, Rabaul, Borneo, Ambon, Sumatra and South Burma. The first party of 3000 Australians, known as 'A' Force, commenced working on airfields in southern Burma along the Kra Isthmus in early 1942.

When their task was completed they were moved to Thanbuyazat on the Moulmein-Ye railway and they commenced construction work late 1942. In the meantime plans were well under way to transfer other POW parties to Thailand; they worked from the Kanburi Base Camp in Thailand. By early 1943, three other POW parties were dispatched from Singapore including 'D' Force of 3000 Australians who left in March.

When it became obvious to the Japanese that they were not up to schedule they conscripted tens of thousands of natives – making attractive promises of good pay and working conditions – packed them fifty to a truck and sent them north.

In April 1943 the Japanese ordered Changi POW Command to prepare a force of 7000 POWs to proceed overland to a new locality where food would be more plentiful and those sick would be able to recuperate in a better climate. They stated it was not a working party – bands could be taken and canteens established.

Colonel Harris of the British 18 Division was to command. The A.I.F. were to provide 3,600 men and the British 3,400. Lt.Col. Dillon, M.C., would command the British contingent, Lt.Col. Kappe would command the AIF which was predominantly 27 Brigade personnel comprising 2/26, 2/29, 2/30 Battalions together with Artillery and Signals support personnel.

Colonel Harris, through the Force Interpreter, Major C.H. Wild, (the unfortunate Officer who carried the white flag for General Percival at the Surrender of Singapore) had several interviews with Captains Miyasaki and Tanaka, officers in charge of Changi, with regard to the fitness and marching. Requests were made for Red Cross representatives to accompany the Force and funds be made available from the International Red Cross representatives in Singapore. The Japanese denied these requests and gave no reason for their refusal.

According to Lt.Col. Kappe, the Japanese said the reasons were a military secret. Kappe would have known that the Australian Red Cross representative was already in Japanese custody – they alleged he was involved in a conspiracy to use Red Cross money to fund an ill-conceived plan by an AIF officer and an RAAF pilot to purchase an aircraft from a Chinese (who was, in fact, a Japanese spy) and escape to India. This group were in Outram Road Gaol at the very time the request was made for a representative to accompany the march.

It seems both Colonel Harris and Lt.Col. Kappe were convinced the Force was destined for "the promised land". Five other Colonels and the elite British Concert party personnel were included in the draft together with a grand piano.

Some AIF groups received their first cholera innoculation on April 13 and were to receive their second cholera innoculation on April 19 – if still in Changi. These innoculations were deferred in order not to change the train allocations which meant many of the British would have arrived at their destination before the AIF and Lt.Col. Kappe was anxious the AIF would get the pick of the accommodation consequently the innoculations were cancelled on April 17. It was then decided vaccine would be sent with individual train groups and given at their destination.[1.]

Earlier, Major Hunt marched his party to where the injections and innoculations were to be given. On the return to Changi Square he stopped and spoke to the men: "We have been told we are going to a Convalescent Camp somewhere up north, the Commanding Officer believes it but I don't. We will be going to a land where disease will be rife so prepare yourselves for the worst – you will encounter diseases you have never heard of and I fear for the future."

'F' Force were dispatched without full medical protection and the slightest hint of their destination or of what lay ahead.

INTRODUCTION

From the medical point- of view the story of F Force can be told very simply – in April '43 three thousand six hundred British and three thousand four hundred Australians left Singapore for Thailand. They suffered very greatly from hardships, starvation, maltreatment and disease – Malaria was practically universal – so was dysentery, both bacillary and amoebic. Epidemic Cholera took a heavy toll and tropical ulcers of frightful severity were common. By reason of the greatly deficient dietary supplied to the prisoners, beri beri was rampant and caused hundreds of deaths. Typhus, diphtheria, smallpox and pneumonia added their quota to the heavy death roll.

By April 44 when all the survivors had returned to Singapore over one thousand Australians and over two thousand British had died died as the result of the almost incredible incompetence of Japanese organisation and the callous brutality and indifference of Japanese guards and engineers. Of the survivors many hundreds were gravely ill and a few have subsequently died. That is the debit side of the F Force affair a debit for which we hope Japan will pay and will pay bitterly – a debit which we must never incur again.

But there is a credit side. Morale was shaken – at times badly shaken – but it never broke. The medical services worked very hard with most inadequate material – they could not do less than their utmost for the thousands of their patients who met disease, starvation and death with a fortitude and patient endurance which was beyond all praise.

The ingenuity and resourcefulness of our Medical personnel, British and Australian were very thoroughly tested. One Australian medical officer contrived by means of a small bamboo tube, a funnel made from an old tin can and a piece of rubber tubing made from his stethoscope to give nearly a hundred infusions of salt and water into the veins of cholera patients and by so doing saved many valuable lives. Nursing utensils of all sorts were contrived from the most unpromising materials – bamboo can be made to serve an astonishing variety of purposes.

Some of the things I saw with F force made me very proud to be an Australian. At one big Australian camp we had had only a few cases of cholera. Suddenly one day the pestilence smote us – 35 men went down with the disease in 24 hours. To supply adequate nursing to these men was far beyond the capacity of the small medical staff. When the labour parties returned to camp after dark that evening – soaked to the skin and tired out, after 12 hours of exhausting work in mud and in incessant monsoon rain, I explained the situation to them. I told them of all the risks involved (for cholera carries a 50% mortality) and then asked for volunteers to help – then and there – straight away – with the nursing of these highly infectious patients. I gave up taking names when I had 75 on the list – there were several dozen more waiting to offer their services – that's the sort of thing that made the medical personnel feel that nothing that they could do for such men was too high.

In a reasonably varied experience of two wars, I have on many occasions seen men tried up to and beyond the limits of reasonable human endurance. I would say that F force was of all these occasions the most searching test of fundamental character and guts that I have ever known. That so many men – British and Australian – came through this test with their heads high and their records unblemished was something of which we of the British race may be not unreasonably proud.

BROADCAST BY MAJOR BRUCE HUNT, A.A.M.C., OF PERTH
FROM SINGAPORE RADIO ABOUT 9 SEPTEMBER 1945

CONTENTS

Chapter One 1

Chapter Two

Banpong – Sonkurai 3

Lower Neike – Neike HQ 28

Chapter Three

Lower Sonkurai June-August 1943 34

Chapter Four

No. 2 Camp – Upper Sonkurai 71

Chapter Five

Tanbaya – 30 July to December 1943 89

Chapter Six

Lt. Col. Pond's Party Taimonta-Konkoita
May-November 1943 100

Chapter Seven

Lower Sonkurai-Sonkurai August-November 1943
No. 2 Camp 111

Chapter Eight

Return to Kanburi-Singapore 124

Tributes 130

Honour Roll 142

End Notes 164

Major Bruce Hunt, A.A.M.C.

CHAPTER ONE

At Neike at night the glow of the funeral pyre reflected in the misty sky above the camp – a constant reminder to the prisoners of the plight they were in.

It was August 1943 when the sick were moved from Neike to Tanbaya, about fifty men who were too ill to withstand the trip were left in the hospital.

Our small group would occasionally slaughter a yak, take broth to the patients in the hospital hut and distribute it to those who could take food. We got to know a little of their background, their families and those who knew their chances of survival were slim; there was S/Sgt. Hudson who was carried four kilometres from Lower Neike on a stretcher – he was more worried about his wife and family who had been evacuated to Australia – we heard their prayers for their families in far away places.

There was Reginald Rennison, one of the members of the elite British Concert party and a well-known pianist, he was frail; occasionally when well enough he would walk up and down the centre of the hut, shirtless, conspicuous by a beautiful crucifix hanging from his neck, his hands behind his back, thumbs linked together, fingers moving as if playing the tunes of yesterday. He was deeply religious and very reserved. After tiring of walking he would return to his bed on the bamboo where, on his haversack, he displayed religious symbols. One evening when he was near the entrance to the hut I motioned him outside to see the glow of the pyre on the hill – he was composed, calm, and said, "Don't worry about me – the Lord will look after me".

And when September came there was sunshine, the nights were cold, the mists had gone and so had Reginald Rennison – the fires were still burning.

There were four major camps – H.Q. was established at Neike to the south was Colonel Pond's group of originally 700 men, known as No.4 Party. North of Neike was originally Lower Sonkurai, also known as No.l Camp, and at one time housed over 2000 A.I.F. The next camp was Sonkurai, originally a British Camp but now a mixed British/Australian; up the road further was Upper Sonkurai, known as No.3 Camp.

'F' Force were placed in Thailand east of the Pagoda Pass from Changkarai by the border south to Taimonta H.Q. at Neike. The British were last to arrive and followed the muddied trail left by the Australians 300 kms to Sonkurai. Now dispersed in the most isolated stretch of the surveyed route for the railway they marched through the native camps and with them came cholera, dysentery, malaria and tropical ulcers. About 250 AIF and 600 British had already died, 2000 were too ill to work and those able to remain on their feet were fighting for their lives.

The senior Officers, who believed they were going to a location where there were several convalescent camps, were now isolated and some of them too frightened to deal with the Japanese.

The Force Commander was located at Neike so the records claim, but at no time did I see him – the Australian Commander, Lt.Col. Kappe, was now known to be inefficient and incompetent and rarely seen by his officers and men. He remained insulated with his senior officers – much to the embarrassment of some of them. He passed orders down the line – the major work was carried out by junior Captains and Lieutenants who carried the burden of camp maintenance, administration and the responsibility in providing the numbers required for the work force.

The Administration had now moved from Combatant Command to Medical. The A.I.F. Senior Medical Officer remained with Lt.Col. Kappe at this time while the dominant figures were Major Bruce Hunt, A.I.F., Lt.Col. F.J. (Andy) Dillon acting for the Force Commander Lt.Col. S. Harris with the assistance of Major C. Wild, Force Interpreter.

Personal written records of fifty years ago have been used as the basis of this account, commencing at Banpong.

CHAPTER TWO
BANPONG – SONKURAI

Alan Charlton remembers:

"Departed Singapore 22 April '43 for 'a holiday camp' and spent five and a half days in a train to an unknown destination, during which we were fed six times, mostly rice and one small dried fish known as "Modern Girls" and a stew made, presumably, by boiling a few bulbs of garlic in a 44 gal. drum of water.

"With 28 men (one Officer) in a very small box-car there was not sufficient room for all to lie down at the one time and during the daytime turns were taken to sit in the two doorways, two men in each. Boots were removed and hung across a wire. The time between the last two meals before Banpong was 40 hours, and was composed of tinned Army food issued to us before leaving Singapore.

"We were dirty by the time we reached Kuala Lumpur and the engine was taking water, so the great Aussie ingenuity came to our aid, and when the men were finished with the water it was turned on once more and we stripped right off and had a shower. Major Johnstone came down and ordered it to cease immediately, stating that we were lowering the dignity of the white race, we poor, thin even then, were guilty in his eyes of the crime of betraying ourselves in front of the natives!"

Harry Weiss:

> Tuesday 27 April '43: Reached Banpong at 7 am, and detrained a funny looking place it is. Japanese made us dump everything we couldn't carry – kitchen stuff, and officers' gear etc., and say the truck will bring it. We marched to Stinking Camp hardly any water and are the Japanese cranky. We are to make a long journey on foot so will have to leave most of our stuff. As the heaps of goods left by previous train loads are still to be seen

rotting in the sun, we are miserable at even having it sent on and a lot of selling to the Thais is going on. I gave my great coat away. We have all been numbered and labelled on our hats, No.548. However we have had quite good stews here but are just glad to march out tonight. We all have too much gear, even yet, and I'm sure a lot will be cast aside.

Wednesday 28 April: Marched at 10.30 pm, but after the long train journey and no spell, soon cracked up. Ground sheets were cast aside and goods sold to Thais who appear suddenly alongside you wanting your pullover or some other thing – watch, fountain pen, etc. By the time we reached half way where we were given hot water and ate our rice and fish many men had blisters and skin off the feet. We carry medical gear and dixies which increase the fatigue of the journey and many chaps have to be helped. Got to the first camp, 25 kilos, at 9 am, and were cheered up as we had sun shelters in the grounds of a Buddhist temple and a good river a few yards off. Thais were selling coffee, bananas, fried eggs (ma-mee), sago, limes, mangoes, very cheaply. The land about abounds with banana plantations and plenty of cattle. I did enjoy the swims in the river.

Jim Ling recalled:

"We marched into Kanburi about the third night on Anzac Day. We had a Bugler, Signalman Kirk, and he marched at the top of the group as we marched each night. On the first night the usual old dog-hour about three in the morning when things were dragging, up struck 'It's a Long Way to Tipperary' and 'The Road to Gundagai' Kirk was playing his bugle and it woke everyone up and people started to sing and move on again. On Anzac Day going into Kanburi he played all the old First World War songs – by gee it was amazing the lift that bugle gave."

Alan Charlton:

"Upon arrival at Banpong about 4.30 am, I could not find my boots and was marched to the camp with the other men and was told by a couple of chaps that our Officers had two pairs each, so asked some of them for boots, but to no avail, and had to march the whole distance to our destination, plus the seven months working time on the Railway, bare-footed. The first night's march of 15/18 miles was on bitumen. A lot of the men who had boots had to drop out at the first camp because of blisters but I did not wish to leave mates so stuck it out. I had a friend, Bobby Bee (who fought in the ring pre-war under the name of "Bobby Fraser") and he and I had trained together at Jack Dunleavey's Gymn., so he and I led the march out of camp each night, singing – 'Bee's Band" Bobby called us. He still sleeps in Thailand. Heroes of that long march were John Taylor, our R.M.O., and Padre Paddy Walsh, who walked up and down the column and covered easily twice the distance covered by the rest of us. Sid Musgrove was Dr. Taylor's batman and carried the gear of that good Doctor, as well as his own. My gear consisted of a thin strip of canvas to lie on and half a blanket to cover me".

Bob Kelsey remembers:

"On the second day on the road Padre Polain organised a yak cart to carry heavy gear for anyone who had the money. I had a very well filled kit bag as a result of some months of working in a Japanese laundry, and accepted the ride for my gear. Next day the good Padre told me that my kitbag had been stolen!!! So I had nothing except the small haversack with dixie and toothbrush, spoon etc. Peter Hendry, whom I did not know, heard of this disaster and came over with his blanket which he tore down the middle, giving me half plus a pair of socks. I never did get another blanket.

"A week into the march we came to the river, and many men plunged in drinking thirstily, for we were parched. I called out to them not to risk drinking unboiled water. 'It's alright sir – it's running water'. Demonstrating the Australian's pathetic faith in the sterility of running water – shared by myself until we had been recently told not to drink it. Most of those men were dead from cholera within two weeks.

"The first time I saw Captain Frank Cahill, A.A.M.C., was on the short and very hot walk from the train to the huts waiting us at Banpong. I noticed a man dumping a portable typewriter beside the track, and asked him why he did so. It was Frank Cahill – he said he could carry it no further, so I picked it up for him, carried it on and handed it back to him when we reached our accommodation. He soon found a buyer but probably did not remember the bloke who had persuaded him not to throw it away.

"I mention this to illustrate his courage on the exhausting walk up the line, when we all were soon at the point of collapse. It was while I was lying on the track during one of the inexplicable breaks that I saw Cahill, still plump and flabby as a result of having never indulged in physical exercise – certainly never on a route march wavering down the line of panting men asking if anyone needed help and asking, 'Any complaints?' I thought, "Here is a better man than I am."

Harry Weiss:

> Thursday 29 April '43: We paid $40.00 to have all heavy gear taken to the next camp by truck, but even so this march saw more sickness and falling out. We left at 9 pm and reached what we later called 'Dry Camp' at 10 am and it was a long time before the stragglers came in. We did 25 kms and I'm glad it was in the cool of the night. This camp stinks – dirty lavatories, or pits I should say, open refuse pits everywhere, and flies! Water can be bought at 10¢ a bucket and the river is 2 miles away. I went with the organised party and enjoyed the wash. We stay the night here. Have made us a brush shelter. Thais here are pretty wild and seem to be getting less civilised as we proceed north-west on a good motor road. I did enjoy the

night's rest and slept. Had another swim today. Thais will buy anything. Before falling out we purchased boiled eggs, sponge cake and beautiful coffee.

Saturday 1st May '43: I had a bad night, sick all the way but I carried all my stuff to half way hot water point. Here I reported sick and was so bad that I was one of eight selected to ride on 2 yak carts which we hired for $40. These carts crawled along and we had to stop them every mile or so to rush off and vomit etc. We reached a good camp on the river in the Buddhist monastery grounds after 24 kms. We call it Temple Steps Camp, as long steps lead down to the river. I built a brush shelter, bathed and slept, and after doses of chlorodine feel better. Even ate a little stew and bought sweet sago with the peculiar native salty sauce. We march tonight and hired yak carts to carry on our heavy gear – cost $300 – but before leaving, found all the stuff wouldn't fit on the carts and many had to get their packs back. Our road is now just a passable bullock track.

Joe Zeeno recalls:

"I was with Major Hunt's party, we marched at the rear of the column and as they dropped out we looked after them, carried them until there was a halt then we handed them over to their Unit mates to be cared for."

Eric Stone:

1st May – Night leave again. Weather crook. Track nothing but mud. Cannot see. Boys tired. This is murder. Help one another along. Arrive at camp by river. Beaut spot. Temple Camp. Sick in stomach. Arrive morning 1st. Leave night 1st. Hire yak carts but only six turn up. Arrive 2nd May at a first class camp half mile from river. Help Mick. Stay here 6 hours rest. Called best Camp. Leave in night.

Harry Weiss:

Sunday 2nd May – Left at 9 pm and did 26 kms to "New Bridge" camp. I was sick at the start, but came good. It was a terrible march in mud, rain and pitch dark. Many had bad falls but we all came in followed by yak carts. I was lucky to get my baggage but the Thais pinched dozens of packs and things so many chaps have little left to them. No more yak transport for us. River is 3/4 mile away and very good. I had a good rest in my bush shelter and am eating better now. Had some more sago. Apart from the Thais selling us eatables we see no houses or inhabitants. Left the good road last night and are now on a jungle track. This is peculiar country, soil seems fertile but covered with bamboo. Flies are very bad. Food is dearer, and no sign of fruit growing. A rest day, so I slept when the flies allowed. Thai vendors are very dirty and terrible thieves. They are just waiting for us to fall in to rush about our shelters in case something is left.

Peter Rushforth :

"On the fourth day of the enforced march into the hills, the road had deteriorated into a steep mountain track and torrential monsoonal rains had been unrelenting, making progress difficult. A number of men had already contracted dysentery and the extra burden of carrying a heavy pack became a test of endurance.

"At this time an officer made contact with a yak driver from a nearby hill tribe with the aim of paying him to take our packs to the next camp. This proved to be a disastrous move. Many of the hill tribe people seemed to treat both the Japanese and the prisoners with suspicion and would exploit any situation for material gain. A deal was made and I was delegated to walk behind the cart and accompany the driver to the next camp. Soon I was separated from the party and the Japanese guard.

"The scene was unforgetable, the heavens opened up, rain came down in torrents and flashes of lightning momentarily illuminated the jungle background and the cart slithered and lurched up the track with the driver yelling and urging the yak along.

"Through the noise of the storm the primitive sound of drums beating periodically drifted through the jungle. Later I was to realise that the drums were a means of announcing our arrival in the district and seemingly a plan to loot the cart.

"Periodically a light would flash through the trees, and then I became aware that the driver was dropping off some of the packs. My yelling and shouting seemed to inhibit his looting and when dawn broke we reached camp with most of the cargo intact. How many packs were stolen I do not know."

Gordon Gaffney:

"As dawn came we had not reached our camp and word came down the column of very tired men – it was "Mother's Day" – so the men started to pick a tiny white jungle flower and drape it over their packs as they marched on to their next stop. "Mother's Day" was never forgotten.'

I arrived on Train 5 – volunteers were called for drivers and I decided to apply. On each train a number of Ford Marmon trucks were sent with the Force with about 4x44 gal. drums of petrol. We were not to know the trucks had been sabotaged probably prior to Capitulation. The engine oil had been sanded – the effect was not noticeable until after some days. The ambulance was not affected, this was used as Col.Banno's staff vehicle and was usually driven by Bert Chamberlain, better known as "Neville".

Earlier I had driven out of a jungle clearing at Tarsoa into a large area of small wooden crosses and I realised that 'F' Force was marching into some sort of hell. The men marched at night and didn't see these cemeteries until they got closer to their destination. Most men remember passing through Tarsoa.

Captain Roy Mills, A.A.M.C.:

I remember Tarsoa – we were fairly exhausted because in the preceding camps if you stopped for a day you would often be working most of the day and you did not get enough sleep and what I remember most of Tarsoa was that I was filthy and Colonel William Harvey, 197 Fld.Ambulance, and Colonel Knight gave me a hot bath in a canvas bath – that sticks in my mind and before we left Reg Newton came along and poured an egg flip into me and away we went. It was good to meet up with 'D' Force men.

Eric Stone:

> 3rd May – Arrive Base Camp Tarsoa – very dusty. See Cush. (Evans). Large camp, river half mile away. Boys feet are in bad condition – terrible. Arrive morning of 4th May. Here food is terrible. We are fed twice a day and given rice with a piece of fish to carry with us on track. Leave here on night of 4th.

By this time a new figure emerged – Major Bruce Hunt, AAMC.,SMO, he walked up and down the column of exhausted men and instructed his medical orderlies how to look after and protect the sick and frail. He carried their packs and where possible arranged for men to be rested for a day or two at the staging camp. Hunt would not have been known to most of the Force but now they were recording in their diaries, "Major Hunt with us thank God".

At Tarsoa, Hunt endeavoured to leave men behind, he stated:

"I was informed that all sick had to be submitted for examination by an I.J.A. MO, who was quartered about half a mile away. The total number of my sick on this occasion, derived from my own and previous parties, was 37; 27 with infected feet, 10 with malaria or dysentery. The Japanese medical officer agreed that none of these men was fit to march. The Corporal of the Guard, however, only gave permission for 10 to remain. A further conference with the Japanese MO by Major Wild (Interpreter) and myself produced a letter of instruction from the MO to the Corporal. This also was resultless, as was a further visit from Major Wild to the MO later that afternoon.

"At the time scheduled for parade I fell in the 37 sick men in two batches – 27 and 10 – and Major Wild and I stood in front of them. The Corporal approached with a large bamboo in his hand and spoke menacingly to Major Wild, who answered in a placatory fashion. The Corporal's only reply was to hit Major Wild in the face – another guard followed suit, and as Major Wild staggered back the Corporal thrust at the Major's genitalia with his bamboo. I was left standing before the patients and was immediately set upon by three guards. One tripped me, while two others pushed me to the ground. The three men set about me with bamboos, causing extensive bruising of the skull, hands and arms, and a fractured left 5 metacarpal bone. After I was disposed of the Corporal then made the majority of the 27 foot-sufferers march with the rest of the troops. This episode took place in front of the whole parade of troops and caused much resentment amongst them."

During this bashing the men were infuriated, there were some who wanted to get in and 'do' the Japanese, Hunt told them, "Keep out of this you blokes – this is my fight!" – the men were restrained.

Soon after, I arrived in a truck and the men were still fuming at what they had witnessed. I saw Major Hunt standing alone amongst the tall bamboos, he was holding his left arm up in pain. There were groups of men scattered around talking about the bashing – I went up to Hunt and spoke to him, he deeply resented the suggestion he should go forward by transport "My duty is to protect the men!", he said.

Major Bruce Hunt recorded:

> At Camp 6 I was again struck and some of my patients rejected – these were the only occasions on which I personally received violence at the hands of the guards. It was the general practice of MOs to march at the rear of the column to succour the stragglers and endeavour to prevent any possible molestation of these by the guards – I saw such treatment on several occasions as sick men were hurried along, but I myself never saw blows struck under these circumstances.
>
> The diseases and disorders most prominent on the march were Senility and cardiac weakness – the majority of men with complaints were left at Camp 2. Dysentery – increasingly common as the march progressed (I was myself held up for a day at Camp 9 by a very acute attack of bacillary dysentery).
>
> Septic abrasions of the feet – many boots were ill-fitting, and very many of the men were totally unaccustomed to marching.
>
> Fever, apart from a few malarial relapses, were of lesser frequency and importance until arrival in the working camps.

No.5 Train came up behind Major Hunt's group and reported seeing men of 'D' Force going to work, they heard from some of those left behind about the bashing he had received, within days the story was passed down the column and everyone knew who Major Bruce Hunt was.

Harry Weiss:

> Wednesday 5th May: After 23 kms, we reached a horrible stinking camp on a poor little creek – flies bad and food scarce. How disillusioned we feel. Ever since we left Changi we have to boil all drinking water and that does not add to our convenience or the joys of life.

Eric Stone:

> 5th May: Along hard track, but rains en route so we slither and slide in pitch dark. I am sick in stomach. Bill Brown has sore heels. Impossible to describe this horrible march where men are little better than pigs. Arrive morning.

Frank Smith was on 'D' Force and at Tarsoa he learned his two brothers, Bob and Les, were on 'F' Force. He called out to men on the march, "Anyone want to swap and stay here?" He changed places with Pierce , Frank Smith became A.W. Pierce and the three brothers went on 'F' Force.

Harry Weiss:

> Tuesday 4 May '43: After a night march of 24 kms., we reached a large camp – Tarsoa – where we saw 2/18, 2/19 and 2/20 Aussies going to work. We are in the sun here, river a mile away and food very poor, but move on tonight. What we miss most is tea.

Eric Stone:

> Arrive footsore and tired on morning of 5 May and at a camp one and half miles past Poms. Little water and everybody dead beat but told we leave that night instead of resting. Captain Taylor doing marvellous job. Leave in night.

It was customary at this locality for native families to hitch a ride from village to village, the guards often slapped on the cabin roof calling me to Stop! and allow some young girls to climb aboard, the guard sitting in the cabin then ordered me to move off. Nearby there was a gathering of Thais, mainly what appeared to be family groups; I had proceeded a short distance when I felt a bump and there was a great call to stop – I saw an older woman screaming, pulling her hair I alighted, looked back and there was the body of a girl, the wheel had gone over her head and crushed her skull into the dusty road surface. I was stunned – the villagers gathered around and soon removed her body tied to a stick two men trotted away with it.

Now I was the target. I was endeavouring to explain to the guard she must have stood on the fuel tank and slipped off it as the truck-moved away. I had done a drawing in the dust and while I was doing that the Japanese started kicking me – boots came from all directions. One of the Thais tried to explain to the Japanese what they had seen, the guards were not interested, they wanted to hold me responsible for the girl's death.

It seemed ages to me but probably was not long before an English-speaking Thai Police Officer arrived, listened to the guards and to a large group of natives who had witnessed the incident. He turned to me and said, "You are not responsible for the girl's death, the moment the people got on the truck the Japanese crowded them and started to interfere with them, the girl killed jumped from the truck." That did not stop Ishima from bashing me until a more senior guard ordered him to stop. It was a long day, the incident was reported at a Police Station further up the road and eventually we were allowed to proceed. Fortunately none of the guards could drive

Harry Weiss:

> Thursday 6 May: Left 'Stinking Camp' and were pleased as the march was only 18 kms to a better halt. Gordon Highlanders, Dutch and Aussies were camped down near the river. They are very miserable in their surroundings. River is good and the Thais bring up good white bait, gula malacca and tobacco in barges. We bought white bait and kept issue onions and made a good stew.

Eric Stone:

> At camp one mile from river where we spend 36 hours. Leave in night of 7 May. Arrive morning of 8th. After pretty big hill climb arrive at camp where we are coralled. Stream close handy. Food pretty crook. So far mixed vegs with rice. Through lack of containers leave on night of 8th. Arrive morning.

Harry Weiss:

> Friday 7 May: A good night's rest, but a poor breakfast of rice and onions. The 6th Train mob arrived and we were a man short, so the Japanese did a bit of bashing, picking on three chaps who considered themselves dismissed and went for an early swim. The lost man arrived at 3 pm, hardly able to stand. Poor old Padre Wallace Dean is staying behind tonight. His feet are impossible. Also Bernie Jenkins. We bought some good gula to eat with our rice on the road.
>
> Saturday 8 May : Believe we are most proceeding north and not too far from the Burma border. It is useless to think of escaping in this awful land. Hardly see a Thai – no clearings – no houses, just bamboo mainly. We left last night at 6.30 pm so had five miles in daylight. There were Aussies in the camp – 4 miles out who gave us mugs of rice-coffee, which isn't bad. It's all we have to give they said. After 23 kms we reached the 'Drafting Pen Camp'. Not allowed to shelter in the bushes, however there is a lovely stony brook, and I feel refreshed. We are quite familiar with elephants now. The track we follow is very rough and narrow and it marvellous how the Japanese transport uses it. It leads right into Burma. I hear lots of Europeans escaped this way when the Japanese came. I am sure this road would be useless in the wet season but hear the rivers are largely used then. There are Japanese front line troops proceeding along the track – some on foot.
>
> Sunday 9 May: Came on 22 kms to 'Discipline Camp' last night. Everyone seems to be marching along a little easier and even feet are better now. This

is a cleaner camp and strictly run. Meals are like clockwork. A lovely river and we have a night to rest and as Peter Henley and Ollie Beach gave us their beautiful shelter, Woody, Willow and myself look forward to the night's rest. We even had a breakfast at this camp. Next march is short, but across the mountains. No fruit or anything to buy but wild mangoes on huge trees are edible. Today was Mother's Day.

Eric Stone:

At camp where guards are of the Imperial Guard. Stay here 36 hours. River beautiful. Try hand at cooking. Mangos very bitter. Guard speaks English. Boys eat mussels from river. A lot now with dysentery. Alf going well. See Bill, OK too. Leave night 10 May. Arrive morning.

Harry Weiss:

Monday 10 May: Have had a refreshing rest here. Some chaps are busy diving for mussels but these are not so nice when cooked but may be nutritious. Japanese soldiers arrived on foot this morning looking tired and weary but they of course have tents to rest in and better food than we get. They had to do half an hour's PT on arrival – I think it was showing off. Alan Cox gave us a cup of tea and it was just perfect. The stews here with rice are very thin. A lot of barges proceeded up the river and we had hopes they might land fresh fruit, etc.

Tuesday 11 May: Left camp last night at 7.30 pm. 17 kms. walk and did not find the climb too stiff. Major Hunt came along with us although he had dysentery. He is a very hard, efficient and popular M.0. I call this camp 'Good Tucker Camp' as we had four fair meals here. Had a bad start off though, as the Japanese Corporal beat up our Adjutant, Mr. Eaton, thinking him disobedient. The stream here is swift and clean. McNickle and I did our washing together. Expected to spend the night here so Woody, Willow and I scraped away elephant dung and made a shelter. However, at midnight the Japanese woke us and sent us on our way. I will always remember the Japanese bully-beef stews here – our best stew of the trip.

Eric Stone:

At camp where bridge going across river. Hill Camp. We are told we stay until receive orders where we are to move to. Lt. Eaton gets beaten up through misunderstanding. Fed little better here. 11.30 pm on night of 11th my dreams interrupted to move on. Boys lumber Pommy trucks up hill and over gullies. Very tired when we reach next camp.

Returning to Banpong to collect medical supplies we were held up at Wampo, the bamboo scaffolding had been removed from the cliff-face and a low-level road just above the river was being blasted. During the delay I watched the elephants rolling large boulders over the river escarpment. Here I spoke to a young Japanese, he told me, in flawless English and a reflective manner, 'This time of the year is cherry blossom time, I'm going home to further my studies at the University. My father was able to have me released from the Burma Army.' He must have had great influence. Nearby I saw two Indians wearing turbans on their heads and with rather darkened skins, as I went past one of them said, "How you going mate!" I was surprised but kept going – from the truck I looked at those two very hard and was convinced they were Australians but were over-dressed for their part.

Returning to Neike the Japanese convoys en route to Burma stuck in the mud for the rains had arrived. I had Lt. Yamata, a Japanese Adjutant on board, with several guards and about 20 stragglers who had fallen by the wayside. The guards were not supposed to pick up stragglers. I remember seeing one Australian, his clothing was immaculate, his webbing equipment was scrubbed, he was regimentally correctly dressed, but he was a sick man and I explained to the Japanese officer that he was one of our party and we should take him on. At first he said, 'No,no, no stop' then he thought about it and he said, 'Stop stop stop'. I never knew the man's name, he was obviously one of those patients from a hospital the Japanese promised would be able to recuperate in Thailand.

That night, when it became dark, we stopped at Brankali; there was no food for the others but the Japanese officer took me into the Japanese Mess. In the dim light he walked in, they saluted him and glared at me, and in Japanese he ordered them to give me a meal. I never thought much about that meal for many years, I had never forgotten the taste, and it was not until Tim Bowden took me to a Japanese restaurant in Sydney that it took me back into the camp at Brankali that night; I asked Tim what the food was and he said, "Bean curd".

Further on we camped somewhere near Tamaranpat on a small plateau. Here we caught up with a party who had completed their task cooking for the group at the staging camp. A large fire was lit, mainly to keep the wild animals away – the Japanese guards were scared of the dark and actually handed a rifle to a POW to guard the camp. During the night hyenas were heard howling and moving around the perimeter of the men sleeping around the fire, no one wanted to be on the outer perimeter and during the night the circle moved considerably.

Harry Weiss:

> Wednesday 12 May : After our late start, we did well to reach 'Pork Stew Camp', 23 kms, at 9 pm. It is the usual camp drafting paddock and bushy area for shelter. The river is handy and good, but very steep banks. This is a nuisance as the kitchen is built on the water level and I was a mess orderly. Except for a fatty pork stew, stews here were extract of liver. Watched the Thais working their light, but large, canoes up-stream against a strong current. They are as good as Red Indians. The pork stew cheered us up but just as we were saddling up the rain teemed down and everything gets twice as

heavy. Some of the chaps bought salted buffalo meat from the Thai canoes before leaving, $1.00.1b.

Eric Stone:

12 May – Morning at camp where water is good but boy, are we tired. Have to wait long while for meals. Drive bamboo into foot. Leave night of 12th. Rains just before we pull out and arrive morning of 13th.

Harry Weiss:

Thursday 13th May 1943: A twenty five kilo march and a lot of climbing to reach this large unfinished camp. I call it "Cholera Camp", but believe it's called Tamaranpat. 29 Bn. lads are here doing roadwork and don't like the place. Although the river is large and clear, it is cholera infested. I was on water boiling fatigue they won't even rely on chlorination now. Kitchen could only feed us two meals of rice and onions so we are glad to move on, especially as the Asiatics, who are roofing the huts, are particularly filthy — passing their excreta wherever the mood takes them. They are said to be (many of them) sick, and two were carried away this afternoon apparently dead. An Indian told us they came from Penang mainly and the Japanese told them this would be a good job just over the Thailand border.

Eric Stone:

At camp where dysentery very bad. Full of Indians and Malays from Penang. 423 Indians of which 200 are down sick with three deaths in 20 days. They cannot leave, and get no medical attention. 2/29 at this camp. Leave night of 13th arrive morning of 14th.

Harry Weiss:

Friday 14th May '43: Clarrie Wood had to stay behind sick last night. We marched 20 miles to Base Hospital Camp, although it is uncompleted yet. Here we can relax for a couple of days. It is a very poor stream to wash in there. An elephant nearly ran us down last night – they are so silent. Only had two meals but towgay and fish is better than onions. A large party leave this Camp tonight, mostly 26 Bn. and we hope to follow in a night or so and reach the end of the weary journey. Huts are unroofed and it is raining. Surprising how the chaps have come through but everyone is thin and old looking. At present too we are very hungry. Indians have been changing Thai dollar and cent bills, but the lads are very silly, as we do not now seem destined for Burma. Some chaps have gathered wild ripe bananas in their hunger, but owing to their being full of large seeds one can only chew these and the flavour is delightful. We didn't get our second meal till 8 pm and it was inadequate so we went to bed.

Eric Stone:

> At base camp Lower Neike Carry Alf's pack as he is very weak with fatigue. 2/26 already here. Pull out in morning of 15th with 1000 men.

On the night of 14/15th May, 1000 A.I.F. from Trains 3 and 4 under Major Tracey, marched out from Lower Neike to their permanent camp at Lower Sonkurai, a distance of 7.5 miles. They arrived on the morning of 15th May, on 16th May all fit men were sent to work. The following day the second group under Major Johnston marched in. After a survey of the camp, Major Johnston pressed for the immediate supply of attap for roofing of the huts in view of the approaching monsoonal season, and stressed the necessity of keeping sufficient men in camp to construct new latrines, kitchens, water sterilising points etc., and for the reinforcing of the huts. The floors of two already had collapsed under the weight of sleeping men, and some showed signs of complete collapse within a week or two.

Harry Weiss:

> Saturday 15 May 1943: At dawn Woody woke me – he had come in with last night's marchers so I rose and used the last of our tea, but in our hunger we did enjoy the early morning cup. We were delighted to get three full meals today. Woody finds he has to remain with his new Coy. and is very wild about it. Quite a lot of chaps have developed bad vomiting attacks and diarrhoea. Some chaps have netted the stream and get buckets of small fish – others are digging and cooking a native root. Bird life is plentiful in Thailand. I hear curlews and dollar birds – crows are everywhere too – probably because of the number of zebu cattle.

Eric Stone:

> 15th May: We had good night's sleep. Abbie still sick with dysentery. Meals very light. Picquet all day on water. Bill arrives. Looks OK. Hunt bananas with Alf but cannot find any. Sleep night of 15th and rest morning of 16th.

On 15.5.43 Captain R.L. Cahill, 13 A.G.H., arrived as M.O. with the original party. Two cases of cholera developed on that day and were promptly isolated under the charge of L/Cpl. K.R. Marshall, 2/3 M.A.C. A general hospital was also erected and placed under control of Sgt. A.J. Buttenshaw; this hospital received 40 patients within the first 24 hours.

I asked Ken Marshall how he became involved in caring for cholera victims – "We had not been at Lower Sonkurai long when the first case was diagnosed by Captain Lloyd Cahill. The Japanese were also informed and their doctor arrived dressed in gown, mask and gloves. There were men standing around when the Japanese doctor asked for someone to roll the victim over so he could look at his eyes. I stepped forward to assist."

Captain Lloyd Cahill, A.A.M.C.

A tent was quickly erected to place the patient in isolation, it was over the creek north of the camp and it became known as "Cholera Hill"; that was the first of several tents to be erected as the Isolation Hospital. Major Hunt later called for volunteers – Wally Southwick was one of the first to join Ken Marshall, he said he imagined what it was like to be a victim and looking around with no one wanting to touch you, "so I put my arm around their shoulders to give them hope."

Major Hunt recorded the names of those volunteering to assist, a large number of A.A.M.C. Orderlies and many volunteers also became victims of cholera and died.

Lieut. Fukuda intimated that the 800 men who had arrived with Major Johnston would be medically examined next day and therefore would not be required to augment the working parties drawn from the original 1000. He linked the arrival of Major Johnston's party with the outbreak of cholera, and, despite protests, persisted for several days in the view that only this party was affected. This officer was to display the same lack of common sense during the second outbreak.

Harry Weiss:

> Sunday 16th May 1943: A good rest day but little food as the cooks have so few utensils. First meal 12 pm, 2nd at 4.30 pm, both light on, so we are ravenous and drinking rice water if we can get it. Chaps are digging roots to eat, others netting little fish and some out finding the poor wild bananas.The Japanese are very lenient as to our wandering about – so they should be. The worst has happened – a cholera outbreak of 8 cases – so we are glad to pull out of this camp tonight.

Eric Stone:

> 16th May: Bill Brown caught fish which we boiled. Night of 16th men suspected of cholera left at camp. We march out at 4 am.

Harry Weiss:

> Monday 17th May 1943 – Lower Sonkurai – After an easy march of 12 kilos we reached our journey's end and are we disappointed. The huts are

unroofed and no early hope of receiving any attap roofing and anyway the structures are falling down. They are built of bamboo tied together with vines, so are pretty bad. The creek is dirty and small and we are sad to think that we have walked over three hundred kilos or 187 miles to reach so poor a camp. Have had only 2 meals and it is all we can expect with 1800 men here and more to arrive and no increase in utensils. On parade tonight we learned of the death of 2 of our mates left behind with cholera. Arthur English I knew well. We have also one case here now so are isolated from 26 Bn. and others. Lads are fencing the camp in – the usual tiger fence. Altogether we marched 301 kilos of 187 miles.

Eric Stone:

Leaving Capt. Taylor, Howells, Lieut. Waite. We are pleased to be on our way. Arrive at camp about 8.30 in morning. Camp without roofs. Very little water and food. They keep us waiting about. Night 17th – man dies with cholera. Capt. Taylor, Major Hunt in morning 3 o'clock. We are quarantined for three days. Cannot wash only with boiling water. Hear of Arthur English, Harry Godbolt deaths day before in night.

Lieut. R. Eaton:

Shimo Sonkurai. Buggered about for hours by one Toyama – finally quartered to huts – no roofs few leaking tents. Everyone very tired and not happy with camp – 12 suspect cholera – general cleaning – fatigues – rain – C.O.'s policy speech – 2/26 party out at work. Rations poor cooking containers inadequate 5 Officers bashed – Major Johnston C.O. Camp. Major Anderson C.O. Bn.

Innoculation for Officers limited vaccine more coming. Each M.O. very busy – hospital establish news of English and Godbolt – cholera suspect – mild outbreak – Isolation – Volunteers to go back to Camp 1 for syringe and vaccine – Japanese say more doctors coming. Both floors of huts collapse – bloody awful quarters.

Dr. Lloyd Cahill recalls:

"Lower Sonkurai – 17 May – We had been in the new camp one day and I had diagnosed the first cholera case in this camp and the fellow had died. I was naturally extremely concerned being the only Medical Officer in the camp – I was wondering how one man could handle the situation.

"I was not to know an urgent message had been sent from Lower Neike to the Senior Medical Officer at Konkoita to come forward. After a hazardous trip, partly by ambulance and on foot, they arrived at Lower Neike where they talked to Captain John Taylor who passed on the rumour that I was seriously ill at Lower Sonkurai. It was decided Major Bruce Hunt and Capt. John Taylor would proceed to Lower Sonkurai.

"That night I had decided to try and get some sleep and my mind wandered back to 1940 when I Enlisted. I had gone from St. Vincents to the Showground, Major John Lowenthal was in command of the Medical Unit and Pete Hendry was his 2 i/c – I was in civvies – I didn't know much about it but they soon got me into it. I had a choice of Units, I selected the 2/19 Bn. which was at Walgrove and someone said, "You poor bastard you have a doctor as C.O.!" Lt.Col. Maxwell –

"I reported on a cold Saturday afternoon, by Monday morning I thought this was no good for me, it was an awful camp, I'll try and get back to Sydney and see if I could do better but I would have to have an excuse. So after Sick Parade that morning I went up to see Lt.Col. Maxwell, saluted the best I could – "Yes Cahill? What can I do for you?" "Sir, I was wondering if I could go back to Sydney for a day or so" "Oh yes" he said, "what do you want? you will have to have a good reason". "Well Sir, I can't find a thermometer in the camp, I've left my razor behind and not only that I left my stethoscope". "Three very good reasons Cahill! Now, you see that hut over there? that is the Barber's Hut and if you go over there I am sure you will get a shave, and you see that camp over there?" I said yes – "That is the Hospital – give the Colonel my compliments and I am sure he can spare you a thermometer" and reaching into his pocket he said, "and here is my stethoscope!" and I thought Oh brother! I know where I stand now!

"My mind went back to the battle of Muar and I must have drifted into a deep sleep for suddenly I was woken and told that Major Hunt and Capt. Taylor had arrived ... I was relieved, one man could not have handled 1800 men – it was the first case of cholera I had seen. I always had a vivid picture painted to me – clinically – as to what cholera was and there was just no doubt what this was, added to the fact that I knew we were in an endemic area. When these two colleagues arrived it was just incredible!"

Next morning, Major Hunt and Captain Cahill innoculated 1400 men with a 1/2cc of vaccine from the limited stocks they collected at Konkoita. This was the vaccine brought forward from Changi.

Major Bruce Hunt recorded:

"Protective innoculation of all troops against cholera was carried out on 18 and 19 May 1943. On 19 May 1943 the construction of an isolation camp for cholera was commenced on a neighbouring hillside. This camp was under the charge of L/Cpl. Marshall with Pte. Staff as his chief assistant and all cases of cholera were nursed in this camp.

"Nursing of high quality was carried out under circumstances of great difficulty, incessant rain, thick mud, and inadequate tent covering over improvised bamboo staging. Extensive improvements were effected in camp hygiene, in particular as regards latrine construction, kitchens, messing points, and the sterilisation of mess gear, and general personal cleanliness."

Harry Weiss:

> Tuesday 18 May: We are all in camp so got to work cleaning up and feel better for it. Have our own kitchen on account of isolation and hope we will be able to continue to cook our own meals afterwards too. I think we are a little happier today, but what we could not do to those Japanese. They knew this is a cholera area, but they don't care if we die.

Eric Stone:

> Some of us injected against cholera. Alf pretty sick with fever.

Lieut. R. Eaton:

> Major Bruce Hunt and Capt. John L. Taylor arrive plus 15 orderlies at 0300 hours plus gear and medical supplies – work on hospital – fires – attap roofs.

Capt. Taylor commenced the erection of a cholera hospital on a hill adjoining the camp. This hospital, which subsequently housed up to 128 patients at one time, consisted of tents or marquees erected on bamboo stagings. Its construction was carried out in incessant rain and despite indefatigable work by Lieut. McKibbin in charge of construction, never until the height of the epidemic was passed was the supply of accommodation more than half a day ahead of the demand. The nursing of patients with cholera was throughout under the charge of L/cpl.Ken Marshall, later promoted to Sergeant, whose faithful devotion to duty in circumstances of great danger, difficulty and discomfort, is worthy of the highest praise.

Major hunt approached the I.J.A. Officer in Charge of the Camp, Lieut. Fukuda, together with Major Johnston, C.O. of the camp, to make various requests mainly in connection with medical supplies, tools, which were at all times inadequate, and for the construction of new latrines.

During this day, 7 cases of cholera were detected, all obviously infected prior to reaching the camp.

On 19th May innoculation of the whole camp was completed. This was extended on 20th May to cover such of the 163 men arriving with Captain Howells on that day, as they had not been innoculated in the lower camps.

Harry Weiss:

> 19th May – This cholera outbreak is very bad, but MOs think that though we had the first injection at Changi, it is saving deaths. All but a few of us – I was unlucky – received the second shot yesterday. A couple of Japanese officers called yesterday just as one of the huts had collapsed. They had a good look and we hope for some action.

Bill Jobe enlisted in the A.I.F. and didn't like the Infantry training – or the Sergeant Major – so he decided to re-enlist in a Unit of his choice. He enlisted under his Mother's maiden name, "Rerdon" joined the 2/10 A.G.H. and was posted to Singapore where he arrived a few weeks before Singapore fell.

Now up in Thailand, he was one of the heroes who volunteered to assist on Cholera Hill with his mate "Titch" Kean.

Meanwhile, down at Port Melbourne about this time the Military Police called on Mrs. Jobe, "We are looking for your son Bill" they said. "Well", said Mrs. Jobe, "so am I! He's a prisoner of war with the Japanese and when you find him bring him back to me!"

Eric Stone:

– Work all day carrying stones and digging pissaphones. Alf feeling very sick. Just remembered Alf's birthday.

Lieut. R. Eaton:

– Cholera admissions growing – work parties return from work at 2100 hrs. – rain incessant – malaria test – no improvement in quarters. Complete apathy in this camp

Eric Stone:

20 May – Work again digging pissaphones. Vic Barnes in charge of party. Officers toss chaps out of hut with roof and take the place themselves.

Lieut. R. Eaton:

Capt. E.R. Howells and 162 march into camp good to see them – brought George Clarke and 80 of 2/30 making total of 570 all 2/30. Rain – more malaria tests.

Eric Stone:

21 May – First day at work. One hour lunch time. Drive us all day until 9.15 at night. Building railway – every bone of my body aches. Go straight to bed. Worked with Mick and Vic. Shovel and chunkel all day.

Lieut. R. Eaton:

Accommodation limited ... huts ... 10 men to bay. 1st Work party – Isolation of camp parties – kitchens moved – men return from work 2030. Work all day pouring rain up to ankles 11/2 cubic metres p. man a day – nominally actually much more – men asleep at work. Japanese hostile over work figures and sick. Men have no reserves. Japanese issue 1 quinine pill per man nightly hence.

Eric Stone:

22nd May – Work all day – railway – on basket with Mick. Raining like hell but we work through it. Cholera very bad. Feel temperature coming on in night. Aches and pains all over.

Lieut. R. Eaton:

Officers work party – Rutherford hit – rain – 1730 return.

Harry Weiss:

Sunday 23rd May '43 – First chance I have had to make an entry here since Wednesday. Japanese working us from daylight to dark. Wednesday and Thursday our huts and everything we had flooded out, and things still damp, although the Thais put the atap on the roof on Friday. At least we can keep dry now. Haven't been allowed near the creek since Wednesday, and have to wash in boiled water so except for being wet all the time at work, we should be filthy. We are working on railway embankments ...

9 pm (dark) was our latest knock-off. We are all wet, tired, hungry and cranky but carrying on. Received second cholera injection. There was another case today and M0 thinks the injections have so far saved a great epidemic. We have lost 10 of the Force which left Changi on 22nd April.

Eric Stone:

23 May – Fever – admitted to M.I.R. – Alf already in there with diarrhoea – feeling very crook.

Lieut. R. Eaton:

C.O. quit duties – rain – rations bad 700 gm per man plus 12 beans per man approx. plus onion water only. Men march 12 kilos return to and work – exhausted – impossible to keep it up. There were now a total of 2014 all ranks in the camp.

Eric Stone:

24 May – Changed from dysentery side of ward to fever. Feel very weak.

Harry Weiss:

Monday 24 May – I am a bit sick today, diarrhoea and loss of appetite, despite this I'm on duty. The Japanese even want all men evacuated from the "M.I.R." and sent to work. No doubt they are sticking it into us. Not half the huts roofed yet, and it is raining most of the time. Such a lot of the chaps have bronchitis. Another man died late yesterday. It doesn't look as if we will ever get fresh fruit or vegetables and beri beri is coming forward once more.

Lieut. R. Eaton:

We all press for stoppage of inactivity. This no action is bad. All the jobs which need doing but we have no fit men to do them – e.g. latrines must be sealed and hygiene improved.

Harry Weiss:

Tuesday 25 May – The rain hardly stops. English and Australian troops halted here today, wet and weary. More of our chaps have died including Jack Heasman, whom I knew well. He had a wife and three children and was so anxious to get back. A chap named Harry Moseley died here today too. A fatigue went up the hill to form up and clean up a little cemetery. I am going to work tomorrow. I read my letters again and feel homesick and miserable, and I'm sure spirits are higher at work. Had another cholera injection. Lads had to carry rations 5 miles from the bogged truck, so we will be lucky if we don't often hunger in the wet season. There is a little fresh zebu and pork meat in but probably we won't get any. Afraid I'm a bit down today.

Eric Stone:

25 May – Receive another cholera needle. Sent out of M.I.R. to make room for more patients. Given one day's N/D. Vic and Clem to hospital with cholera in night. Ray Mosely died same complaint. Heard of death of Jack Heasman and Nolan.

Lieut. R. Eaton:

2nd cholera innoculation 1cc per 100 vol. 10 march to Neike to carry back rations – only 1 day carried here – 12 kilos 25 bags each 220 lbs. ankle mud. Arrived at Neike and truck available – could not have carried it.

Harry Weiss:

Wednesday 26 May – Back to work and they even knocked us off at 7 pm. We arrived to find 5 more chaps had died and this casts a spell over everything – you can't help but feel there is a plague on us and I'm only using the camp lavatory when forced to. The road work is not so bad as the railway. March flies are very bad and give you such a sting. Bees too seem to run all over you and when you brush them, of course they sting. The butterflies of Thailand are gorgeous and we all feel would make a great collection. Bird life is much more plentiful than Malaya.

Eric Stone:

On N/D. Hear Vic very crook. Clem a bit better. Feel very weak myself. Japanese commander says unless he gets 70% to work he'll take over camp administration himself. I only hope they have to pay for all of this. Clem passed away today. Vic very low. Feeling very weak through fever.

Lieut. R. Eaton:

Wednesday 26 May – My birthday – not well – Fukuda tells C.O.

Engineers will demand 70% fit men to go to work. Unless we increase figures soon they will come in and take anyone.

Harry Weiss:

Thursday 27 May '43 – Road work again. It's much better and healthier to be out of camp. More deaths today, so the camp M0 and C0 saw the Japanese Lieut. and told him they must have all the men left in camp for at least three days to make new lavatories and do all the jobs necessary to keep down cholera, otherwise they would hold the Japanese Government directly responsible for all future deaths. Hence we are in tomorrow.

Eric Stone:

Go to work on road about one and a half miles along road. Carry stones all day. Met at gate on return by Abbie and Padre Walsh. Alf passed away this afternoon. Receive his personal gear.

Lieut. R. Eaton:

There have been 22 cholera deaths to date Alf Stone today admitted after 1000 hrs died at 1600 hrs. Brother Eric out at work still. Total cases at present 55 – situation now all but out of hand medically. Major Hunt, S.M.0., places responsibility on us to help ourselves. He and John Taylor and Lloyd Cahill have been lion men – marvellous show – goodness knows how they keep up. Bob Howells after chat with us in which we agreed if any action were to be started it would have to come from Bruce Hunt and selves. Went to B.H. this morning and put position frankly. Whole show just plainly up to us alone. Recce of area – jobs to be done at which camp C.O. plus Bn.

Alf Stone

Eric Stone
Pics: Betty Stone

COs attended then straight Japs. B.H. put fear of death into them.

Immediate result – 300 men in camp remain in camp and put to work in camp for balance of day plus assurance of staying for 3 days to put camp in liveable order – whole camp. Priority complete sealing latrines and construct new banks – construct attap hospital and huts – inclusive of hospital fumigation of camp – burning of all surface soil – construct mess tables – sterilisation of all gear brooms and kitchens. These were the things which were forcefully impressed on the powers that be days ago when total cases were 10 and well in hand. So we ourselves have to answer for this. Even now there will be a period of 14 days in which time anything may happen. Today has been sunny – may it please be sunny for 4 days to come. B. Hunt now has hospital as follows: Cholera on hill – Dysentery ward, Fever ward, total patients 586, which compares with an A.G.H.

These facts are accurate for a very definite reason and full use will be made of them. Personal note not warranted in these circumstances. Am in one day – result – collapsed fainted last night 2130 – but feel better today – forcing food down – have fears for home – hope there is no link – cremations have been awful task. The cemetery has been established NNW of camp. More definite location related to features later. Numbered from top to bottom in order L-R. Men showing more spirit already since they have heard of this chance to recover what has been lost or rather to keep what we have – Two yaks killed for rations – just a taste.

Harry Weiss:

Friday 28 May '43 – We are all working flat out today. I was up getting bamboos near the crematorium and saw a poor corpse being hoisted in. Twenty five deaths up to last night and four today since we arrived which is really serious and has one very worried and upset. A chap in my hut lost his brother.

Eric Stone:

Major Johnston arranges to keep everyone in camp cleaning up. Go to Alf's burial after lunch. Move back into platoon in night. Sleeping next to Jack Greenwood and Dave Tate. Japanese promise us three days in camp off duty. Talking to Dick Lumby.

Lieut. R. Eaton:

Friday – Lt. Fukuda down with malaria – very sick – promise broken. 720 men asked for work party – spoils whole camp work plan – whole scheme of work. Men return to camp late. The whole damn show is very bad. To see the Cholera Ward is an awful sight. The cheeks hollow in, the eyes sink back, and the pulse almost stops, the voice sinks to a whisper. All the fluids leave the body.

Gordon Gaffney:

"We were put straight to work on the railway and it was not long before cholera broke out and I was unlucky enough to cop it. A mate, Noel Blackwell, led me to the sick parade and when we were about 10 yards away from Dr. Lloyd Cahill, he said, "Take him away" meaning to "Cholera Hill". We were put in leaky tents in the pouring rain. If you lasted 24 hrs. with cholera you had a chance of survival, however I lasted 9 days up there ... After a couple of days someone took my boots, I could not talk but I heard them say, "This bloke won't need these where he is going". That was fair enough as some poor bugger could go to work in boots.

"The Orderlies would come around each morning to collect the dead and wrap them in their blanket to be put on the fire, when they came to me I heard one say, "This poor bastard has had it" and he started to take my 'meat ticket' off and I winked at him! After coming off "The Hill" I think I only had about two weeks No Duties and then back to work. We worked from before daylight and it was after dark when we got back to camp, it was about a 3 mile walk in pouring rain. At night we would stand around a big bamboo fire and try to dry our clothes, before lying down. Wal Eather and I came from Garah, just out of Moree, I used to talk to him every night but I didn't see him in the daylight because he was on another working party. One night Lieut. Norm "Killer" Couch handed me a pair of boots taken from a dead mate, he said, "Gaff, I think your mate would have liked you to have these". Unfortunately they were too big and rubbed my heel and started a tropical ulcer – which eventually had just about eaten my heel away. Luckily I knew Phil Bailey from the 2/30 who had a R.A.P. (so-called) and he had no medicine or drugs, so he put a small piece of rock salt in the centre of the ulcer and it corned it and saved my leg."

Eric Stone:

> 29 May – Japanese break their word and send large party out to work. I go to work with Ernie Willis who invites me home any time. Also with Bill, Jack Ellis, shovelling gravel out of creek all day. Very hard work. Still feel fever. Receive news Dick Lumby passes away also Merv Shore and Philps.

Lieut. R. Eaton:

> One hell of a day. They have broken their promise and we sent out 750 men to work thereby leaving many works not yet completed. One bank of top latrines was filled and has been burning ever since. The others are being prepared ready for filling today. Work at cholera hospital proceeds – floors are being built and tents pitched over them – over 90 patients there now and there have been over 40 deaths. Bruce Hunt came up today and sitting in corner wrote a classic document putting clearly forward to Japanese our demands or rather HIS demands and signed by Johnston, Hunt, Anderson and Tracey. Immediate results – no men to go to work tomorrow.

Demanded one copy be sent to Col. Bannu and to Col. Harris. Feeling better – no rain – rations same. Dick Lumby, Bill Borlase died – tragic no less – Command very upset.[2]

Harry Weiss:

Sunday 30 May – Of course the Japanese did not keep the their word and we were worked till dark last night. This morn, when our deaths total 38, a letter was sent to the Japanese CO to be forwarded to the Red Cross at either Rangoon or Bangkok, stating the dreadful state of things here and our parlous plight and bad treatment by the Japanese. I'm not very hopeful of the Japanese sending this. We have lost Merv. Shaw, Sis. Phel, and Stan Marsh of our Company. One thing, the Japanese have not done anything today about our refusal to work, and we are feverishly building new lavs. and burning the old.

Eric Stone:

Japanese presented with note from Majors Tracey, Johnston, Anderson, Hunt for more drugs etc. Go on sick parade with fever. Jack also sick with runs. Given N/D, Jack L/D. Lay on back most of day resting and going through Alf's stamps and sorting them.

Lieut. Ron Eaton

Lieut. R. Eaton:

Fine day – work goes well – L/Cpl. Bayliss to cholera ward – very ill. Church parades tonight if fine, 1530 hrs. pouring rain – stops after a while. Thoroughly scared of whole situation which could not have been worse – actually don't blame them entirely.

Eric Stone:

31 May: Still on N/D. Feel OK. Morning still sorting stamps. Afternoon I am running a temperature and so is Mick. Both admitted to M.I.R. All dysentery and diarrhoea cases have to move to Con. Run fever all night. Mick and Scotty's birthdays.

Lieut. R. Eaton:

Further demands made for whole party to remain on camp works until further improvement. 300 work party went out but returned almost at once and whole camp now on essential work – heavy rain set in stopping work on latrines. Maj. Johnston to hospital – extreme nervous stomach upset – vomited for 10 hrs. – thought at first cholera – needs rest – now much better. Anderson also in hospital – malaria and beri beri. Better to have them there than out NOT fit and trying to carry on. Major Hunt O.C. Camp but under medical dictatorship advisedly so. Captain E.R. Howells O.C. Bn., Reg Swartz 2 i/c C.O., Adjutant Eaton and Eales.

Lieut. J. Cooper

LOWER NEIKE – NEIKE H.Q.

May 15 '43: I had just arrived and I spoke to a group of men, they looked exhausted and in a state of shock. I enquired what had happened and was told cholera had broken out.

It was now just on dark, the camp was situated in a horseshoe shaped valley surrounded by hills on three sides, there was a layer of low cloud with smoke below. Up on the canopy of the jungle the birds and animals seemed excited about the activity below.

I had not suffered the 300 kms. march; for the first time I noticed the gaunt expressions of the men with that soon to be common, far away look …

I learned Captain John Taylor, A.A.M.C., 2/30 Bn., had been up the previous night worrying and going through his book on tropical diseases and had announced he had diagnosed two cases of cholera. Here in what was a skeleton of a camp with only a small section of the huts with a roof Sgt. Gordon Nicholl, 2/3 MAC, Senior Medical Orderly with Sgt. Alan Buttenshaw, had just arrived.

Gordon Nicholl:

"We were in the Advance party, Pat Wolfe was with us also, and we arrived to find that the huts were incomplete, no roofs or wall, just the bare flooring, so Alan Buttenshaw and I put ground sheets over the flooring part and slept on the ground underneath. This gave us some shelter from the continuous rain for the monsoon season had just commenced. We had only been there two or three days when the first outbreak of cholera took place, there was a young fellow who could speak Japanese and acted as interpreter, he died of cholera. The ration was very very poor and the fellows were very sick. There were only about 100 men reasonably fit, some of the men were unable to keep what meagre rations they were getting in their stomach and were puking them up, they just did not want to eat, Major Hunt ordered that these men be force-fed and he detailed fellows to make sure they were. When the sick men vomited up the food Major Hunt said, "Well catch it in the dixie and feed it back to them! that food is too valuable to waste, make them eat it!"

The road to Neike was impassable and no traffic was getting through from the south; ration parties were forced to walk to the main Japanese staging camp to draw rations. The terrain was a series of steep ridges and gullies. When I saw one of these parties struggling back through the mud I suggested to Cadet Officer Onishi a truck should be used with extra men to assist it through the bogs. He agreed with the suggestion. We took four hours to do the 4 kms, at times leaving the vehicle in low drive on its own while we kept on shoving small bamboo under the wheels to improve traction. On the return journey the added weight improved traction. Onishi anticipated trouble, at Neike he acquired a long, heavy rope and placed it on the truck, he was obviously considering getting back over the river by the camp.

When we reached there, just on dark, the river had risen; I walked into the water to estimate the depth and was confident I could drive across but Onishi said, "No! no!" and he ordered a guard to cross the river and pull all men out of the hospital to get on the end of the rope. Gordon Nicholl was in the camp and remembers Major Hunt strongly objecting to the men being pulled out. When they were placed on the end of the rope I was ordered to drive over – the bottom of the river was sound. I flashed on the lights and saw all these men wearing their ground sheets, their wet, white, gaunt faces I will never forget. Onishi had no mechanical knowledge at all and because of his stubborn attitude he created many problems.

Warrant Officer.I. Assistant Surgeon Pat Wolfe, Indian Medical Corps, reported:

"Arrived Lower Neike mid May. The following day cholera broke out and an isolation ward was immediately established. I worked in this ward until the arrival of two more medical officers. The next day, under orders from Lt.Col. Dillon, I and four nursing orderlies proceeded to Konkoita. On arrival there I saw a horrible scene. In one tent on the bank of the river fifteen patients were lying helpless, eight of these were suffering from cholera with nobody to attend them. The whole area was polluted with infectious stools and vomit, and full of flies. A report was made to the Japanese Medical Officer (Major) who removed us to the coolies' cholera camp. In spite of repeated requests, this officer refused to give any transport to move these patients to hospital. He also refused to give any drugs or adequate accommodation (most of us were left out in the rain). I treated these cases with M&B, $EmN0_4$, and saline by a transfusion set improvised from stetho-scope rubber and funnel. These drugs were soon exhausted and I sent an orderly with an urgent appeal for help to 2/29 Bn. A.I.F. camp at Taimonta, 7 miles away.

An officer was sent next day with necessary drugs etc. I then received orders from Col. Harris to proceed to Taimonta to relieve Captain Mills, MO, who was ill. I could not leave my patients and go to Taimonta, so I suggested that all of us, including patients, should go to Taimonta. The Japanese MO refused permission for the move.

"On 5 June '43 eventually after a great deal of representations from 2/29 Bn., I was told I could take all my patients to Taimonta. No transport was provided. I raised subscriptions amongst ourselves and promised to pay the hire of 2 or 3 bullock carts. This was refused. We improvised bamboo stretchers and carried 5 stretcher cases, two men carrying a stretcher. The rest of the patients had to struggle along somehow. It was impossible to carry the patients very far in the heavy rains and boggy roads. Lt.Col. Dillon had told me that on the authority of Colonel Banno, I would get all the necessary help at Konkoita from the Japanese hospital. The Japanese MO not only refused to give me any help but treated me most callously and only smiled when I remonstrated to him that we would all die there if we were not given drugs, help and transport. He did not seem to care. Fortunately, there were no sentries and we managed to get out of the camp area and hide ourselves in the jungle. I then sent an orderly to Taimonta with an appeal for help. The 2/29 Bn. immediately sent an officer and 50 men with stretchers and food and carried all our sick to their camp. L/Cpl. R. Somerfield and Pte. Bill Carlton of the A.A.M.C. gave great untiring and unselfish help under most exhausting and dreadful conditions.

"On my arrival at Taimonta I found the M.O., Captain Mills, sick and still working very hard. He was forced to go to bed and I carried out his duties. This unit was under great hardships, on half rations, and there were about 400 sick including cholera cases.

"After a week's stay here, I left with half 2/29 Bn. to Neike, Captain Mills remaining behind with patients and unfit men. This march was one of the worst I have experienced. I reported to Colonel Harris on my arrival at Lower Neike hospital and marched with Col. Harris and patients to Neike."

Lower Neike was a staging camp to look after those too ill to move and they remained in the care of medical orderlies who had volunteered to care for them. In June it was decided to evacuate the camp and carry the sick to Neike.

Neike was Force H.Q. Camp located on high ground and below on the river flat were two regulation huts – Cookhouse and Store – to house 1200 men. Above this camp on a drift sand ridge a couple of metres above was the H.Q. Camp where Colonel Banno and his staff were located; also a hut where POW Command was also present. The POW Camp was commanded by Lt.Col. Dillon who became the effective Commander of F Force.

Captain Hendry probably saw more of Colonel Banno than most medical officers and found him a gentleman. He retired from the Army and was recalled to duty when the war broke out, he often visited the camp and hospital. Colonel Harris was in the Administrative part of the camp and never was seen near the hospital or working areas. However he was seen by Colonel Banno walking with his arms behind his back and Colonel Banno told him to 'straighten his shoulders'!

Weather was overcast, misty rain, the men's boots were wet, falling apart and in many cases men did not have boots and ulcers became common. In the incessant rain the men were ordered out of the Long Hut to be paraded. Wearing old World War I rain capes draped over their shoulders and a great assortment of hats, the mainly English prisoners were addressed by Lt.Col. Dillon. He was angry and disgusted at the way the British had been stealing from each other and he told them, "You are a disgrace to the British Empire! your conduct cannot be condoned, this practice of stealing must cease!" A group of Australian prisoners cheered him after he spoke, the British officer was not accustomed to being cheered by Australians, often described as 'Colonials', and whatever his reply was to them it only encouraged them further ...

W.O.I. Asst.Surgeon Wolfe: "After a few days work in Neike hospital, cholera broke out again and I was detailed by Major Phillips, R.A.M.C., S.M.O., to be i/c of Cholera Isolation Hospital, three furlongs away from the main hospital. In addition to our troops, I was obliged to treat Burmese patients here. One incident here is worth mentioning: when under orders from Lt.Col. Dillon I objected to admitting Burmese coolies to our hospital, the Japanese threatened to hit me and gave me a long lecture about our "superiority complex", and about our being fed and paid by the Japanese Government and as such we have to obey and work for them. The little success I have had in treating cholera was I think due to the following treatment. Large saline transfusions (about 4 pints on the first day, 2 or 3 pints on subsequent days depending upon the condition of pulse, dehydration, vomiting, diarrhoea etc.) M&B tablets, $EmN0_4$ (weak solutions orally), cordise stimulants when necessary, plenty of fluids, rest, nursing etc.

"At the end of the cholera epidemic I worked a few days in the malaria ward at Neike."

I was selected by Lt. Yamata, the Adjutant, to drive to Moulmein in Burma in order to obtain medical supplies and lime; cholera was rife and the Japanese Administration was deeply concerned. The road was almost impassable and only the odd 'A' Force vehicle was getting through with supplies.

The Burmese had abandoned their yak carts and commenced the long walk home, the track was strewn with bodies left where they fell, small amounts of food were left on leaves near their mouths.

It was a very sad sight.

After entering Burma beyond the Pagoda Pass it was down hill all the way and when we arrived at the first obstacle the bog had been filled in with green bamboo – the bamboo rolled up under the vehicle and in no time an elephant was sent for. The mahout instructed me to start the engine which was contrary to normal practice but this bull elephant wouldn't work unless the motor was assisting. Once he heard the motor running he just leaned forward into the harness, rocked back and forth once or twice, loosened the vehicle from the bog and walked off away to high ground.

Some distance away was another bog but this time no elephant. Suffering from malaria, head pounding, I was praying for a miracle when a similar type vehicle fitted with winch equipment appeared – it was manned by an American from the USS HOUSTON, sunk in the Java Sea with the HMAS PERTH. I didn't have to ask for help and in no time the winch was hooked on and we headed for Moulmein. Between Thanbuyzayat and Moulmein I saw a never-to-be-forgotten scene – just on sundown – of an elephant train moving along a padi field bank, their trunks and tails linked together and all reflected in the still water of the padi field.

At Moulmein I drove past the local Masonic Hall – the same design as ones I had seen back home ...

After many calls, Lt. Yamata was only able to obtain lime and a large number of fibre mats with which we returned to Neike.

At this time we made room in our tent for Captain John Frew from 'K' Force – a medical party recruited at Changi to assist, I believe, the native forces in the area. Known as 'Jock' Frew, he was a very popular figure. Officers were not forced to work but Jock could not see his men struggling unloading barges – he always removed his epaullettes and helped the men, arriving back in the tent in darkness. We shared much of our scrounged food with Jock, he was a fantastic man, later to be knighted and become a well-known figure in Melbourne medical circles.

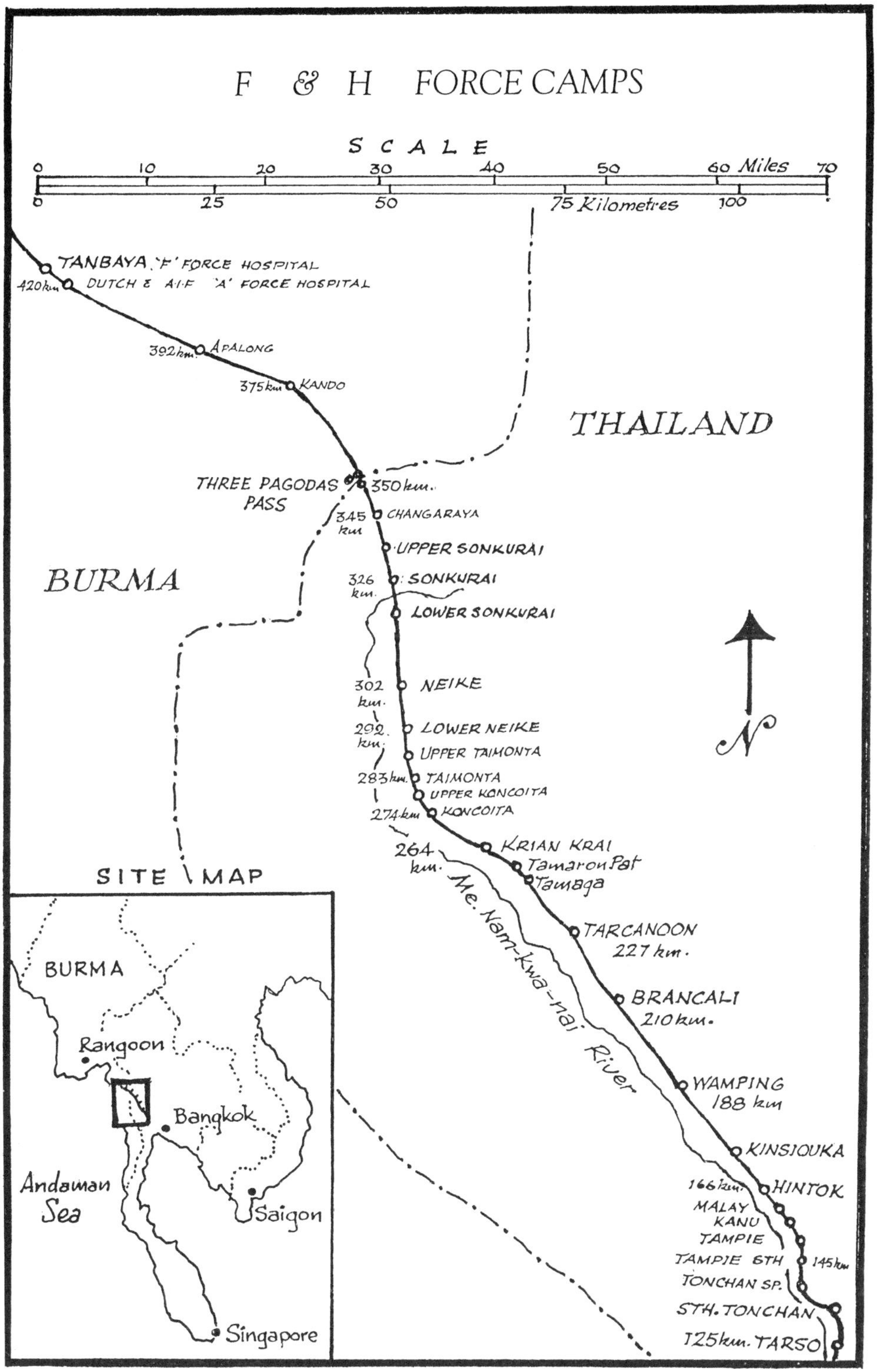
F & H FORCE CAMPS
SCALE
0 10 20 30 40 50 60 Miles 70
0 25 50 75 Kilometres 100
TANBAYA 'F' FORCE HOSPITAL
420km DUTCH & A.I.F 'A' FORCE HOSPITAL
392km APALONG
375km KANDO
THAILAND
THREE PAGODAS PASS
350km.
345 km CHANGARAYA
UPPER SONKURAI
BURMA
326 km. SONKURAI
LOWER SONKURAI
302 km. NEIKE
292 km. LOWER NEIKE
UPPER TAIMONTA
283km. TAIMONTA
UPPER KONCOITA
274km KONCOITA
264 km.
KRIAN KRAI
Tamaron Pat
Tamaga
Me. Nam-kwa-nai River
TARCANOON 227 km.
BRANCALI 210km.
WAMPING 188 km
KINSIOUKA
166 km. HINTOK
MALAY
KANU
TAMPIE
TAMPIE 6TH
145km
TONCHAN SP.
STH. TONCHAN
125km. TARSO
N
SITE MAP
BURMA
Rangoon
Bangkok
Andaman Sea
Saigon
Singapore

CHAPTER THREE
LOWER SONKURAI
JUNE – AUGUST 1943

Harry Weiss:

We have all been working in camp for two days, but over half the men are sick and the rest of us just dragging ourselves around. Deaths now total 51. Our CO is ill and Major Anderson malaria which made the Japanese think a bit more. Last night seven of our 30th Bn. men escaped, if it can be called escaping, as we are practically unguarded. Everyone wishes them well but I'm afraid the odds are better to take your chance with the cholera and whatever may lie ahead, although anything seems preferable to this present life. Still forced to do all washing of body and clothes in our own small mess gear with boiled water and this most most miserable and clothes and selves all smell. If we could only get a fine day our spirits would rise. The Q.Sgt. toasted rice and boiled coffee at 11 am, and it was a bright spot, also the zebu meat we had in the stew last night.

Eric Stone:

Cholera seems to have eased – maybe needles have taken. Only three deaths last night. Raining like hell. These monsoons seem to be starting properly. Seven of our unit went through yesterday morning. Sgt. McGregor, Ptes. Mawsley, Landow, Wilson, Franklin, James. See Capt. Taylor in night. He tells me I have malaria again also Mick. Tells me Alf did not stand a chance when the cholera hit him as he was so weak from illnesses.

Lieut. R. Eaton:

June 1: Complete re-organisation once more – this time along the only lines possible in these circumstances. The camp has now been divided in half. A block all Hospital and men too sick to work and Cholera Isolation Block. Figures are today: Cholera 104, Dysentery 576, Fever 180, Skin 76, Accidents 30, Respiratory 3, Beri Beri 2, Miscellaneous 8. Not diagnosed 1 = Total 950; larger than the AGH at Changi serving 15000 men has ever been – B. Hunt certifies that these men are all such as would be in AGH some for considerable periods. There are amoebic dysentery and malaria. Cholera admissions have been only 5 in 48 hours and B. Hunt considers that the epidemic is in hand. Deaths to date are 70. Sgt. Vic Barnes died today after long fight. Thank heavens the Old Man is not here to see the Greyhounds hit in this way. Japanese insisted on 500 work party today and cleaned out camp.

Wednesday 2 June – The new latrine, constructed of bamboo attap and having hewn squat hole timber opened yesterday. Today completed closing of old latrines – burned and sealed. The fly menace to decrease at once. 2 kitchens doing a good job. The fit men are one Battalion. Capt. E.R. Howells, C.O., Lieuts. Eaton and Eales, Joint Adjutants. Fence between areas and no traffic between even for mess orderlies. Lt.Col. Dillon and Colonel Banno passed through yesterday on way to Japanese HQ. Reports everything OK back further, but next camp neck and neck with us. Some definite results should come of this – atebrin to key officers. Whole camp now clean. All mess gear sterilised before and after meals in boiling water over fire. The only water used for dixie washing is boiled water. Whole camp now covered/roofed. Continual rain makes whole place quagmire of mud. Damned uncomfortable. We hear many rumours and hope for the best. Japanese say all out of here by July. The rations continue to be bad – butter beans and onion water. No tea, sugar, salt, or any vitamins. Men in weak state generally. The loss of valuable cooking gear, looting of men's personal gear en route is insufferable. Medical stores lost and wasted. Disciplinary measures and Japanese control of march were definitely difficult. Japanese call for complete nominal roll of camp, typed and parade state by ranks – also all non-combatants. Major Bruce Hunt's staff at moment 192, including all the volunteer orderlies – response for whom has been grand. The escapees (all 2/30 Bn.) have not been heard of since leaving last Monday (31st May) S/Sgt. McGregor, Ptes. A.J. James, C.M. Wilson, M.L. Landow, J.A. Franklin, M.J. Maudsley. We have much yearnings for any sort of food with some weight in it, a little sugar and salt, vegetables and some good simple things. Bread would be a luxury. Hope to heaven there will be some chance soon. Fruit, coconut and banana there are none. Nothing grows near this God-forsaken spot. The Japanese orders are headed for POW and Coolies. Exactly the same conditions apply. We have learnt to appreciate all those little things of every day civilised life we yearn for. This life is uncivilised. This section of the Japanese nation is not civilised. I have learnt for the first time to fully appreciate family. What a holiday was Changi – where we had some of those little things – even peanuts.

Eric Stone:

2nd June – Hear of death of Vic Barnes. It seems but yesterday that we were working together. I hope I can get Alf's ashes sent to Changi and buried next to Dick's. I know he'd like that. Had a bad night last night in that I was dopey. Started 12 days course of quinine. Tablets 8 per day.

Harry Weiss:

Thursday 3 June '43 – Yesterday and today the Japanese worked us till 7.30 pm from 8.30 am and are we tired? This may go on for days. Sgt. Jack, too, was so badly bashed up for disobedience he had to go to "Campo" for medical attention and is in hospital. The MOs think the cholera under control, probably through the second injection now being effective. Less cases and milder, and only three deaths today and last night. The Japanese bought a few more zebu cattle for killers, but we won't see much of it. So far we have had two meat stews. Food is really terrible and no wonder three-quarters of the camp are sick.

Sgt. R.W. Jack:

"I was standing over knee deep in water shovelling gravel from the creek for the road surface, we were about 200 metres from the roadway and the gravel had to be carried in flat baskets strapped across two hand-poles by two men over very swampy ground.

"After two hours work on the baskets one of the men complained of very sore feet and I took over his job with Pte. V. Barrett. We did one trip and because my partner was elderly and not well we had to stop twice, each time the IJA guard yelled at us. For the next trip I asked the L/Cpl. to put smaller loads on the baskets as we were unable to carry them and as a result he doubled the loads and would not listen to my request. At that time a 'smoko' was called but we were ordered to keep on carrying. I refused to pick up the basket load and tried to point out how difficult it was but he immediately became a raving lunatic, picked up a heavy sharp-pointed shovel and forced me to lift the load. As we staggered across the swamp he followed us and, with all his force, struck me on both arms with the shovel about five times each arm and dealt several body blows. My arms lost their sense of feeling and swelled up considerably. I was forced to finish this load and also another one.

"I tried to reason with the Japanese soldier in charge of the party to let me get medical attention but was refused. I lay down and the L/Cpl. saw me and began to come towards me with murder on his face; the other men in the party, seeing his intention, closed in on him, causing the Japanese in charge to stop the L/Cpl. Lieut. Bill Douglas was with the working party and tried to intervene but he was knocked away and threatened with the point of the shovel.

"After half an hour the Japanese in charge gave permission for me to return to camp where Major Hunt and other MOs examined me. I was immediately admitted to hospital; my arms by this time were completely stiff with broken blood vessels, bruising and possible splintering of the bones above the elbow. It was six weeks before I recovered. Major Hunt furnished a report of the whole incident to Lieut. Fukuda."

Eric Stone:

> Bill in Con. with runs. Looks pretty thin on it. Had a talk with him this morning. Cliff Bayliss passed away today. Cholera seems to have eased nevertheless. Major Hunt does the rounds today (3rd June) and takes me off quinine. Case not yet diagnosed. Mick seems better today. Talk with Fred, Butch and Mick over old times.

Lieut. R. Eaton:

> Thursday 3rd June – Bruce Hunt, John Taylor and Lloyd Cahill should all receive highest Award for their wonderful unceasing efforts. They alone have saved this camp from almost complete destruction. Rain sets in, very heavy. 400 out to work under impossible conditions. The men have to work on road and railway embankments up to ankles and knees in mud, carrying earth on bags between poles for about 1.5 miles 12 hours per day. Cutting bamboo under same conditions plus damnable mosquitoes and flies. Inhuman to the highest degree because the result achieved is negligible. 4 more gone through – 3 AAOC and Pte. Golding, J.B. from 2/30.Bn. Cliff Bayliss ('I' Sect.) has passed away. Lloyd Cahill was doubtful even last night, and the fight lasted until about 1600 today. One more of the whitest men one could ever hope to meet. Lloyd Cahill has been down with malaria, as has John Taylor and Bruce Hunt and Frank Cahill carrying on. John Taylor was only down for a few days, he is now up and about again. Thin as a whipping post but full of life as ever.

Harry Weiss:

> Friday 4th June – Worked hard from 8.30 am till 7.30 pm and are we tired? Being constantly wet is gradually undermining the best of us but Japanese don't care. Woh! News – Col. Harris just arrived with the Japanese Colonel and we have tomorrow off. Troops are instructed to keep dry – what a laugh. Still it is said that these Japs have now received instructions to go easier on us and we earnestly hope they will.

Eric Stone:

> Sid Tyson, George Coote pass away today. Major Hunt came around today and told me I had debility. Feeling weak otherwise seem OK. Mick progressing nicely. Jack, Ken, Eric and Sid all seem to have runs badly.

Cholera eased. If only they would feed us properly.

Lieut. R. Eaton:

4 June Friday – Colonel Banno passed through on way to higher Jap HQ. Lt.Col.Dillon visited 2 camps north,, believe conditions on a par with here. Cessation of work for 2 days ordered. Glass rod tomorrow. General appreciation made by Jim Rutherford, Howells, Geikie and self consider that (!) severe reaction must soon take place when we have to explain the death of some 500 men in 2 weeks. Bad situation all through. More of this later – must mean the total evaluation of Force "F" as ineffective.

Harry Weiss:

Saturday 5 June – A day in, but I'm on a bamboo cutting party so that ends the dreamed of rest. Up to 9 am yesterday we have lost 84 men with cholera and I hear 3 died last night. These wet days, the sandflies worry you constantly and the big March flies drive you mad, but mosquitoes in camp are not too bad. How gladly I tick off each of these days and look forward to the start of each new month but things will brighten and one glad day we shall be free – and really contemplate a return to Australia and our loved ones. Can't imagine what that feeling will be like.

Eric Stone:

Captain Taylor around today again. He didn't have much to say. Major Hunt has been sent on to another camp further on where cholera is said to be out of hand. Cam Owens goes to cholera ward as suspect.

Lt.Col. F.J. Dillon, M.C.
Pic: Dr. W.J.E. Phillips

Lieut. R. Eaton:

Funeral C. Bayliss – a very fateful day. P. Jones reports back from village of Neike with some medical supplies and Dr. Frank Cahill – one chap has cholera badly. Major Hunt has gone forward 2 camps to put things straight – could be away 2 days. Hospital here is now 1280 – fit are only 630 and the change is different about 30 a day.

Harry Weiss:

Sunday 6 June – Have just

returned from church parade, which was spoiled by a shower of rain so that we had no message. Still I felt that everyone felt the power of prayer more than we ever have done and I'm grateful indeed to God, who alone could have helped us in this cholera outbreak. This epidemic is so well under control here now that Major Hunt, who was marvellous from the outset, has gone on to the next camp, where we hear that the English MOs cannot get the disease under control at all. Today we are all in camp again, so perhaps it is true that Col. Harris got a promise from the Japanese not to work us till we are properly fit.

Major Hunt was instructed by Col. Banno to visit the forward camp and advise on hygiene, sanitation and other matters of health. He found conditions deplorable at the British camp, No.5 Changaraya. Later he called on Sonkurai and spoke to the British SMO, Major Hanbury, who obviously resented Hunt's intrusion. They disagreed on the treatment of dysentery, Hanbury informed Hunt he had the medical position under control – this British camp was to have the highest losses.

Eric Stone:

6 June: Just realised it is my birthday. That's how things are. Never want to spend another one like this. Discharged from M.I.R. and back to Coy. Still feel weak. Max Cook – cholera. Bunk in with Abbie. Sneaked down to the creek for a wash and washed my clothes. We have been cut off from washing in the creek ever since we have been here so one doesn't feel dirty – much! I bet it would take a fleet of trucks to cart all the dirt away especially as we have no soap.

Capt. John Taylor, M.C.
Pic: Alex Dandie

Lieut. R. Eaton:

Church Parade. No tools issued because 2 saw blades broken Glass rod for hospital. No work. All fit men leave tomorrow – 250 only. Major Johnston still ill back from hospital but quite ineffective. Ferguson bashed. We study Bartholomew and think of plans. First Church Parade cut by rain. Padre Polain, Padre Walsh disappointed. No work only collection of firewood and cleaning. Give men 1 days rest much needed and appreciated. Major

Tracey in charge of hospital area from Admin. side – expansion daily. Wards controlled by Officers – now 11 wards and complete hospital organisation. Another tribute to B. Hunt.

Harry Weiss:

Monday 7 June: What optimism – we went to work alright – 11 hours of it in the rain and up to our waists getting gravel from the stream. Other chaps had to carry gravel 500 yards across the slushy paddy fields to the roads. There will be soon no fit men for the Japanese to work. Only 200 out of 1800 now and we will be required to look after the sick. This malaria unfortunately is the malignant type and may prove fatal. Poor Al. Cox, who gave me tea along the road, died today and it did cast a gloom over us.

Eric Stone:

Cracked a good job. Cpl. of wood party. Hope I can cling on to this until I get better as I am very weak. (7 June) Saw chaps feet sticking out of fire. Japanese send boys to work. About 250 out of 2000 fit.

Lieut. R. Eaton:

7 June – Major Johnston back to hospital – nervous dyspepsia – not well and obviously needs rest. E.R. Howells takes place and there is not very much one can do. 300 men sent to work today and only on the road – the object being to make them passable for ration supply purposes – absolutely nothing being achieved by perpetuation of this Force –

Harry Weiss:

Tuesday 8 June – Three deaths of cholera yesterday, one of heart. Cholera is less worrying now, but fevers are on the up. I am now clerk in Hospital Ward II so was pleased to work hard in a new ward, but at least I'm dry. We started this fever ward with 13 cases and ended tonight with 68.

Eric Stone:

Work on cross cut saw for first time. It is useless to try and explain my disgust for these yellow animals. Men have now been passing us every day hauling carts. They are certainly buggered – mere animals. Have to walk two miles out with party of 70 and pull large truck out of mud. Takes us about three hours. They would have made us carry the rice back otherwise.

Lieut. R. Eaton:

A yak promised today – we now have 39 yaks tethered and that may seem a lot – 3 are killed at intervals of 4 to 7 days allowing one piece the size of a shilling per man. At least 3 yaks die per week and the animals are simply skin and bone – no more – in addition the Japanese take a good proportion of each kill – 4 men with Stan Arneil sent to Neike for medical supplies – weather bad.

Harry Weiss:

Wednesday 9 June – One cholera death last night. Bob Surtees is very bad. The roads are so bad that rations are not getting through but we did enjoy a yak stew for tea. Fifty of our best men have to set out with 5 yak carts to the nearest depot to pull rations and these carts are heavy and the road indescribable. Every day it rains and every night, but mosquitoes are not bad and one wonders how the malaria is contracted. We are trying to build bamboo corduroy tracks everywhere, but everyone is sick or busy. Three fires have to be kept burning in each hut. All water has to be boiled and boiling water ready for sterilising mess gear before each meal, which all means a lot of firewood. All the roofs have slipped and leak. A couple of drivers from camps up Pagoda Pass gave us a little information about 'A' Force and other news. The men arrived back with the carts and had a very strenuous time.

Eric Stone:

9 June: Japanese grabbed 50 men from camp and make them pull yak carts for rations in mud waist high at times. Boys arrived back footsore and weary. I cut wood all day and saw. The boys will never forget this slavery.

George Castle:

I am down to 11 stone in weight so no one at home would know me. Major Hunt is keeping up the good work and has got all work outside cancelled until the camp is put in order. We now have roofs on the huts and latrines have been erected as the hygiene is considerably improved although still not 100%. 50 men detailed to draw rations in a yak cart about as heavy as a dray about 12 miles daily. Food is now disgraceful as we get only 6 oz. of rice per day and very weak fish water now and again a few hard beans or towgay.

Lieut. R. Eaton:

Cholera 157, Fever 23, Respiratory 3, Dysentery 427, Malaria 493, Beri Beri 7, Skin 48, Accidents 1, Mixed 11 = 1170. These figures speak for themselves. Deaths now 93. There have been 2 last 2 days malaria or weakness. One has to watch ones fellows being carried out on pieces of bamboo with that horrifying appearance never to be forgotten. One becomes hardened to these sights of cruelty results.

220 work yesterday 150 today. At 1500 hrs. order 50 men to go to BR camp 17 kilos march to bring back rations in yak carts. The 10 men to a cart was ridiculous in the extreme as these fellows had to pull the things over roads that were impassable to trucks (Marmons). 2 men sent to Neike to get oil for broken down truck. Absolutely no organisation. The ration party changed to go to Neike instead. These people simply don't know what they are doing and meantime 7000 persons who are still British Best are being

quickly weakened to a point of desperation. Of those 7000 men only 1000 are still fit. The situation is serious – cholera is in hand here but rife in next two camps. British camp 120 deaths out of 200 cases and they had 5 days less than us –

Harry Weiss:

Thursday 10 June – Our ward patients reached 115 this morning and I am waiting on more now. My beri beri is worse so I am on double issue of stew and the envy of many. Most of our fever cases are not too bad and many can still eat well. Another yak party left for Neike camp again today.

Eric Stone:

Had a dry day for the first time in weeks. Gee it was great to see the sun or Sol as the bushies call it. Mac has fever and is trying to throw it without going into hospital but everybody is getting it so we may as well be in fashion. Nobody will ever realise how much Alf's death hurt me. Greater love hath no man for his brother but there is nothing we can do about it.

Lieut. R. Eaton:

'A' Force arrives – tell us of news of their Force being 30 kms north. Cholera starting there too – death rate over 12 months has been 2.5% – not over high. They are being well treated in so far as they have a Canteen at their base camp where practically anything can be purchased in way of food. The ration here is half as good. Onions enough for juice only – about 12 butter beans or black beans – a merest taste of salt and a gravy of salt fish mostly bad – any one of these additions to make the meals. These men cannot live on this diet. There are no vitamins in it. Deficiency diseases which were rife even in Changi are now prevalent and there is no immediate prospect of relief from this situation.

Eric Stone:

11 June – Spent all day on cross cut saw. Well up on kitchen wood now. Mac and I still bunking together. He's a great scout truly the whitest man I know. One lives day by day. Only 80 men went out to work today and 70 on yak carts to haul food again. The yaks the Japanese gave us are dying off fast. Have to run butcher down to kill them while they are still alive. Talk of home with Abbie.

Lieut. R. Eaton:

Friday 11 June '43 – Stirred by the good oil – I believe 'em all – the Marmon truck attached to this camp which should be getting the damn rations of which we now have 2.5 days supply has seized owing to lack of oil and broken rings. Dick Tompson trying hard to get through to the right places – again 50 men to the next camp for rations and 80 men to work – slight improvement in food situation, now have a four daily issue. Control

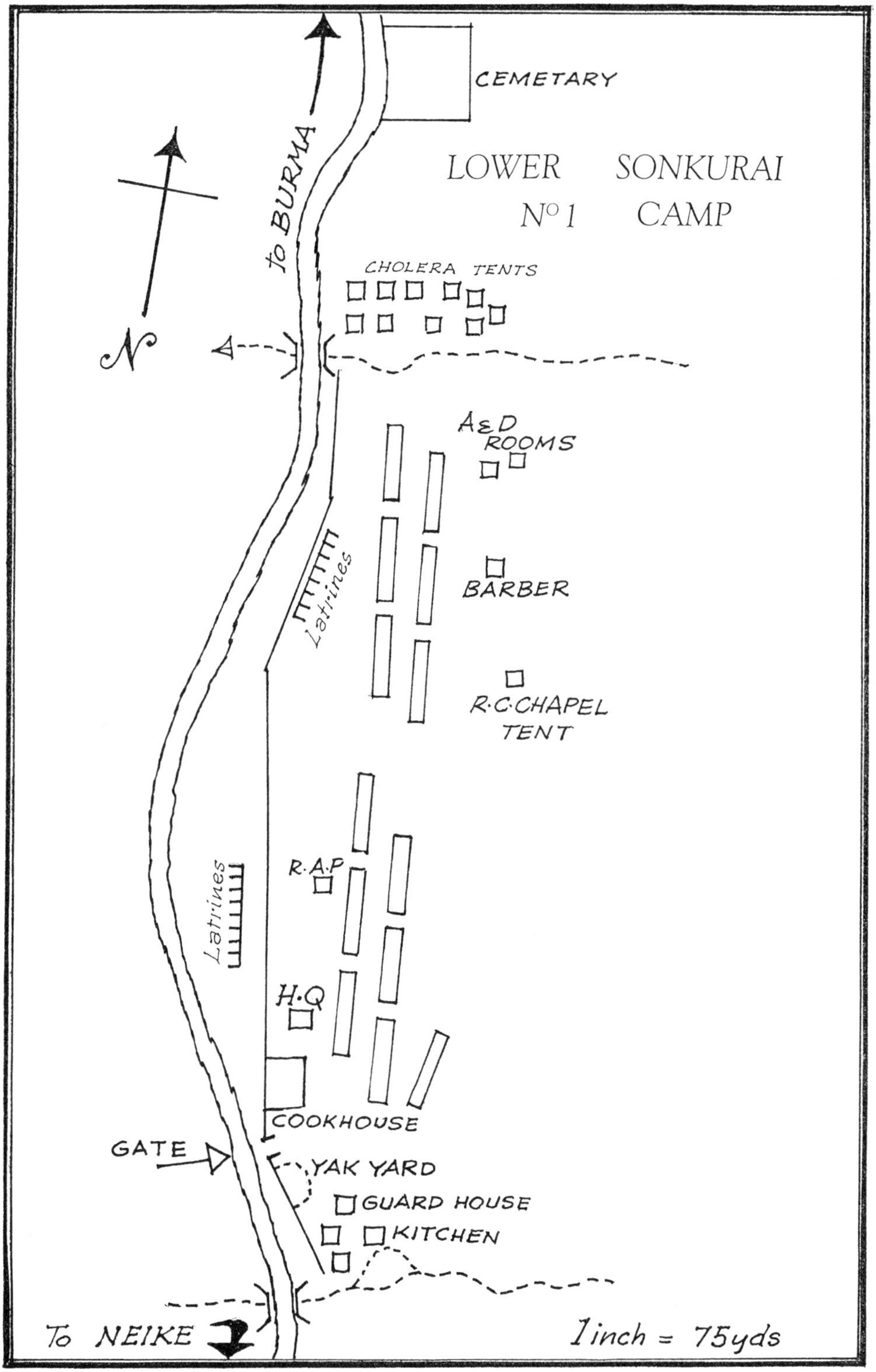
CEMETARY
LOWER SONKURAI
N° 1 CAMP
to BURMA
N
CHOLERA TENTS
A&D
ROOMS
Latrines
BARBER
R·C·CHAPEL
TENT
R·A·P
Latrines
H·Q
COOKHOUSE
GATE
YAK YARD
GUARD HOUSE
KITCHEN
To NEIKE
1inch = 75yds

of camp now vested in Major Bruce Hunt – Tracey – Howells – Rutherford we have discussed today the problems and need for building a Chapel and have the direct symbol of all it means in our midst and also the work necessary on our cemetery which must be left in as permanent a state as possible with the large cross in the dedication crematorium. Ground and the whole area to be cleared and lined crosses for graves with names and Nos. engraved and burned on them also the A.I.F. insignia over the gateway. W.O. Crawford has done a wonderful work in this regard.

Harry Weiss:

Saturday 12 June – Our deaths now total 101 since arrival. Had a small amount of yak stew for tea – it was tasty. My beri beri and sores are pretty bad, but I'm feeling much better and happier today and my hospital job and colleagues are all that could be desired.

Eric Stone:

Had argument with wood choppers in morning. Used cross cut all day. Rained all afternoon. All fit men had to go to work on road. Very few men left to work. All going down with malaria. More into hospital than coming out. Sacked off job as too many on kitchen staff.

Lieut. R. Eaton:

Major Hunt back to Neike for medical supplies. Went back with 3 Orderlies and then on to HQ Camp. Whacked knee cap in mud – roads impassable –

300 sick 2/29 HQ Camp 150 sick clearing out to Neike. Rations bloody. 6 oz. rice onion water 14 days cut off from Siam 40 trucks bogged to tailboards – bridges washed away – stayed away 2 days returned 13 June with stores Cpl. McCormick with oil for truck. Today Japanese Engineers called conference – P/Duties cut to half – 120 for Camp Hospital staff cut by 100 – Reason road has to be opened or we starve. Throws us into tail-spin. A good thing in one way only 80 sent out today and bugger-all achieved.

Harry Weiss:

Sunday 13 June – The Japanese are demanding more workers for the roads, so I should not have been surprised if I too had been put back on the active list, but am prepared for it any day now. See McNickle each day in the Dys. Ward but he is doing well.

Eric Stone:

Spent day on road. Just staggered in at night and flopped on bed. Drilled holes in rock with Bill Bailey all morning and carried baskets all afternoon full of rock. It is an effort to move my feet. Rained like hell but we just work in it. Remark – "You wouldn't work a dog in it".

Lieut. R. Eaton:

We have to co-operate or go down. Burma our only supply source. Raise 80 men for ration party to pull carts to Border camp and 200 for road by supreme cutting down and forced to use unfit men for camp duty. 50 cooks for 2000 men all in. F. Songenson died on 11 June. B. Hunt returns in time for discussions – we rely a lot on him – He commands this camp tells us that we have the best camp in line and is true. Pams birthday today – Many happy returns Sis.

Eric Stone:

14 June – Out to work again. Carrying baskets over paddy fields knee deep in mud. I crack up. My feet won't work. I receive light duty from M0 in night time. Left leg worse than right. We take over administration of road day after tomorrow. Food shortage acute. Japanese tell us we starve unless the road is kept open. I feel very weak and weary. Another party sent for food with yak carts. Have to travel 20 miles (about 300).

Lieut. R. Eaton:

Monday 14 June – The yaks go to Border camp. Bert Sabin, Dick Tompson – 9 officers 72 OR – 10 carts – return 0200 absolutely finished. 16 bags of rations – a good thing – we have 4 yaks – both last 2 days – wonderful to get a little taste of meat. The yaks collapse from exposure and then we kill them before they die. We hear George Ramsay 'A' Force is well – also Pryde – only 30 k up – spirits are good today – Special Mess – many laughs – Jim Cooper Mess orderly. M.O. Officers inspection – L.D. Diarrhoea and Geikie Beri Beri – given M&B – feel better but weak.

Eric Stone:

15 June – One day's light duty. Classed as beri beri. Cpl. McCormack passed away before my very eyes today with malaria – cerebral. This makes the second case of death out of three cases with same complaint. Saw Stuart Plowes out of 'A' Force today. He said Kreckler and Frenchy OK. On L/D sweeping up the hut.

Lieut. R. Eaton:

Cpl. McCormack passed away – had fever and slightly ill at 0900 lay down and suddenly went red and died in 10 mins. Malaria cerebral – a tragedy and one more white man gone everyone saddened. Rations now 9 ozs. for patients 15 ozs. for fit men. We have suggested to Japanese yesterday and Japs agreed would be possible to grant a trial. We to take section of road and do repairs in our own way and generally get the thing done. The result would be more work achieved and road opened quicker. Recce by Lt. Nin Gibson and Japanese Engineer Officer. They give us 100 yards and give us tools we require. We are delighted because whole thing depends on our result. We can get the men to work for us and get the road open – with Japanese over them they will not work. If success the whole future association will be good and whole situation improve. Work on railway is carried indefinitely. They have had their rations cut too. Permanent duties cut down to 220 for whole camp including Hospital.

Harry Weiss:

Wednesday 16 June – I'm still in Ward II, but we have lost all our hard workers to road work or malaria, and consequently apart from clerking, I'm wood getting, water carrying and mess helper. Now this should be in bold type – we have been on 9 ozs of rice since Sunday, and are we ravenous, but fortunately the butchers have been busy on the yaks and we have had some meat stews which greatly helped some to keep the pecker up. I should say that the yaks are so poor that as soon as one looks like passing out the butcher gets busy. The reason for the starving is that the roads are well nigh impassable and this camp is even favourably situated compared with those further south. We are advised now for our own sakes to do all we can go to work and help keep the road open. Today the Japs have been induced to give the Australians a free fling on the roads to do the jobs in their own way and we all hope that they will be satisfied with the result as these Japanese are woeful to work under .

Eric Stone:

16 June: On T./D again. Billie boiler – spend pretty hard day. On guard rations in night for two hours. Boys start on trial party of their own. Hope they do OK as will go under our own administration. MO very decent towards me.

Lieut. R. Eaton:

Gibsons party 5 Offrs 120 OR away OK – Job to corduroy about 100 yards of road to be completed 2 days. Completely under our control. Men very pleased this change and keen to work. 3 Offrs 110 OR under Japanese control. Further demand for more men on road. Japanese stress must be finished by 20 June to be open for supplies. Capt. Mudie passed through on way to Neike from British Camp. (Capt. Mudie and Capt. Knowles were the official operators of the secret wireless at No.2 Camp.)

Eric Stone:

17 June: Spoke to Japanese today who had been in Java. Given L/D but I tell MO that I will go out to work tomorrow. Japanese say that our officers are not to eat tomorrow. Spend day water boiling. Job finished – satisfactory.

Lieut. R. Eaton:

Gibson. 5 Offr. 120 OR. 11 to Burma 164 to Japanese. Discussion P. Duties hospital staff. Result approx. 220 OR. Duties total in addition and do Duty as required.

1600 hrs. Japanese QM – he had ordered to issue rations on scale. Men at work Offrs at work duties – all 600 grams. Patients & Offrs. No rations for day – Protests lodged – 1600 Fukuda left camp for No.2 with situation now that hospital would not be fed tomorrow also Offrs. Capt. Gibson party return 2130 hrs. task completed – Japanese engineers very pleased.

Eric Stone:

18 June – Officers not fed all day. Hospital light and N/D 6 ozs. for day. The situation is impossible. Something will happen at any time – it must. Went to work and knock off at 8.30. Just absolutely buggered. Job should bring lunch things back. Carry rock in afternoon.

Lieut. R. Eaton:

Conference sought with Engineers to point out success (of road building) and to request whole road work to be left to us our appreciation that only way road can be ready by 20th is to leave it to us plus 5 elephants – Japanese will never do it – ration threat effective – No Offr. eating except five going to work.

Harry Weiss:

Sat. 19 June – I came into Ward II yesterday with malaria, but feel fairly well today. The Japanese are turning it on these days kicking all fit men out to work and leaving the hospital to carry on with the best of the sick. Hospital patients receive 2 ozs rice a meal and a little stew. Yesterday the Japanese made all officers and officer patients starve. Of course men are collapsing on the job and returning straight to hospital.

Eric Stone:

In charge of party for day – 30 men. Have to keep moving around so that I do not have to work. Feel very tired in night. Ration light, one cup rice, little dipper of stew. Home 8.30 pm. Hours too long. They are killing us.

Harry Weiss:

Sunday 20 June – Had my worst attack from 4 pm yesterday, shivering and sweating and thank goodness, unable to eat. I'm afraid this record is nothing but a tale of woe these days and anyway I'm much steadier on my pins tonight and the camp truck is at last repaired and so far thank God little Bob Surtees is holding his own. Poor chap started with dysentery then got cholera, then black water fever and we all fear he will be left afflicted. To add to my troubles I have a great red lump on my foot, which is soft and so far the Doctor is leaving it alone.

Eric Stone:

20 June – Work on shovel filling baskets with rock in morning, Japanese slapping and pushing all day. They cannot keep rock up to us. Knock off

8.15. March back to camp. Long hours – little food – sickness – being driven all day. Heavy work. We just simply cannot keep going like this out of 1900 men 390 go to work. The others are sick or on permanent duty. Men come out of hospital, go straight to work and back into hospital in two days through terrific work. I have been without soap since about 10th May. I stink – so do our clothes. Tinea of the feet through mud is increasing.

21 June – Dig drains all day. My back nearly broken using little Japanese shovel. I can hardly straighten it. Work in wet clothes all day which happens every day. Japanese say we must keep ration parties going so we send 70 men every second day six miles to bring rice back. Home 9 pm. Rumour of move. Where and when ?

Harry Weiss:

Tuesday 22 June – Much better today. Fever seems to have left. Also the boil on my foot has come to a head. Japanese won't let the sick play cards or read now and prowl through the hospital trying to catch anyone who doesn't appear sick. Even here we are not free from the little yellow brutes.

Eric Stone:

Feel very weak and weary. Walk 5 kms to work. Job axe all day. Eight men carry logs which are too heavy for them. I cannot go on working as I can't raise axe much longer. Can scarcely drag myself home from work. Half hour for lunch, home at 8.30. How men stand up to it I do not know.

Harry Weiss:

23 June'43 – Feeling weak but more cheerful and my last day of treatment is tomorrow, then five days light duty, then work. My ulcers on the legs are very slow at healing up and I want them healed for work. I've been thinking of the short days at home now and the long nights and the fires and lovely food I used to think so little about. Our rations are still 2 oz. of rice a meal and a little stew of sorts, not even yak meat to help the last few days – dried fish and lima beans – but three yaks were killed today. Fortunately I'm not hungry yet. The sun will shine again.

Eric Stone:

23 June – Have to go on sick parade. My muscles feel as if they are all tingling. My head aches and I can scarcely stand up. Sent to M.I.R. with debility. Admitted. Do not know anyone in my bay. Meal for night, four spoons of rice, ladle of stew (e.g. rice water). See Fred and Jack. Look weak. Scotty to hospital.

24th June – Three spoonsful of rice today plus stew. Do not feel any better. Truck arrives back with food. MO gives me three days L/D. Tells me I want to cheer up. He doesn't realise it is only bodily I feel weak.

George Castle:

24 June – Little better today – Ben McFarlane came and cut my hair and shaved me so I feel a lot cleaner. No more deaths or admissions to cholera – food still the same.

Harry Weiss:

Friday 25 June – My first day off quinine – weak, but more fit. Now weight about 8 stone 7 lbs, the thinnest I've ever been in my life and I'm fat to many. Bob Surtees is in a good way to recovery, but to our great grief, Fred Breeze of our 13 Pn. died today of peritonitis – nothing could be done for him. Made a shirt out of bits of rag and a sea kit bag, and it will save my good shirt and be just the thing for work. The lads are all boiling edible leaves, herbs and roots, and for the second time the Japanese allowed a work party to kill a stray yak so some lads are more cheerful tonight tending their stews over small fires. Last few days are much finer.

Eric Stone:

Japs give us an extra ¾ bag rice which means that we have four spoonfuls today. Jack and I go out before breakfast, pick grass and pig weed to eat for lunch. Banana stalks also popular. Three years in Army today.

Chaplain Patrick Joseph Walsh.
Pic: Catholic Weekly

Lieut. R. Eaton:

25 June – Ration party Offrs. 25. Capt. Howells to 2 Camp for rations. 7 bags rice 5 klms. – Started 1330 Retd. 1900. Conditions No.2 Camp apathetic. Morale low. Increase to 7 bags for camp. More beans. Yak killed. Rumours rife for moves etc. Reports continue – weather fine.

Harry Weiss:

Saturday 26 June – This record certainly will not get such daily attention when I rejoin work parties. Even yesterday one party worked till 10 pm. Our rice issue is some grains more today, but the stews are very thin and watery.

Eric Stone:

3 spoonfuls rice for breakfast. 4 spoonfuls for dinner. Major Johnston took trip up north. Rumour of 1000 men to move very strong. Jack still has pains in stomach. I feel no stronger than when I came in. See Capt. Taylor today. He says it's just lack of food which is making me like this. Capt. Howells tells me he has a letter of Alf's. Bill feeling better after malaria.

Lieut. R. Eaton:

Fine – 321 to work – Maj. Johnston on ration truck Toyama to border for rations. Report in preparation by SMO for Maj. Johnston returned 0100 Truck left at No.2 Camp – rations 7 bags – slight increase – work 320 return 2100 – slightly better conditions in Japanese handling on road.

Harry Weiss:

Sunday 27 June – I've been shifted to Ward II, as the MO is not satisfied with so many sores on my legs and thinks they may turn to ulcers, some of which are almost frightening in this ward. Tucker is so light I can't hope to feel strong, but rations are expected to improve a little tomorrow.

Eric Stone:

Dish rice out now by little half pint mug. Capt. Taylor puts me on special backup, also three days N/D. Tells me he will run over my nerve centres later. Still feel as if I want to flop everywhere.

Lieut. R. Eaton:

Heavy rain then fine – work 320 – ration party 50 to leave for No.2 at 1300 – Increase in rations from 6½. 7 to 8 bags rice plus slight amelioration Beans Fish (whole meal) supply. Effect on troops most pleasing. Weather today bright sun and presents totally different complexion on life, the whole being fresher and better.

Harry Weiss:

28 June – The better I feel, the hungrier I get and its terrible to feel so

hungry. I could eat anything and everything and find it hard to think of things apart from food. Still, my fever has gone and legs almost better so I'll be out at work soon and get a bit of extra tucker. Even now the Japanese think the sick eat too much.

Eric Stone:

Jack and I spend our last dollar on 1 lb. yak meat. Make two weak stews. Make up menu for feed at Jack's place when we get home.

George Castle:

Rations rose slightly today – 3 extra spoons of rice. Ben McFarlane made some yak broth and brought to me, also Pete Hooper gave me a cup and few spoons of yak bought from the Thais. Very tasty. Another chap died here a few hours ago, been bad for some time with typhus. I feel slightly better but still have dysentery bad. Another fall over last night. Raining very hard as usual and our fellows out working in it without any covering outside a pair of shorts and some have shirts. A large number are barefooted but guards have all waterproof clothes.

Harry Weiss:

29 June – Last night we had a rice rissole with our meagre ration and did it taste good. Each night and day the lads have been catching stray zebus – killing and selling them around camp. They make a profit of over $100 from each beast which is understandable, seeing a little piece of meat for the cost of a dollar. Now an order has come out that all stray yaks will be dealt with by the butchers and it is illegal for anyone to be caught selling meat, as it will all go to the kitchens from now on. It is expected that shortly about 500 of the worst hospital cases will be moved to a large base hospital 80 miles north, near Moulmein, Burma, and I believe there is something in this as we had a special classification today and a Japanese came along looking at the worst cases.

Eric Stone:

29 June – Make up menu for night at Australia to be approved by Splinter. Feel just the same. 600 men put on list to move 30 miles into Burma. Jack and I put on it so far.

George Castle:

Much the same in health. Rations increased a little and tonight we had a doover extra that is fried rice flour and seasoning, 1st we've had, told it will be issued to 1 ward daily so that means get 1 every 11 days. Another Japanese inspection today by one of the Chiefs of the I.J.A. Some talk of sick men being removed to receive treatment.

Lieut. R. Eaton:

Japanese Doctor Tanio from Changi called with staff to give information and make prior arrangements for move of all sick men within certain classes up to Camp Base Hospital 80 km north from here. Major Anderson John Taylor to forward base camp to complete arrangements. Why Andy I can't say as he must be considered unfit – we expect subsequent move of all fit men work parties kept out till 2245 – strong protest made by Bob Howells to HQ.

Harry Weiss:

30 June – Half-yearly balance day in the old C.B.Coy. of Sydney Ltd. and here am I lying on back on a blanket in a leany, leaky, rickety hut in Western Siam, and how grateful I am for this long rest off road work. Last night the road workers reached camp at 10 pm, so I'm not looking forward to resuming the job.

Eric Stone:

So endeth June. Still feel very tired all day. Food is now the general conversation. Bill and I have good old yarn about camping. I don't know when this party will be moving out. Boys working harder than ever on road arriving home at 10 o'clock at night. Nobody can realise just how hard work here is.

Lieut. R. Eaton:

Fine weather – work parties 270 Ration party 50 – 17 Offrs. No Duties and L.Duty – damn shame to see unfit men go on duty like this. No job such as this for them – hard enough for fit men.

Lieut. R. Eaton:

1 July '43 – Lt.Col.Kappe arrived to take over command of camp. Major Anderson, John Taylor returned from north. Work parties returned at 2000. J. carries on. Request 2 men 24 hr basis to patrol camp.

Harry Weiss:

A new month and may it soon pass. My sores are looking much better and I await the MOs verdict. Clarrie Williamson went to work today and Allan McNickle thinks he may tomorrow, all of which makes me want to get out too. I boiled up greens yesterday (pig-weed) MO said it was OK, so I fed Bob Surtees some and he did enjoy it. They were lovely with ginger and peppercorns which Jack Haskins added. Poor Bob can't even lie on his side yet. I'm going to make him tea today.

Eric Stone:

Yak situation reached crisis tonight when six chaps were caught killing one by the Japanese. Bomb Happy – given slapping.

George Castle:

Slight improve today. Food still very light and am very hungry now. Heard other camp south have moved further down for food purposes. No deaths at their camp. Major Hunt and four orderlies went on a trip from here today. Hope they do some good for us. No further word of any move. Sold pair of crowns (badges) for 1 dollar today to buy something to eat, may get a cup of broth for it. Looks certain to spend 2nd birthday in captivity also 3rd in this god-forsaken hole.

George Castle
Pic: John Castle

Harry Weiss:

Friday 2 July – Six of the chaps from Convalescent Ward wandered down to the Thais zebu corral in broad daylight yesterday and slew a yak. Of course, they were caught and now we are to do without meat for a few days. Another chap knocked down a Thai tobacco vendor and took his goods. Yet another man (a Sergeant at that) was caught going through the worker's mess when he had already fed in the hospital, so we really had a bad day and this makes the Japanese worse to us, and shows how adversity makes animals of some men. After writing this I went to see Clarrie Wood and what should be his worry but of all nights he chose the last to buy the first yak meat he has ever bought. On top of this he has a relapse and wanted me to throw it out as we are not supposed to have it. As it happened, I saw officers cooking meat, so I took courage and cooked it among the bushes and am to share it for tea but we both agreed no more yak meat bought like that.

Eric Stone:

Allen Cameron stood up to attention all day because somebody stole a pick. Japanese are a nasty lot. I worked on pay books all day heading name camp Shimo Sonkurai. Wakened up at 3.30 in morning to be told that we did not eat again until pick and culprit had been handed over to Japanese.

Lieut. R. Eaton:

Capt. Burne hit by Toyama. Inspection of all lines for cooking of yak. 2230

Maj. Johnston sent for at HQ for extensive enquiry into missing pick. All Staff Offrs. called for – forced to squat on floor while Fukuda belted with words – result work party fed – sick fed and no Offrs. until pick found.

Harry Weiss:

Saturday 3 July – Two days ago a pickaxe disappeared from camp tools loaned by Japanese engineers. Yesterday they checked and found out and had the officer responsible stood to attention in front of the guard house all day. Last night they took a serious view of the loss and at 1 am all men were awakened and told if the pick were not produced by the morning, all men except those who did not work or were on the road on Tuesday would starve. This morning road workers fed, also our Ward and No.III – all others starved. They not only want the pick, but the man who took it. Just now the pick was found placed under the tool shed so we don't know how we stand. Now the hospital staff has all been herded into the staff hut and all other men except patients are confined. McNickle went to work for the first time yesterday and in the arvo. a stray yak came along so the Japanese said kill it and give us hind quarters and tongue. Each man got a piece of meat (35 men) and the rest went to the kitchen. Mc. gave me a piece and now as we cannot leave the ward, I'm having a lot of trouble to cook it. Another yak came along as they were leaving for camp and this the Japanese led in and put with their herd. No wonder the Thais resent the Japanese. At 4 pm the Japanese allowed all men to proceed as usual and those that have starved all day had a light meal and will have their tea as usual. Feel quite sure I shall be discharged tomorrow. I shared my meat with 4 others so didn't have too much and it was tough. Made Bob Surtees a cup of tea after 4 pm, and he still has a little tea left.

Eric Stone:

No breakfast (because of pick) for hospital and others. Only workers fed. However, they sneaked us a feed at 3 o'clock. The pick turned up about 11 o'clock. Japanese called it off about 4 o'clock. Men on road came home tired out.

George Castle:

2 o'clock this morning we were awakened and told we would receive no food until a pick which is missing is found. Was eventually found and took back at about 10 am but would give men no food until 4 pm. Allowed our ward and cholera and bed patients in other wards to eat so I had little but could not enjoy it knowing other men were hungry. Just got another tablet for my head aching that way. I think I'll go mad if it keeps up.

Lieut. R. Eaton:

Pick located at 1000 hrs – fast continued until 1700. All men confined to quarters under guard – 2 meals 2 hrs about 700 no less – nothing achieved by either side. Major Hunt returned from Neike with medical supplies and orders for Burma Hospital.

Harry Weiss:

Sunday 4 July – The men who starved yesterday received so much rice for tea that they could hardly get through it, so how can one understand these Japanese? All of us in hospital are becoming very thin, but I feel cheerful, and look like going to work. Unfortunately, the incessant rains are on again after a fortnight of light showers. An increasing amount of thieving is going on. I was moved to Ward 5 today, and hope for discharge tomorrow. Food in this ward is even lighter, and I am very hungry tonight. It's American Independence Day.

Eric Stone:

Had to interview Major Hunt. He asks me why I am weak. Jack not very well. Still starving. Food is the general conversation now. I spend a lot of time with Jack talking about food and camping.

George Castle:

Had very good night and have been alright today. Head is a lot better. Rations are still very light. Major came back with a fair supply of medical necessities. Things should change to the better soon.

Lieut. R. Eaton:

American Independence Day – so here's hoping it can't be long anyway – Men returned from work at 2245 having completed 200 metres of corduroy and gravelled surface under rainy conditions. Men driven all day and not given one minutes rest except lunch 1 hr. and in one party 4 hr. Whole party exhausted after 13 hour day messing in dark, bedded down 2400 for 7 hrs. rest – this set of conditions can only be described as ... the details are in fact beyond description. One does not want to describe or even dwell on the thing he wants to forget. I wonder how the men possibly keep up –

Harry Weiss:

Monday 5 July '43 – The workers did not get home till 11 pm last night, so I feel a little less anxious to get out today and will leave it in the hands of the MO. Exactly 49 days since we arrived in this beastly Sonkurai. It has been 7 weeks with few bright spots but we are thankful for the cholera outbreak being under control and for the Japanese leaving our hospital alone, thanks to Major Hunt. Next camp, north, the English troops are often turned out of hospital if the Japanese want more workers and we hear it is a pitiful sight. Even here yesterday the Japanese made 5 weak men carry a log one foot thick and 20 feet long and when one chap slacked and vomited, he was beaten. Ten men had to pull a loaded timber cart and when they stopped the Japanese whacked them just as they would oxen. The engineers here will stop at nothing and are furious that so many men are sick. Hence the light hospital rations, and so soon as one goes on light duty his ration is promptly cut.

Eric Stone:

Pommy Colonel and eight officers from camp No . 2 escape today. Japanese make us put 75 men on picquet so we won't escape. Boys still on late hours even as late at 10 . 30 . This is worse than slavery especially as food is so terrific! Boys do not get a chance. Talk with Jack about Minnamurra.

Lieut. R. Eaton:

Wet weather – heavy rain – 271 to work – ration party 50. Kappe still Hors de Combat or reportedly so – Rather amusing to see how the tall poppies have bent so easily and some others who having bent return to temporary straightness. Just another source of wonder.

Harry Weiss:

Tuesday 6 July – I am mess orderly today, and finding out how weak I am. As a result of the English officers' escape from No.2 camp, the Japanese have placed all other officers there in confinement and without food for five days. As a consequence too we have to build a tiger fence all round this camp in three days with convalescent labour, and the Japs patrolled around all last night.

Eric Stone:

I am starting to pick up again. Japanese give us three days to build tiger fence around camp, otherwise 600 sick men might not be moved. I hope I am on the party as I know I'll not last as a workman on the road in this condition i.e. I mean I'd be a frequent visitor to this hospital. Rations the same. Small half pint of rice, ladle of so called rice water stew.

Lieut. R. Eaton:

Work parties returned 2030 – slightly easier day. Cholera convalescents paraded work party from hospital.

Harry Weiss:

7 July – Think I'm trying to do too much and using up all energy on this small ration, as I've had two blackouts today. Have only one more day in hospital now and am a little worried about the hard work ahead.

Eric Stone:

Bill brought me a dixie of rice today. He comes to hospital again with fifth attack of malaria today. Japanese still moving out the camp, also working the boys until 10.30 which is terrific as they rise in the dark. I have an annoying feeling in left breast.

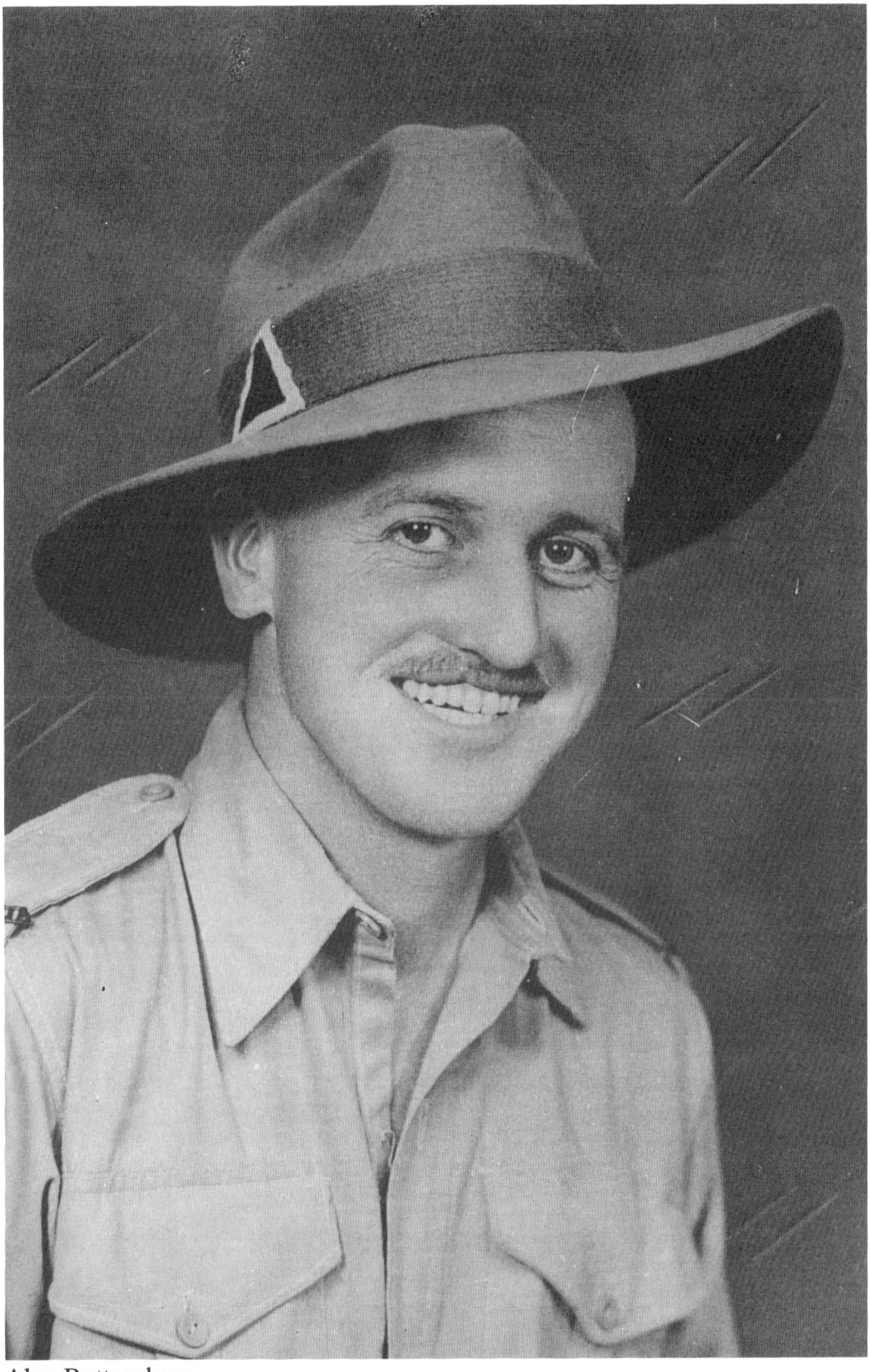

Alan Buttenshaw
Pic: Family

Dr. Lloyd Cahill:

"About this time I had to do an acute appendix at Lower Sonkurai. It was an interesting event – the man had peritonitis and if I didn't operate on his ruptured appendix he would just die. We got the little pot we boiled the rice in for breakfast, a few handkerchiefs to use as side towels and the dentist in the camp gave the anaesthetic; we got a green mosquito net to keep the flies out and we just put the patient on an ambulance stretcher over a few sticks of bamboo. I had few tools and it was going to be a hectic operation. We told the Japanese what was going to happen and they pissed off, they did not want to see us. But the man survived and all we could do after the operation was to nurse him the best we could and get him to sit up so the pus would go down – fortunately I had some M&B but that was all."

George Castle:

> Nothing to write yesterday only food was bad also 2 meals today but tonight had very good meal, cup of stew with a fair issue of yak meat. Rice still very light. Have not been too bad last few days but still have bad headache. Getting used to them now. Heard today 500 deaths on this F Force alone to date. Let's hope things change for the better. I try not to think of the kiddies of nights but my mind always wanders to them, still I know they're in good hands.

Harry Weiss:

> Thursday 8 July – Saw the MO and he has put me on three days more hospital so it is not mine to reason why. Rumour says that a statement by Knox says that all future war production of America will go to the far East. How I hope so, as we may get out of this awful life sooner. Also says the Japanese are being driven from Solomons.

Eric Stone:

> Have to go before Major Hunt today. He includes me in Burma party. Get pay book back – Jack has runs badly again. Talk with Bill about holiday also remember curried egg recipe which I gave Jack and he told me it was the best one I'd given him yet. Rumour of better rations tomorrow.

Harry Weiss:

> Friday 9 July – I'm to go to a new Con. Depot tomorrow and to eat 18 ozs rice instead of 10 per day, which is expected, under Japanese inspiration, to fit me for work in three days and I do hope so as I grow weaker and thinner daily. Hospital rations have gone up two ozs a day to 12 ozs too. Eight men were caught thieving rice in their water bottles on the rice carrying party yesterday. This party goes daily to the next camp north and carries about 60 to 70 lbs of rice per man, and the thieving is hard to control. The names of the culprits were read out to all and they were also paraded. The party of

sick men for Burma has been warned(includes Clarrie Wood) but they don't expect to make an early departure. It will be wonderful to get the very old and sick men out of this awful spot. One of our work parties unloaded A.A. guns and ammo. from the river barges at Neike yesterday reaching home at 1 am which is a sin. Another party failed to come home at all and we think were made to spend the night at a village at Neike.

Eric Stone:

Rations only a shade better as far as rice is concerned. A11 day job on hut – absolutely buggered. Left breast bone still worrying me. One chap expressed the road as "In here, it's heaven, out there – hell, and it's hard in here". Rumour Burma party off. More Japanese arrive in our camp.

Lieut. R. Eaton:

Lieut. Tanio returned from recce north Japanese HQ Moulmein. Proposal move of sick cancelled indefinitely – no move until after wet season end of August. Two and a half cases of quinine delivered at Camp plus half a case vitamin tablets. Disappointed at move falling through – meant more to this force than any other thing.

Harry Weiss:

Saturday 10 July – Con. Depot is much better fed and I feel a new man already. Had to spend the day sorting good onions from rotten ones. More than half are rotten, yet the Japanese count every bag as good 'makan' (food). I'm marked three days light duty. Bad luck the hospital Burma party is cancelled. The driver who brought back the Japanese MO said that a bombing raid was experienced at Moulmein – planes too high to see.

Eric Stone:

Japanese promise us better rations if Burma party cancelled. Go before MO with chest. He tells me my heart O.K. More Japanese arrive at our camp – now 80 guarding us (1900) which is most ever since being POW. The ration is between ours and the road ration. Off preference backup list. Hope things are moving. Boys still working like hell outside. Do not feel so well today. See Bruce and Jack.

Lieut. R. Eaton:

Work 208, Ration 50 3 Offrs. Con Depot 150 – Dean Wardmaster. No sick in Coy. lines. Conference Lt.Col. Kappe, Johnston, Japanese. Japanese ask for more money to be recalled from officers. Alas I have never had any. No buying party.

Harry Weiss:

Sunday 11 July – I had to do MP duties all last night, but as I had so much rice for tea, felt quite strong. The Japanese regard the recent escaping of prisoners very seriously, and told us last night that for every man who escapes now a man in camp will be shot. Our chaps are forced to build and dig gun pits and A.R. shelters at Neike these days and hardly ever reach home before midnight. This afternoon I did 2 hours of light rice handling and carried a load of dead bamboo into camp. Bamboo is cleaned out in an area of about half a mile all round the camp.

Eric Stone:

On wood job. Feel very weak and as if I'm getting a cold. Slight temperature and headache. Talk with Jack Buckham most of the afternoon about work, clothes etc. He comes from 15 miles outside of Moree. 1450 men now in hospital. My hips are so sore I can hardly lie on them through bamboo. Receive Alf's diary back from C Coy. chap.

Lieut. R. Eaton:

2200 – Address by Lt.Col. Kappe and Maj. Johnston to all Offrs. General blah excuses for Senior Officers –

Harry Weiss:

Monday 12 July – Did a hard days work and feel well. Saw the MO tonight, so I'm off to Bn. tomorrow and work the day following. Had a good tea tonight, which should help me on my way.

Eric Stone:

Looks as if Burma trip definitely off as Burma party can now be discharged for road. Still don't feel the best. Jack comes up and we talk of holidays at Katoomba and about cars. Talk of decent knocking off hours outside. Our food in hospital a little better although we are still hungry and the vitamins are totally inadequate. Jack's idea of flat for honeymoon seems 100%.

Lieut. R. Eaton:

220 to road work – no ration party. Have decided small small men have small ideas. That lack was one long excuse for all that has gone before.

Harry Weiss:

Tuesday 13 July – The Japanese insisted on a ration party and ten of us from the Con. Depot had to make up the number required. The MO granted us another 24 hours in the Con. Depot as a result. It was quite an enjoyable 9 kms walk to the next camp, although the roads are a quagmire at the English end, but coming home with 1/3 bag of onions on the back was very strenuous and my muscles are very sore tonight. We have had extra rations all day and I feel well fed but the exertion has given me bad diarrhoea. The English have not done nearly as good a job on the road as we have, and they have elephants and a tractor to aid them.

Eric Stone:

No news at all today. Do not feel extra well. Talk with chap from 26th Chatworth on money making. He tells me that he considers a Pie Run as the best money making concern. I believe they operate in Qld. Talk with Jack also Bill who has some good recipes. Meals still light. Vitamins none.

Lieut. R. Eaton:

Work road 220 – Ration 30 – Self and Geikie are punched.

Harry Weiss:

14 July – A hard day's work and drafted to Bn. at 7 pm. Feel I have at last shaken the hospital atmosphere off and only hope that I can stick to the road work. So many go out for a few days and then back to hospital.

Eric Stone:

Had to see M0 today. I move to Con Dept as soon as vacancy occurs. Japs putting on more lousy acts on road. Food very light today. Talk to Bill and Jack Greenwood. Rumour we go back to Changi about September. Hope it's right.

Lieut. R. Eaton:

0500 sugar matches tobacco to be purchased by Japanese and carried home by work party.

Eric Stone:

15 July – Moved to Con Dept and given 24 hours A class duty by Capt. Taylor. Feeling weak but much better. Food very light. 16 July – Given job by Mr. Couch (the Div. killer) carting tents back to Japanese. (Lord only knows how many are missing. The boys have been cutting them up – also Japanese blankets. But the cholera is a good blind for that). Have bad night and day with side. 24 hours Class A again. Major Hunt's lecture tells Japanese have come into open, say Hague Convention means nothing to them – that they are prepared to die if necessary and POW will do the same if necessary.

Lieut. Norm Couch
Pic: E. Couch

17 July: Whatever was under my rib burst with relief today. Work carting wood for Jap kitchen – sweet beans. Given 24 hours then discharge from Con Dept.

18 July: Had to go out on road. Cart wood to Japanese kitchen in morning. Carry mess afternoon then on pick and shovel getting road ready for corduroy. Got my first hit for dropping Japanese dixies. Discharged from Con Dept.

Lieut. R. Eaton:

18 July – Ration party again and Geikie and I are punched to boards B. awful road – load very heavy – we are very tired – clothes soaked mud to knees. Some people getting fat – don't know how wonder why – whats the use! Fear will not see home again – it's all a bad show. Geikie and I probably next to go – have put up outline of plan for some co-ordination in this area to Johnston for passing on to Kappe and Harris – but not registered – a great pity because it is so necessary.

On 19 July 1943 the Commander of F Force wrote the following letter to Colonel Banno:

"Sir,

I have the honour to inform you that yesterday I was told by Lieut. Yamada that some British officers had been arrested for escape, that they would probably be condemned to death and that I must hold myself in readiness to witness their execution.

If this is so, then as senior British Officer and therefore the representative of the British Government on the spot, I wish to make a formal appeal to the Imperial Japanese Government (on behalf of the British Government) not to exact the death penalty.

While I have no information as to the reasons that impelled those officers to escape, the basis of this appeal is:

(a) It is contrary to the Laws and Useages of War to exact the death penalty from prisoners of war who escape, nor is capital punishment imposed by other Great Powers.

(b) There is a feeling of despair among some officers at their continued inability to mitigate the severe and unprecedented hardships of the men of whom they have been put in command by the Imperial Japanese Army. These hardships have already caused in the space of three months the deaths of over 600 men and sickness of 90% out of this force of 7,000 men. I have no doubt that this feeling of responsibility weighed heavily on the minds of these officers. In the meantime I urge that immediate action be taken to postpone execution until such time as a reply to this appeal is received."

Harry Weiss:

19 July: My first chance to record anything in daylight, but I haven't had a bad time really. I worked hard on Thursday carrying timber – in for tea at 9 pm. Friday worked on hammer and drill (for blasting) and got sore hands – tea at 2100 pm Saturday, a much easier day. Sunday, in the quarry breaking stone – tea at 10 pm. Today ration party carrying 60 lbs rice my feet very wore. We were knocked off at 8 pm – very early but as we are one hour's walk out it isn't too early. The Japanese treatment is indescribable and I'm sure no one in Australia could credit it. So far I have been hit on the head with an axe handle and an iron drill, and bashed with a shovel, but I'm lucky.

Eric Stone:

Dave Tate and Denny had to hold rock; chaps and logs. Home at 10.30. Terrible day carrying rocks over corduroy!

Lieut. R. Eaton:

We have break today and called to do Hygiene work I am writing the diary and Geike is working out some personal problem. Some men are low, very low. Kappe has choice so have I but not in the same place.

Dick Tompson looking better these days so has J. Rutherford.

Wal Southwick

Herbert Shields, 10 AGH
Pic: W. Southwick

Harry Weiss:

Tuesday 20 July – A job still further away – I carried logs all day. The Japanese say two to a log or six to a log, or whatever they think and bash you till you somehow managed to get on the shoulder and stagger across bamboo, etc., sometimes a quarter of a mile to the road. If you have to rest they are at you again. Working under them is real hell. Had our tea at 11 pm.

Eric Stone:

Carry logs all day that an elephant would jack up on. Shoulders sore as hell. Stomach sore. Home at 9 o'clock.

Harry Weiss:

21 July '43 – Worked on the same job, but with picks and shovels and the Japanese were not so bad, except five of us had to get on "the hands down" for a quarter hour for something, and every time knees touch ground came a smack from a shovel. I felt pretty tired after that lot. Another chap had to hold a crowbar above his head. However, as we had to carry all tools in, we left the job at 7 pm and had our tea by 9 pm.

Eric Stone:

Home in daylight. Oh boy isn't it good. I have washed all my clothes. We completed a corduroy job 35 yards long before dinner. Dug drains all the afternoon. Feet starting to get sore. Am feeling well. Tate made to hold iron bar for one and a half hours.

Lieut. R. Eaton:

Have done 7 Ration parties on 10 days back breaking business – boots worn through – a good show – work commenced on railway.

Harry Weiss:

22 July – Worked close to camp, but carrying gravel half a mile across the boggy paddy fields was no chop – 11 hours of it. One Japanese said 'no speedo' to my fellow carrier and self, and the next thing I copped a woeful crack on the back of the neck, so did poor Bunny. It was so hard that water gushed out of my nose, and I've got a bump like an egg. We had a Sergeant in charge of the party, and at lunch they beat him up badly for supposed disobedience.

Eric Stone:

Start building railway again today. Given an impossible job to do. Rains like hell all day. Cold as hell, shivering. Did not finish until 9.30. Mud and slush everywhere.

Harry Weiss:

23 July Friday – A similar job, and I can hardly walk with beri beri, but we

have three good Japanese with us. Came home and went on sick parade, and was sent to hospital again. It is fairly reliable news that 500 sick men are to proceed to No.3 Camp in a few days – I look like missing out.

Eric Stone:

Work all day in creek dragging gravel out then have to carry it about 600 yards in chunkas along the road. Finish at 7.30. Very tired. See four of our chaps having to grovel before Japanese Cpl. Makes me sick in stomach – just for emptying basket in the wrong place.

Alf Staff, 10 AGH
Pic: W. Southwick

Lieut. R. Eaton:

Have malaria rather bad dose – admitted hospital have dysentery also feel poorly – Ron Maston Dick Tompson have same. News of move of 500 to 3 Camp. Kappe to go, Natives come on here. Boy this quinine knocks me.

Harry Weiss:

24 July – It was wonderful lying in bed at reveille, I'm to transfer to Ward III for special treatment today. I am placed on special diet and had a stew full of tripe, liver, heart and brains not much, but it's beautiful twice a day.

Eric Stone:

On railway clearing. Good job with axe but rains all day. So cold and miserable. Told that I am on party to go 15 kms further north. 500 men. Bill from hospital to make party.

Lieut. R. Eaton:

Still hot and cold feel anyhow most of time. Strange malady malaria. Takes all ones strength – hell of a headache – no appetite – 7 tabs. quinine takes all ones resources, makes very hard to think clearly – losing weight fast.

Major Bruce Hunt recorded:

"Major Phillips was to have accompanied Lieut. Tanio forward to other camps, but as he fell suddenly ill I arranged for Major Anderson (2/30 Bn.) and Capt. Taylor to accompany the Lieutenant and to make the necessary arrangements for him with forward camps.

"Lieut. Tanio returned from forward camps on 1st July and I then accompanied him to Neike learning en-route that the allotment of patients from No.1 camp was likely to be 750. Lieut. Tanio went forward again from Neike into Burma on 2nd July to inspect possible hospital sites.

"Immediately on return from Neike to Lower Sonkurai on 3rd July I commenced the classification of prospective Burma hospital patients. As it appeared likely that there would be an entirely inadequate allotment of fit men to do the routine camp work, I arranged for an appreciable proportion of semi-fit men to be included in the lists.

"Lists were practically complete when on 8th July, Lieut. Tanio again visited the camp on his return from Burma, and announced that the whole scheme was postponed indefinitely. Naturally the announcement produced much disappointment. However on 21st July we were informed that the scheme would go forward, but that the camp allotment was reduced to 500 – the total number of patients now being reduced to 1250.

"On 24th July I was suddenly informed that Lt.Col. Banno, with Lieut. Saito, prospective commandant of the Burma Hospital Camp, was proceeding forthwith to Burma to inspect the hospital site, and I was instructed to accompany him (at twenty minutes notice). This I did, spending 2 days at Tanbaya, situated 77 km NNW of Lower Sonkurai on the railway to Thanbuyzayat, where I made a thorough inspection of camp and environs, and returning to Lower Sonkurai on 28th July. I found that in my absence Capt. R.L. Cahill, despite an attack of catarrhal jaundice, had done a tremendous amount of work in preparation for the proposed move, and that arrangements were well in hand. I had been informed by Lieut. Saito that no move was likely for at least a week, but two days later I was suddenly summoned to the Japanese hut and informed that the advance party from No.1 camp (about twenty of us in all) must leave on foot within the hour. We had been informed a few days previously that the whole camp personnel would shortly be moved to No.3 Camp."

Harry Weiss:

> 25 July Sunday – Beri beri swellings much better, but tinea as sore as ever. It doesn't look as if the 500 lads will march out today. The Burma Party of 500 is on again, but they can't take the stretcher cases.

Eric Stone:

> Clearing railway towards Neike. Home at 8.30. Good job on parang. Feet very bad. Afraid I'll have to go on sick parade. Cannot hang out.
>
> 26 July – Sick parade. Admitted to hospital with bad feet. No.5 Ward. The starvation ward they call it. Talk all morning with Snowy who is also going

in with runs. Jack has another attack of malaria. News of 500 Burma party to move shortly.

George Castle:

Well, 37 again today, bad place to spend a birthday and also believe I am not on the Burma Party as number has been reduced and I improved for a few days. I am not feeling too well again now. The MOs have things well in hand now but still on rice. No birthday cake for me today but rice and yak soup. Working pay arrived in the camp and each man is to receive 1 piece of soap and some tobacco, 40 cts., 80 cts., about 2/2. All we have got in last 3 mths. Heard prisoners in Australia were receiving 14/9 a day where here the most we have got has been 15 cts., i.e. 4½d a day.

Lieut. R. Eaton:

Only 2/3 days left Major Hunt to Burma with Banno. 500 natives to come in here 500 to Burma 500 to 3 Camp Balance to ? Camp if possible. Rolls confusion. NO activity. Hospital site OK. Looks as if Johnston will have his Bn. split to 4 Wards?? without any consideration?? at all – Proportions of NCOs etc. not observed very carefully. We are impotent now and out of favour. Bad show. Weather improves – sunlight good – Bridge goes at No.2.

Eric Stone:

27 July – Given 24 hours L/D. Work all afternoon mending boots. Les Gallard kindly gave me a left one. What a windfall. Cooking Jack's rice for him to make it edible as he is off his tucker. Also sleeping with Andy Noble who lives in Bank. Martin Place. Given an issue of one cake of soap from Japanese. Talk with Bill who was building bridges all day about pie business.

Harry Weiss:

28 July Wednesday – I've been too sick to write for three days. Besides beri beri I've had a rotten malaria relapse and diarrhoea, but feel better. Beri beri is so much better visibly that I'm afraid I'll lose the special stews. The 500 men leave for No.3 Camp this morning, and we now learn that the whole camp is to follow, but it is only 7 or 8 mls. although all kitchen gear, etc. has to go on our backs. I don't suppose we will be left here long. Saw the sun – first time for days, but later the rains came again.

Eric Stone:

300 move out of Con. Dept to AIF camp 5 miles away. Jack glass rodded for Burma. I move to Con. Dept. Feet healing. Do all my mending. Given A. 24 hours.

Lieut. R. Eaton:

Party 300 from Con. Depot left to No.3 Camp under Lt. Col. Kappe. Bruce Hunt returns.Burma Hospital OK being built should move in 10 days –

4000 natives coming in here – all this Camp to No.3. How long O Lord How long –

Eric Stone:

29 July – Exactly two years since we sailed today. Sent out on road and work under new Japanese. Best day I've ever had in Thailand. On shovel. Home 7.30. Food very light – others building bridges.

Lieut. R. Eaton:

Persistent reports from Japanese that all POW move back to Changi end August beginning September – would be good thing. The fat gentlemen of Sin'pre seem to be in a spot of bother right now. There will be another shortly we hope. Things are definitely looking up. Geikie much improved – just a helpless big bear. Dick Tompson looking old 40 – he will be OK out of here. Jim still away.

Harry Weiss:

30 July – Our 500 sick for Burma are now standing by. The rest of this camp looks like 'staying put' for a while. The Japanese hinted to Major Hunt that they expect all AIF and British troops to have finished their job and be out of here and be back in Malaya by October. The railway track here is being rushed along. It is to carry very light motors. A small party left for Burma this afternoon.

Eric Stone:

Was to go out on road but one of lucky three who stayed in camp. Carted wood all day with Cec Plewes. Advance party for Burma went today with Major Hunt. Discover Alf's roneo diary in A&D Room, so try to get paraded to Major Johnston but he is out.

Harry Weiss:

31 July '43 Saturday – The end of another month, thank goodness, and we all wish it were the end of August, which is sure to prove a hard working one, the Japanese being determined to finish this railway at the earliest date.

Eric Stone:

Out to work on railway cutting – crew with ant bed. Very tired – too late to be paraded so to go first thing in morning. Bill to hospital with beri beri. 23 Sgts. to go on Burma party. Give Bill bamboo shoots to cook.

Lieut. R. Eaton:

Plenty to be done these days. 30 July Advance party including Major Hunt, Harry Riches, Don Garner, left for Burma Hospital. Remainder due to move 2 Aug. Weather continues excellent. Have permanent headache these days.

Harry Weiss:

Sunday 1 August '43 – My feet and legs still very swollen but body nearly normal today. I'm certainly missing a lot of work and won't deny I'm glad of it. I'm eating better again and feel quite cheerful and hopeful tonight.

Eric Stone:

Should only be another 30 days to do. Rained all morning. Discharged from Con. Dept and back to lines at 9.30 pm. As 216 of us move to Australian camp five miles away tomorrow, worked all day on embankment. Broke my heart. Paraded to Major Johnston – very unsatisfactory – in morning over Alf's diary in A&D Room. Spoke to me while he lay in bed behind mosquito net.

Harry Weiss:

2 August '43 Monday – Three hundred men left for No.3 Camp this morning and 200 for No.2 Camp this afternoon. I tried to get on No.3 Camp party as nearly all my pals were on it but my beri beri just happened to be bad then, McNickle, Williamson and Wood are all at No.3 now and I'm still hopeful of joining them soon. 130 men are still standing by for Burma. Our meals are very light and I'm hungry which shows I'm well again.

Eric Stone:

See Major Johnston. Nothing done re diary. Started on our way on mug of rice. The hardest, toughest journey I have ever done, carrying our sick. Only four men on a stretcher made of bamboo with all his gear – carrying our own and also a large Japanese mosquito net. The road is impossible to describe as it is knee deep in mud, straining our muscles. A nightmare.

Harry Weiss:

3 August – I'm on draft for No.2 Camp, unfortunately, and we are to have an early lunch and may leave early. Jim Pratt and Bill Wallace are with me so things could be worse and it seems I'm intended to go to No.2 Camp.

Eric Stone:

Poms also arrive yesterday just before us. Camp a mud pool. Food good to what we've had. More Poms arrive from Neike, Fever – temperature 102°. Terrible night. Go to hospital at 3 o'clock tomorrow. Good dry yak stew in night. Could not eat it all. Hut full of holes but hopes that it won't be for long. Make it bearable.

George Castle:

Yesterday morning we were given orders to move all hospital patients by foot. We moved 4 mile carrying stretcher cases. We are now camped with English who are losing 6 men per day. Hygiene is bad but there is plenty of food more than the cooks can cook with utensils available. They are very hard here re work as they take sick men from wards and work them as long as 16 hrs. per day. 500 more marched in today and we had no midday meal but were compensated with dry rice to cook for ourselves. Norman Nosworthy of our unit died morning of 2.8.43 also Col Phillips at Neike camp.

Harry Weiss:

4 August – Owing to rain our party for No.2 Camp postponed till 10 am today. Then after waiting, Jim Pratt and I were knocked off. Natives (500) have been in residence two days and already four have died of cholera. That makes us all want to get away, and unfortunately the Burma party is held up again.

Eric Stone:

Feel a little better today. Admitted to hospital. Japanese interpreter Toriama arrives from No.l Camp. Things will be crook here now. Back on my meals. Japanese start building on old railway again today.

Sid and Mick Porter

CHAPTER FOUR
NO. 3 CAMP – UPPER SONKURAI

Lieut. R. Eaton:

5 August '43 – Pulled out of hospital half hour notice to go with Geikie to No.3 Camp at 1430 with 30 ORs. Remainder camp to follow after Burma party leave. Considerate of Johnston to send Geikie and me together.

Harry Weiss:

I came on to No.3 Camp quite suddenly today and had to leave Jim Pratt and Bill Wallace behind. Had a very slow 12 km. trip carrying kitchen gear, etc. Found all my old friends here and slept with the Bn. after a big rice meal.

Eric Stone:

Blood type taken. Another 80 of our chaps arrived from No.l camp including Bill. He has malaria again. Tells me 18 deaths with cholera of the natives who moved into No.l already.

Harry Weiss:

6 August Friday – Had the day off, but went back to hospital at tea. I didn't object as the road and rail work is heavy here too.

Eric Stone:

Had bad night with fever last night. Received blood type BT. Bill in same ward with malaria. Three hashes a day. 120 of our chaps who were supposed to come here stopped on account of cholera.

Lieut. R. Eaton:

No contact by our people at all – John Taylor very worried about whole thing. Expect 3000 or 75% of natives to die. On arrival at No.3 Upper Sonkurai it was a sea of mud. Small camp not prepared for recent trebling in numbers. Lt.Col. Kappe completely despondent. Toyama and Fukuda doing just as they please. Reg Swartz doing hell of good job in fact doing everything. English abt. 650 had arrived from Neike and 5 Camp without any cooking containers or gear or medical gear and about 60% sick. Capt. Wilson, RAMC, Cross in hospital. Maj. Stevens, Capt. Juttner all fit men taken from camp for rail work – none allowed for setting camp in order. Hygiene inadequate and generally a bad show, whole camp in complete disorder. Obvious unless something done fairly fast there will be a tragedy here. Camp in two halves – English & Australian. English definitely showing nonchalance and antipathy. Separate English hospital and officers quarters. No excuse for rotten attitude of Kappe and Stevens toward the Pommies. They have no morale and want boosting a bit but only place it can is from Australian side. The kitchen which previously worked for 450 is still working for 1600 now. Hygiene there is appalling. Lt. Ray Tweedie working under terrific handicap. Scarcely any tools issued by Japanese Interpreter – Scotty Wroe – doing good job. In fact everyone works except tall poppies who do nothing. We feel bad about going away from Camp 2 but as rest expect to go tomorrow alls well. We feel buggered – one hell of a trip. Arrive new camp to find Kappe completely "Jap Happy" and the place one large amount of chaos and confusion. Reg Swartz doing whole task himself. Kappe completely non-active and not accepting any responsibility for camp. No plan latrines huts hell of a mess. Kitchen hell of a mess. Camp on one sea of mud.

Harry Weiss:

7 August '43 – Still in hospital. Japanese snatched 30 patients from ward and made them work. Our last chaps arrived from Sonkurai and I hope Bill Wallace has my bucket with him. Rice boiled with beans in plenty is our sole diet since arrival.

Eric Stone:

Japanese take 20 out of each ward to work. Things are just starting to get tough again. 120 of our chaps march into camp today. Has been raining every day so far. These monsoons ought to ease soon.

George Castle:

Slightly better today, have put in for transfer to Australian camp 2 kms away. Some mongrel bastard pinched my boots this morning, I can't walk more than a few yards barefoot so don't know how I'll go. Another one of our fellows died last night. English are dying off like flies. 16 last night. Fever is lot better but still have dysentery bad.

Lieut. R. Eaton:

Native latrines and hygiene rotten. Fukuda demanding ridiculous figures for work. Plenty of rice but rottenly cooked and no supply store of rations, should epidemic break out will run like wildfire. Sleeping 12 to 14 a bay. 650 British and 900 Aust. – different feeling – a bloody show – Kappe hopeless – no organisation whatever – hospital hell of a mess straightened out partially by Geike and self. Send out Offrs on Rd 2 to 50 in some cases – averaging 500 m p.day. Engineers not too bad – work from 0800 to 2000 – Reveille 0600 – turmoil.

Eric Stone:

8 August – Took another 50 out of our ward for work today but was very lucky. Fever seems to be getting better. Just a matter of waiting now.

Lieut. R. Eaton:

Ron Maston – Jim Rutherford plus 80 arrive from Lower Sonkurai – Good to see them – Ron M. 2 i/c Coy. Rutherford O.C. Coy. Kitchen still chaos – these people are hopeless – Juttner overruled by Camp SMO entirely incompetent – under these conditions no adaptability whatever.

Eric Stone:

9 August – Japanese drag 50 out of our ward to work. I'm one of them, carrying bamboo all day. Japanese guard tells us we go back to Changi in ten days time. Discharged from hospital. Last parties to arrive isolated because of cholera.

Lieut. R. Eaton:

10 August – Cholera broke out – Bobbie Bee first case died – fine men in good health – things are serious – we are moved to isolation quarters – farcical idea in keeping with general trend of show. No further news of Burma move. Looks very much as if the other party will stay down here where they are. Wish Johnston would come here and feel we could pull up the show together – almost immediately first case of cholera evident. Vaccine produced by Japanese about 2 weeks too late in typical fashion. Japanese engineers easier than previous lot. Return to camp 2030 – 2100 Austin Ellerman, Geikie and I force a few ideas of Bruce Hunt hospital on to Scotty Wroe the one officer in charge of hospital. Medical staff damn bad – only about 50% effective. No drive or organisation from the top. No ideas as to how to adapt their work to circumstances – we suggest many things – 1. Parade on dry ground instead of mud – a bit of order into it.

Harry Weiss:

11 August – Worked now for three days. Reveille at 6 am. Knock off on the job (railway) averages 8.30 pm. but the engineers treat us much better. We have also had some salt yak stews. My beri beri is bad again. Now today a

bad blow has struck us again. One man (30 Bn.) has died with cholera and our party (112) is off work and isolated. Tim Johnston died also last night with dysentery. This morning Andy Anderson, who worked in my pit and drank out of my bottle yesterday is stricken down.

Eric Stone:

Out to work today on railway line. Had runs pretty badly. Work on contract. Four of us have to move a slice of earth with two baskets, one chunkel, one pick, two shovels – 4 metres by 2 x 1 deep. Carry of about 25 yards. Snowy working with me also Harry Bailey, Tom Lee. Finish about 6.30. Cholera starts again. Bobbie Bee dies.

Lieut. R. Eaton:

2 more cases cholera – one death – vaccine 3/4cc arrives – God sent.

Eric Stone:

12 August – Working on large cutting today. Finish 7.30. Still upset stomach.

13 August – Given cholera needle. Finish contract 7 o'clock on same cutting. Natives arrive today. Meals very plain – nearly plain rice. Everybody getting beri beri. We have to cross three swamps and go down a jungle track to get to this cutting. Very few of the boys have boots. All with bad feet. We are not allowed to wash because of cholera. Impossible to describe white men living like this. Have glass rod.

Lieut. R. Eaton:

There have been 6 deaths today from various causes.

Harry Weiss:

14 August – Up till today I have been in quarantine, but am now in hospital with b.b. very bad. Still only 5 cases of cholera and the Japanese have given us another injection, so we hope it is controlled. A poor chap collapsed and died alongside me at the lav. last night (cardiac beri beri). Seven were interred in the neat little cemetery on the hill. Andy is doing well. Toyama sent a ration party to No.5 Camp yesterday and the lads were very exhausted last night but it is said that the Japanese are short of petrol and oil so it may often be necessary. Rations are terrible, and 50 per cent have beri beri. Strong rumour of us leaving this place was strengthened by the arrival of 500 coolies last night. How marvellous it would be to leave this awful N.W. Thailand.

Eric Stone:

Draw crook piece of earth – worked like hell but could not move it before 8.15, just as knock off went. Bill Bicket to cholera. Still sick in stomach. Mick from hospital. Took food to Bill.

15 August – Working on old cutting throwing dirt. 12 feet high and higher in places with small handled shovels. Very hard on stomach. Have to walk home at 3 o'clock for glass rod, then have to walk back to work – terrible march. Feeling very sick. Go ten times in night to latrine.

Harry Weiss:

16 August '43: Three cases of cholera in the English section last night. My beri beri is much improved with the rest, and I also get a little boiled grass and rice polishings now. Japanese got more petrol so we hope for more rations soon and no more ration parties. 18 months and 1 day a POW today

Eric Stone:

Start for work but very sick. Broken off party. Got beri beri above knees. Bad feet, runs and fever. Given one day N/D. Also have blood slide taken. 17 August: Spent bad night and day with slight temperature and plenty of running for latrine. Feel pretty crook. Blood slide not ready. One day's L/D in camp. Spent two and a quarter hours on picquet with bad fever.

Joe Zeeno recalled:

"We were trained as Field Ambulance, our duty was to patch up a wounded soldier, put him on a stretcher and get him to a Casualty Clearing Station – now we were nursing orderlies, lives depended on us. The doctors needed sleep and during the night when we were working we would be needed to certify and remove the dead. Each man lay on his side, when one rolled over everyone followed, and if one died we would have to drag him out and place him under the bamboo until he was removed at first light. The only light we had was bamboo, we had a fire going in the hut but when we needed a light to inspect a patient we would light a bamboo stick and hold it high over the man."

Harry Weiss:

18 August: Isolation ends today and the fit men go back to Bn., so will the best of us. I feel better, but find it so hard to eat this mouldy rice and grubby beans which has been our only food for days. Coolies are to be billetted in our first row of huts today, so we have to all cram into this line and the huts are to be converted to double decker. We fear more cholera, living alongside dirty natives. The railroad goes ahead speedily, some of the elephants on the job being simply marvellous and the coolies are much better workers than usual.

Eric Stone:

Given day off as on picquet last night. Could not move fast enough to latrine – two pairs trousers. 14 times between 6 and 3 o'clock. Did not eat two meals. Feel very sick. MO tells me to take charcoal. Move to another hut. More natives expected.

George Castle:

I have now contracted beri beri so may be back in hospital again.

Eric Stone:

19 August: Do not feel well. The double decker broke last night on which 14 were sleeping to a bay. Nobody hurt below luckily. I slept on floor for night. Go to hospital tomorrow.

Harry Weiss:

20 August '43 – I'm still pretty crook and finding it hard to eat this filthy rice and dirty beans. Wish I could get well and go back to work. Coolies are now in our former huts and one long hut is now completely double decker, and congestion relieved.

Eric Stone:

Missed out four times on latrine. Feel a bit better today. Admitted to hospital with diarrhoea. 21 August – Discharged to Con. Dept. The shortest stay I've ever had in hospital. Feel 50%. Runs stopped a bit but cold making me feel off. Run temperature all night. 14 men to a bay – measured it with ruler – exactly 1 foot three and a half inches per man to sleep on. A little off my food.

Harry Weiss:

22 August – Oh! How glad I am to feel better and to be able to eat our meagre ration. We had salt meat in our stew for tea, the first change from beans for days. Our death rate, especially among the English, is terribly high, mostly dysentery, beri beri and cholera cases.

Eric Stone:

On sick parade again. Passed blood. MO marks me back to hospital. Fit men glass rodded. No admissions as we weren't done. This fever making me feel off colour. Give some food to Don MacIvor. Rumour tomorrow last day on railway. Deaths every day from cholera and dysentery. Arthur Stater passed away.

23 August – Max Cook passed away today. Ran fever in afternoon. Feel very weak but runs not quite so bad. Rumour of only one more. day's work then march to Changi. Hope it's right.

Harry Weiss:

24 August – There seems to be a revival of the Burma party and all the bad beri beri were paraded and to my surprise I am so far on the list, and they at last inform me definitely that I am a cardiac case and must be careful. I have asked particularly of several MOs previously and they have always said there was nothing to worry about.

Eric Stone:

Boys worked on railway today again. Moved back to hospital again today. Creek opened up again for washing. Sun shone again today. Looks as if weather may be starting to break. Feel pretty weak. Meals very near starvation pitch as far as anything but rice goes.

Harry Weiss:

25 August – All Burma Party chaps are now in a building of our own. I'm feeling terribly weak and sick – another glass rod.

Eric Stone:

Frank Hudson passed away today. Start quinine treatment today. Feel very weak and sick. Scotty Godley looks bad.

26 August – Still weak with runs and feel pretty sick. MO attacks all ulcer cases with silver spoon – some horrible sights. Poms down at No.2 Camp. Dying rate of 12 a day already. Over 500 deaths. Burma party from No.l passing through. Jack amongst them. Burma party from here standing by.

27 August – Abbie and Butch in hospital with ulcers. Men look weak and sick. Lot of them are just holding on.

Harry Weiss:

28 August – It transpired I had a mild cholera attack and I came across to this cholera ward this not caring if I had lost my Burma ticket or about anything.

Eric Stone:

MO moves me to dysentery ward as I went 15 times yesterday. Feel pretty weak but still manage to eat as it is the only way of survival in this Godforsaken hole.

29 August – Feel a little better today. Japanese put on a kit inspection at tea time. Take some jack knives but mine escapes. Also have to watch Alf's diary but this is OK. We all wonder why this is on. We cannot speak to native lorry drivers or have any rice in our belongings. Think a lot of creams, home, Betty and of good times to come.

30 August – Blood in motions and plenty of them. Do not feel very well. Scotty Godley passed away tonight.

Eric Stone:

31 Aug. – Dr. still using silver spoon on ulcers. Pitiful sight. Abbie, Butch, Don, Ken – all have them. Happy Baker tells me things about Sydney I never knew. I must pay a visit to the railway and markets and see for myself. Started on four sulphur tablets for dysentery today.

Sept. 1 – Val Guy passed away this morning. Had another four sulphur tablets today. Feel very weak but as I finish my malaria today this might help me. Hear Togo Johnson very sick.

Sept. 2 – Put onto Mis Diarrhoea today, a liquid which tastes very crook. Runs have eased considerably thank goodness. Butch has very bad feet. Paid $1.50 today, the first we have received since leaving Changi. Rumour of Red Cross rations coming. I still have hopes for Christmas.

Joe Zeeno remembered:

"I was one of the Orderlies who used to hold the ulcer patients down – we had no anaesthetics, no other treatment, the dead flesh just had to be scraped out; it was just as hard on us as the patient – we were nerve cases."

Harry Weiss:

Sept. 3 – Friday – How wonderful to feel better, I'm eating too, even this food, but sleep poorly, and I'm thankful to God and grow stronger each day. So many poor lads are dying. Ken Forward and Andy Anderson of my old C Coy. are here and doing well. Four years today since the outbreak of war. Loads of sick Burma personnel are passing here daily. We had a glass rod test today, and for what it is worth the Japanese said if we prove negative we, too, may journey to Burma Hospital.

Eric Stone:

Four years ago today. Ernie Hurry passed away today. Feel a bit better. Runs have almost stopped. Feel weak. Given another dose of Mis Diarrhoea today. Russ Mansfield passed away today. MO would not leave him off the road.

Sept. 4 – Runs stopped. What a relief. Discharged from hospital. Four Pom officers, one corporal captured and brought to our camp. Have to carry bamboo to make prison. Did not know I was so weak.

Sept. 5 – Up like a balloon with beri beri. Up to navel. Put on bridge pile driving. Given an issue of cigarettes, six packets for me, 15 was most one man could get. Also issued one sweet potato at afternoon smoko. Very nice.

Sept. 6 – On bridge again pile driving. Sweet gruel for breakfast but not very sweet. More rations coming in.

Sept. 7 – Runs still stopped. Have ticker tested. M.O. says OK. Marg for breakfast, one spoonful each. Pile driving again.

Harry Weiss:

Sept. 8 – Nothing very much happens on our cholera side of this camp, and we are not worried very much by the Japanese and the days are passing. Last test showed me not even a cholera carrier now, but my beri beri has never been worse. I'm rolling fat all over and very short of breath and uncomfortable. The rations are a little better, and we had a little sugar for the first time in both Sonkurai's. There is also some condensed milk for the very sick and we have had a few sweet potatoes. The Japanese have also issued us 4 packets of fair cigarettes.

The furphies commenced to circulate during September that soon they would be returning to Changi within six weeks. Suddenly, in October, an official announcement circulated that they were not returning to Changi for at least six weeks – and the death rate suddenly rose. Those who felt they could hang on for a few weeks could not last another six – no one wanted to hear bad news.

Colonel Dillon gave me the news of Italy's Capitulation in September – "Make sure the men in the hospitals know about it" he said. Arriving at Upper Sonkurai I was blocked by the heavyweight Australian A.S.C. officer in charge of the Cookhouse, "You are not going to talk to anybody!" he said. (This was the camp Lt.Col. Kappe was cloistered in on the top deck with other senior officers.) I informed the officer my orders came from Colonel Dillon.

Eric Stone

> Home at dark each night now. On No.3 party putting up piles ready for driving. Beri beri bad. Heart OK says MO. Our section of railway to be finished 15th.
>
> Sept. 9 – Half pint of broken down condensed milk with gruel this morning. Other meals pretty plain. Things will have to liven up. Still pile driving. Rains each afternoon but morning fine last two weeks.
>
> Sept. 10 – Plain gruel with chillies and pepper and salt. Lunch fairly good, rice and prawns (shrimps) mixed up. Pile driving again today.
>
> Sept. 11 – Pile driving again. Rains like hell. Wet and miserable but we finish another bridge by driving 22 piles. Beri beri still up. Plenty of wagons passing up and down with rations although ours are still cruel. Dutch move past us toward No.2 camp.
>
> Sept. 12 – Spend day building scaffold for another bridge. Japanese hit chaps on bad feet with spikes. Set up ten piles for tomorrow. Snowy to hospital with bad feet. Rains again. Still get sweet potatoes for afternoon tea.

Harry Weiss:

> Sept. 13 – Lived here so peacefully till today. Than the Japanese sent all but 30 of us over to hospital again. I'm terrible sick with beri beri (cardiac) and as all of our persons and belongings had to be soaked with disinfectant, we were miserable from the start, then it took us till 9 pm to get a bed, by which time I was like a balloon all over.

The officers in charge of working parties were informed that work on the railway earthworks and bridges had to be accelerated and accordingly the men would have to remain on the jobs until the work was completed, a period estimated at between 72 and 96 hours. On the grounds that this was a certain way of killing many men a protest was lodged with the administration by the Camp Commander who was informed that superior orders had stipulated that the railway must pass No.3 Camp by 15th September at any cost.

Heavy rain fell throughout that day and in the evening conditions became so bad that the flares by which the night work was to be performed were doused by the rain, resulting in the men being returned to camp at 2130 hours.

Next day – 14th – the weather conditions were little better and working hours much longer. The men went out to work at 0630 hours but did not return until 0230 hours the following morning. Before turning in they were ordered to parade again at 0630 hours which meant at the most, three hours rest. Sixty workers had to be replaced by men from the hospital, the medical officers being kept busy throughout the night examining and classifying men with the object of saving the worst cases from further hardship. All camp duties, with the exception of cooking and nursing of the sick, had to cease.

George Parfrey, wheat farmer, accustomed to hard work, worked 127 days straight. Half the total period he was at Sonkurai, he said he had a bit of a headache and went to see John Taylor who diagnosed malaria. He gave him a week off and during that time the small ulcer on his leg healed up.

Eric Stone:

> Sept. 13 – Drive 22 piles before lunch. Have great wash in creek but I think we will get a wash before day goes. Drive ten more piles completing bridge. This is a record but not satisfied with this. They make us move to another and give us a further ten saying we work until finished. Natives also working on other end. Rains like hell. Japanese treat natives like dogs. Knock off at 10 o'clock in the rain. Very tired.
>
> Sept. 14 – Start to make for bridge but broken off on culvert filling job under the person who gives us no smoko in morning. 30 minutes for lunch, 10 minutes for sweet spud in afternoon. Beats one on head with bamboo and is very unpleasant. Made to move back at dark to first bridge and start night work under bamboo fires and one electric light. Very tired and buggered. Knock off about 12 but it is 2.30 before we get to bed and up again at 5 o'clock. They are certainly making us work night and day.

George Castle:

> Sept. 14 – Vegetable and meat coming in big quantities. We don't seem to get much though. Never had more than 4 small pieces in meal so far. Am feeling a lot better. Have to rest as beri beri is in region of heart.

Eric Stone:

> Sept. 15 – Work all day finishing job of night before. In night move to two bridges and start filling in approaches. Beri beri very bad, so are feet with tinea. Home 2.00. Given duty by M0.

Sept. 16 – Up again at 5 o'clock filling in next bridge approach. Scotty and I allowed to be down most of day as we are both sick. Home at 9.30. What a break. Given L/D.

Sept. 17 – Given job putting up a further deck in hut but as feet are so swollen officer breaks me off. Feel pretty sick in night so get L/D again but had to go on sick parade twice to do it.

Sept. 18 – Feel better today. Job at kitchen and makes it very easy. Rail roars past our camp today. Isn't it a relief – talk of holiday tomorrow for workers. Saw Butch. Abbie looks very sick with ulcers. Abb has fever which is throwing him back.

Eric Stone:

Sept.19 '43: Detailed to work in camp. "Yasme" for all workers. Had to go on bamboo party for Japanese guards.

Harry Weiss:

Sept.20 '43: A week of terrible beri beri and I find it so hard to eat this food and have even got despondent. Then I think of our workers who have worked night and day lately (5 hours sleep) on a little better food, but the Japanese have been giving them good boiled sweet spuds and tea. Yesterday the railroad truck passed the camp and the light motor skips are already rushing rails southward, we may get out of here some day. Wish I could eat and feel well. Was the only one given a shot of Vit.B1 today, so the MO couldn't have liked the ticker. We get no treatment except rest.

(Here Diary ends ...)

Harry Weiss. Died 30.09.43.
Pic: Glen Weiss

Observant Harry Weiss recorded he had heard a Dollar bird in Thailand. Each spring they come down from New Guinea and Asia to breed on Australia's east coast – in Thailand they could be heard but rarely seen as their deep green colours match the jungle. When I hear the birds at Pittwater they remind me of Thailand.

Eric Stone:

Sept.20: Out to work again. Spend day cracking rock in quarry with Bill. Not feeling very well. Off my food. Issued with one pair white PT shorts, one pair cotton socks from Japanese issue, the first clothing they have given us. Shorts made in Rangoon.

Sept.21: In quarry again working with Bill and Lloyd. 'A' Force moving through us working on line. They are putting it through at a fair bat now. Missed Cec Ramalli when he went through.

Sept.22: Work on railway raising line and sleepers. Do not feel well today. Think it is just general debility. Given L/D. Overcast most of the day.

Sept.23: Spend day in kitchen cleaning spuds. See about a job. Tell him I can cook rice.

Sept.24: Out to work on embankment. Fetch mess. Rains like hell. Major Johnson, Captain Taylor expected tomorrow.

Sept.25: Captain Taylor arrives. I'll be eating No.l ration by February. Work under the Bull. Home early. Fine day for a change.

Sept.26: Told we leave for Changi 10 to 14 days time. Simms lose leg. Fred Bladwell OK. Work on railway. Fine day again. Just building fallen embankment.

Sept.27: Work under the Bull – three and a quarter hours for lunch. Ken Reid loses two toes but doing well considering. Given a vaccination against smallpox as some of the natives have it. Also given $1 from last camp – back money.

Sept.28: Work on cutting with the Bull. I am mess orderly so spend most of the day getting rations. Paid $1.80 for work on road.

George Castle:

Finished quinine today, now on light duties, feeling well again although still with diarrhoea and scabies. Food not bad. Camp short of medical supplies.

Eric Stone:

Sept.29: Carrying rations all day to our kitchen. Have haircut and shave, first time for three weeks. Paid $1 in cigarettes from Camp No.l – back money.

George Castle:

Feeling extra well today, only mild dysentery and heart improving. Issued with 2 bananas per man. Working as mess orderly. Eating all my food so all's OK – hope it lasts.

Eric Stone:

Sept.30: Working in quarry cracking rock. Ken Reid passed away today. Big shock as I was talking to him this morning. Having fair weather now. Natives carrying stones to railway.

October 1 '43: Working in quarry again. Joe Carew passed away. Major Johnson was talking to him as we went to work.

Oct.2: Day off – canteen party goes to No.2 Camp. Officers get most of stuff. Had to dig latrine.

In October 1943 Brigadier Arthur Varley arrived at Neike. Dressed in faded and weathered khaki, his tan boots polished, he called on Colonel Banno, saluted him and Banno returned the salute. They had one thing in common – both wore British World War I ribbons. Colonel Banno had served on a destroyer in the Imperial Japanese Navy which escorted the A.I.F. to Egypt. One of the A.I.F. men standing nearby said of Brigadier Varley, "He makes you feel proud".

Ron Johnson:

> Oct.2: We have been told, officially, that we are to move back to Changi in 14 days. Everyone is terribly bucked up to hear this news and are waiting anxiously for movement to commence. Discharged to the Con Depot now, it should not be long before I am out working again. Today is typical summer's day with not a cloud in the sky, sun is burning hot. The dryness brings flies. They swarm on to your meals and all over body and face. A few canteen supplies came in from Neike, peanuts, towgay, tinned sardines, milk, sugar, gula malacca, oil, tobacco and papers. Officers gave the hospital 1000 dollars, which included the peanuts, sugar and towgay. Despite this, they took ample for themselves and many chaps could only buy gula malacca.

Eric Stone:

> Oct.3: Work on basket with Snowy in quarry. Spend one hour in bush talking. Very tired and would like good rest.

Ron Johnson:

> Several patients in hospital now are blown up like balloons from beri beri. The blasting in the quarry still continues. A whistle blows and the next minute the hospital is showered with big lumps of blue metal. One chap had his arm broken and smashed from a big rock. Holes are being torn in the roof. Once again word of move back to Changi has been given and it should be any day now. The railway line is completed, more or less, and we have been pushing ballast under the sleepers. Steam trains have been running for a week, the lengths of trains are bigger each day.

Eric Stone:

> Oct..4: Got $1 soap and $1 coconut oil. Had wash with soap and oh boy nobody will ever realise the difference. Work in quarry breaking rock.
>
> Oct.5: Day off. Carry rations from No.5 camp. Two cases prawns, also get on to spuds. Have tea with Bill and a feed of spuds.

Oct.6-7: Work in quarry cracking rock.

Oct.8-9: Work in quarry cracking rock. Given L/D but have to return to work. Mess orderly.

Joe Zeeno recalled:

"The best kept secret occurred at Upper Sonkurai in October. A couple of medical orderlies were out gathering wood for the funeral pyre when they met natives with their faces covered and realised they had smallpox. Soon some of the Australians contracted this horrible disease but the Medical Officers worked quickly to isolate those stricken with it; as the move south to Changi was imminent they kept close security on the outbreak for if the Japanese had discovered it all movement of POWs from No.3 Camp would have been cancelled. A number of deaths occurred due to smallpox."

Lieut. R. Eaton:

"John Taylor gave the order to Alan Gilbertson, 2/30, to make long bamboo litters and carry these poor men out into the scrub, just away from the hospital in the main camp area. They were left there with just the minimum protection from rain, a ground sheet or whatever was there. Capt. Taylor had ordered this because he said it was his belief, if the Japanese discovered these smallpox cases they could just as easily order all patients in the hospital to be shot. The smallpox cases were left there till they died about three or four days later. Alan said it would have been much more humane if we had been told to knock them on the head really and kill them, but Taylor had to do it for he had absolutely nothing to treat the infection with."

A similar outbreak occurred at Tanbaya and Major W.J. Phillips was of the opinion these victims avoided their original smallpox vaccination.

"As the season started to dry out, the water started to dry up in the stream, the Japanese ordered our chaps to build a dam over the creek at the higher point and about 8 ft. below that another dam. The Japanese washed there, about 10 yards further down stream they kept two or three pigs around the water plus some ducks, then about 10 yards further down the water supply was available for the camp!

"The prawns that came in the ration party were just shells; there was whale meat in 56 lb butter boxes, we were told it was whale meat but it was absolutely rotten and full of maggots. We had to carry each 56 lb box on our shoulders and the maggots would crawl down your neck as we struggled along. All we could do was to put the meat in whatever water was available, wash the maggots away and then cook it.'

Alan Charlton:

"It rained every day while the monsoon season lasts, we were cold and miserable out working and every man had the same illnesses. It was possible to have 2-3 types of dysentery plus diarrhoea at the one time. At one stage I was so swollen with beri beri I was given a job in the Blacksmith's shop in the Japanese compound opposite our camp. Another man and I worked the bellows for the forge where all the tools were sharpened, sometimes the Japanese guard would give us breakfast and also sweet potatoes roasted in the fire, but every few days he would get a News Sheet telling about their great victories at sea and then for the whole day he and another guard would slap us hard across the face while shouting about how mighty they were. Next day would be back to normal.

"It was rumoured when we left Singapore that Lt.Col. Kappe had been given thousands of dollars of Canteen funds to use for our benefit in setting up a Canteen for us. One day we were told that several elephants were being allowed to go to Neike to purchase supplies for our Canteen; when they arrived back they brought many tins of herrings in tomato sauce and the ORs were permitted one tin to four or more men. It was then found that each officer had been allowed a larger quota. I took a tin from the supply of a British officer and took it down to mates in hospital; there was no protest because he was a Padre and never went near his sick men anyway but sat under a mosquito net all day playing chess with a colleague.

"Toyama made two of us hold our mate, who was unconscious and dying, up while Toyama viciously slapped his face for not sitting up when commanded to do so. I felt ashamed of myself for not having the courage to attack Toyama for doing that. We were soon suffering from malnutrition-caused illnesses made worse by hard work. There was a terrible air of misery, gloom over the camp, the fire raged 24 hours a day on the hill, a constant reminder, "Will I be there tomorrow ?"

"The monsoon rains commenced soon after we arrived at the camp and malaria became a common illness. The latrine, being higher than the huts, was soon running over down into them. Eating was difficult because of the blowflies, millions of them – one would see men everywhere trying to eat their food whilst continually waving one hand over the dixie."

Lieut. R. Eaton:

"Up at No.3 Camp was Toyama, he was a sadist and a fiend, also an educated Japanese. He would come in and have a discussion on metaphysics and all these things he had somehow picked up; if anyone misunderstood him he would thrash them with metal golf sticks he had, really vent his spleen on them – and I copped a couple of those!

Gordon Gaffney:

"Eventually we had to move to another camp and had to carry all our possessions including cooking utensils. By this time I had had 32 relapses of malaria, an ulcerated heel, and was poorly from cholera and I kept going down in the mud.

My mate, Ray "Lofty" Ferry, a big bloke, skull-dragged me most of the way and saved my life."

Keith Meakin:

"The bulk of the men who died at Upper Sonkurai were carried in on stretchers from Lower Sonkurai; up to that time our casualties were average. We would be advised there were stretchers on the way and we would walk up the road to meet them. The patients had their hats over their heads, I noticed one with a Sig. colour patch, I lifted his hat and didn't recognise him until someone told me who it was, he was so emaciated. We carried him into the camp but he died that next day in hospital. Joe Fenner from Inverell was with me.

"There was a good looking bloke, Cpl. Fred Gory, he was always neat and tidy, he came to me one day and said, "Curly, the Japanese are killing me, I'm just about done in, can you get off for a day?" That night he dropped dead on the way to the latrine.

"During this period in August it was still raining, rumours were beginning to filter through the lines that it wouldn't be long before they would be going back to Changi. Jack Solomon died in his sleep and in his haversack he had a couple of tins of condensed milk and a tin of bully beef – they would have saved his life. I handed them in and often wondered what happened to them".

Alan Charlton:

"After some time we were moved to No.3 Camp and were told that the fittest men would have to carry camp gear. Wally Starr and myself were given some matting slung on a bamboo pole, we were not well and were just about done in about two miles from No.3 Camp when a young lieutenant caught up with us and told us to get a move on. He was only carrying his water bottle, so I said to him, "If you want this stuff in No.3 Camp carry it yourself!" and I said to Wally, "Come on mate, the gear belongs to Officers!" and we dropped it –

"Life in our new camp was not much different to No.l, we still had Fukuda and Toyama, as well as our own officers, and, happily, our good doctors. We missed Bruce Hunt though."

"The elephants used for shifting timber on the job would knock off on their usual time and go home, and the Japanese would say, "Two men" – that is, two men had to shift logs in place of one elephant, and I can still hear our groans as we lifted huge logs.

"When work was first commenced on the embankment of the railway we had to work a set number of hours. Then the Japanese had a brilliant idea, two men had to dig and carry on the stretcher one cubic metre of dirt per day and we could knock off when we finished. When they saw we could finish early, the task set became two cubic metres."

Ken Marshall

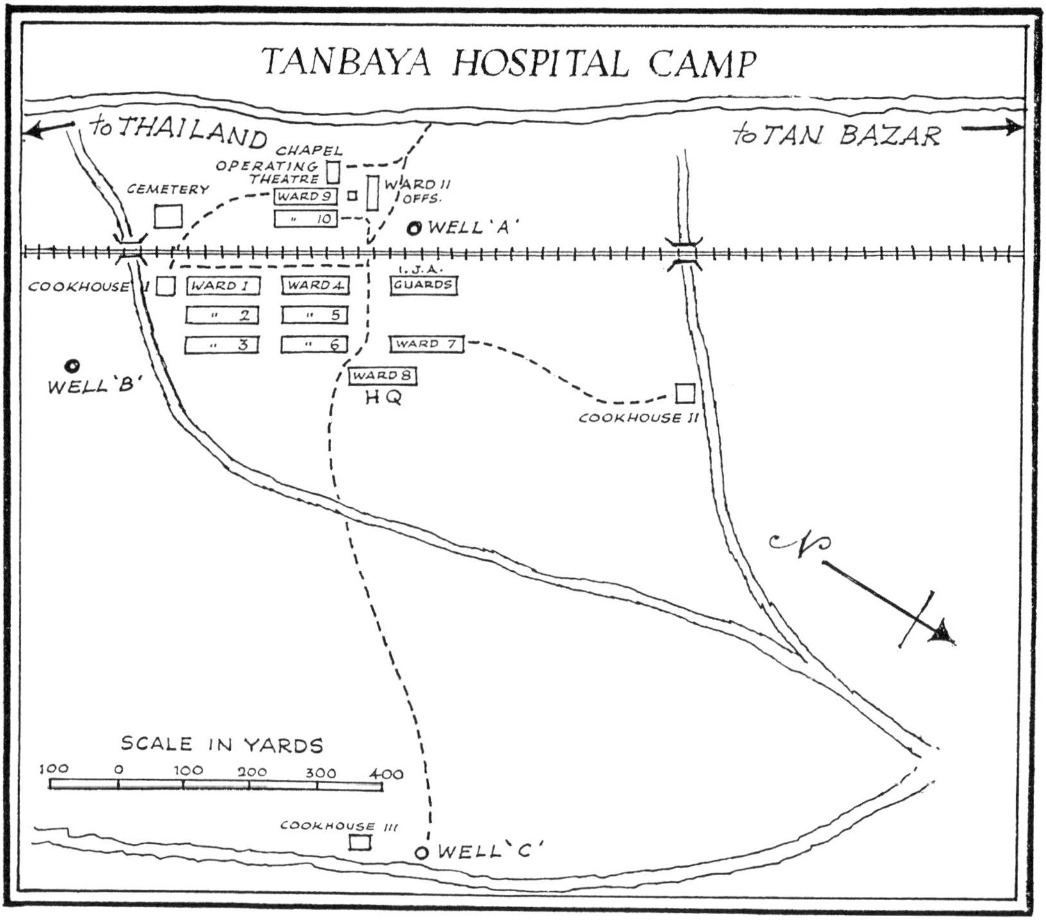
TANBAYA HOSPITAL CAMP
to THAILAND
to TAN BAZAR
CHAPEL
OPERATING THEATRE
CEMETERY
WARD 9
WARD 11 OFFS.
" 10
WELL 'A'
I.J.A. GUARDS
COOKHOUSE I
WARD 1
WARD 4
" 2
" 5
" 3
" 6
WARD 7
WELL 'B'
WARD 8
HQ
COOKHOUSE II
N
SCALE IN YARDS
100 0 100 200 300 400
COOKHOUSE III
WELL 'C'

CHAPTER FIVE

TANBAYA – 30 JULY to DECEMBER 1943

Gordon Nicholl:

30 July '43 – Left Lower Sonkurai after notice of ten minutes heavy rain – march of 14 kms along route of railway line through jungle mud and slush – later along corduroy road – logs being carried by troops – paused for smoko at No.2 Camp Sonkurai. Continued on to No.3 Camp Upper Sonkurai – saw some of our Unit all very fit and well. Marched on to No.5 Camp Changraya reached at 1900 hrs. Marvellous feed of rice and stew – first satisfactory since Banpong. Very unhealthy camp – death roll 200 out of 600 from cholera and dysentery.

31 July – Left by truck at 1230 – 12 men and 2 Japanese per truck. Arrived at Burmese border Three Pagoda Pass at 1400 – lunch – Japanese shared his ration of rice and fish. Arrived at Kandu after travelling 18 kms over very rough road at 1800 hrs. Very mountainous country. Coolies quartered in same hut. Half mile trek to cook house – food good and plentiful.

Aug.l '43 – Reveille at 0330 hrs. Moved off 0430 on march of 10 kms. Pitch dark – very muddy slippery dangerous track column often astray – way felt by holding pack of man in front one requested light for cigarette from firefly – another asked tree to move. Boarded motor trucks at big Japanese transport camp 8 men and 2 Japanese per truck, open truck, deluge of rain completely wet through – Covered further 19 kms through continuous rain and bad road parallel to railway line. Many English, Dutch, American, Australian and Burmese working along line. Ingenious engine – heavy 6-wheeled motor trucks with detachable tires – draws light narrow gauge train – loads of rails, food and men. Quaint headdress of natives combined hat and raincoat made of attap – extensive tattooing of thighs –

inveterate smokers of cigars and huge cigarettes rolled in leaves. Arrived Ronji Stn. 1130 hrs – walked back along road to Ronji Camp (2 kms) – settled down – bought packet of delicious Gula Malacca for 5 rupees. 1230 party of 14 to proceed immediately to Tanbaya. Walked back to station – boarded train. Alan Buttenshaw and myself detailed by Japanese to walk 5 kms to Japanese Hospital where we waited one hour then returned empty handed to train. Immediately after reboarding train ordered 12 men to return to camp. Arrived back just on dusk very tired – all food eaten – retired to dilapidated hut and slept like a log.

Aug. 2 – Camp working party in rain – 2 men slapped for damaging Japanese hut – food excellent – tasted pork first time for 16 months. Good night's sleep. Don Garner knocked off some dried prawns.

Aug. 3 – Reveille 0700 – left on hike of 15 kms to hospital site at Tanbaya. March along railway line through blinding rain. Wet through to skin once again. Railway bridge washed away – perilous crossing. Picturesque mountain peaks – hospital huts in virgin jungle 50 yards from railway line which we reached at 1400 – rest until

Aug. 4 – Cleaning up around camp – drainage etc.

Aug. 5 – Flooring cook house. Detailed by Japanese to work on their cook house. Unloading rice from railway truck until 2100 hrs. Exhausted – tea eaten in dark – slept like log.

Aug, 6 – Again unloading 70 bags rice and huge supply camp stores etc. in teeming rain. Huge crowd of natives in camp – very filthy people. Fire picquet for 2 hours at night.

Aug.8 '43 – Arrival of 50 patients – English and Scotch in very bad way.

Major Bruce Hunt recorded:

These roads were hellish to ride over as I found out when I went to Tanbaya partly by truck. Partly, also, by flat-top train carriages, made a bit miserable due to the constantly falling cinders from the engine. It was easy enough for a fit man to brush the burning embers off, but a serious matter for a helpless patient, as so many were.

Gordon Nicholl:

Aug.10 '43 – 70 yaks driven in – dying off. Picquet watching. Tons of meat. Steam trains commence running Japanese clientele for treatment.

Aug.21 – 23 – Second and third batch of patients arrive. Change of Japanese administration for the better. Letter delivered by one of the lads from Alf Malcom and Tom Schell.

Aug. 31 – Developed malaria. Very busy organising each new ward. Pitiful conditions of English patients, many without even clothes. Very much emaciated and filthy dirty, forced down to stream and scrubbed with brushes.

Major W.J.E. Phillips

Lt.Col. Hutchinson
Pic: Dr. W.J.E. Phillips

Arrival of several corpses – witnessed cremation. One cholera patient – precautions adopted.

September 1, '43 – Cessation of rains. Very hot sunny weather. Patients arriving day and night, many men lousy with huge lice. Appearance of snakes and huge centipedes and scorpions.

George Castle:

Sept.2 '43 – Have been too sick to write. Am now in Burma hospital, left No.2 Camp 2.9.43 walked 8 kms to No.5. Motor truck from there to railhead and then by train arriving here night of 4.9.43. Only had 2 meals on trip of plain rice. Food was not bad when we arrived here but are now out of rations and on plain rice. Plenty of it though and looks like improving. Men died in this camp 134 in last month.

George Morgan:

"After two nights without food we eventually arrived at Tanbaya. The camp was situated on both sides of the railway and we were greeted by a myriad of flies and the overwhelming stench of supurating ulcers emanating out of the ulcer ward on the western side of the railway. My work commenced there and the most devastating experiences of my time on the Burma railway began.

"Stricken men were found with gaping ulcers on legs, arms and backsides.

Almost every man in that ward of thirty had ulcers, malaria and dysentery – their only relief was a merciful death.

"Firstly began the clean up – blankets filled with lice – bed bugs ran unchecked through the bamboo slats – excreta ran underneath the hut. The blankets were placed on the ant hills of the red ants who feasted on the lice and bugs; supurating ulcers were scraped with spoons and those whose limbs were beyond repair were amputated by Captain Frank Cahill with a carpenter's saw and very little morphine to deaden the pain. Walking patients were taken to the nearby stream where the little fish cleaned away the dead flesh in the ulcers."

Gordon Nicholl:

> Sept.9 – Promoted to Asst. Supervisor of nursing with rank of Acting Sergeant. Move to Officers Ward – assisting Capt. Frank Cahill with operations.

George Castle:

> Sept.9 '43 – Have struck bad luck re food as have been eating last and living on rice and rice water for last few days, evening meal at 12 o'clock in dark. I have been ordered to bed by M0. Beri beri has reached heart so if I don't get vitamins soon will not need them.

Gordon Nicholl:

> Sept. 10 – Assisted with amputation of two legs – amputations every day. Total deaths for camp now approaching 200.

George Castle:

> Sept. 10 – Fresh vegetables arrived last night and more today so we should soon be getting some. Had few at lunch but hardly noticeable.

At this stage Major Hunt was pressing the Japanese for more beans, rice polishings and other food rich in vitamins; feeling frustrated he wrote to the Japanese on 20 September 1943:

> "I regret to have to inform you that the health of the men in this camp, instead of improving, is steadily getting worse. This is in spite of all efforts on your side and on ours to make things better. The number of men well enough to carry on the essential services of the camp – nursing, cooking, woodcutting, hygiene – is becoming daily smaller and very few are well enough to be discharged from hospital to take their place. Seventeen of the working staff were admitted to hospital this morning. It is much to be feared that unless a marked improvement takes place at an early date the whole camp service may break down.
>
> "If we had been taken prisoner by a barbarous race unaccustomed to the usages of warfare between civilised nations, complete lack of medical precautions and the failure to supply to the sick the drugs which they so

urgently need, would be readily understandable. But we find it very difficult to understand why such treatment be meted out to its prisoners by a great and powerful nation like Japan, whose doctors and scientists are amongst the best in the world and whose proud boast is of chivalry to the vanquished. Is it too much to hope that even at this late date these poor, helpless, suffering prisoners may receive that consideration, the food and the medical supplies which they so badly need and which I know – because I have personally inspected many POW camps – are always supplied by Great Britain and Australia to the POWs who are under their care?"

Gordon Nicholl:

Sept.19 – Arrival of further supplies of surgical equipment. Musical profession – deaths of Bandmaster Ashton, Gordon Highlanders, Reginald Renison, leading pianist, Aubrey King, tenor. Appointed to J.C. policy of drugs for the living with reasonable chance of recovery. Ward 9 – death of Cpl. Jenkins, 2/30 Bn., late of Mosman, following amputation of right leg.

Sept.28 – W.O.II Wally Shand, amputation of right leg – death rate steady at 10 per day. Death of L/Cpl. Jenkins, NX.39335 Sept. 26.

At this time I visited Tanbaya. I found the camp one of the cleanest I had seen, the patients enjoyed more space, there was Maurice Ferry, suffering from dysentery and ulcerated hands, he kept waving his hands to keep the flies away. He was bright and I knew he would survive. The creek by the camp was fully occupied with scabies patients allowing the small fish to feast on the sores. Angus McDougal was still cranky about the fact he had fallen into the latrine at night; his Scottish mate helped him down to the creek to wash himself and on the way he asked him, Are you superstitious? Angus said Why? Well his mate said, It's good luck to fall in the shit!

George Castle:

Oct. 1 – Wedding Anniversary today. Bad place to spend it.

Gordon Nicholl:

Oct.5 – Permission by Japanese to erect a red cross in hospital grounds 60'x60'.

George Castle:

Oct. 14 '43: We are now getting 3½ bags of beans per day instead of one. Major Hunt says these are cure for beri beri.

Oct.17: Many happy returns tomorrow Glady, will get you present if and when possible.

Gordon Nichol:

"There were no lights out call at Tanbaya – no bugle. Ward 10, which I was in, was just a hut across the railway line. Bruce Hunt couldn't get across there

Captain Frank Cahill
Pic: Irene Whitbourn

very often and the fellows in my hut were getting very down-hearted, things were grim, I put it down to the fact that they had not seen Hunt, so I went specially to see him and told him the fellows were very very despondent, and he said, Well, they are everywhere, but I said to him I think if you could find time to come across there, just to walk down the Ward and say How are you doing? How are you? it would boost their morale. He said, Right, I'll be over this afternoon.

"Down the centre of the hut we had the odd fire going to give a bit of light and keep the water boiling, the smoke went out pretty well but there was always the faint smoky air about and when Bruce Hunt appeared that afternoon at the end of the hut you could hear the whisper The Major's here!. He had a powerful figure and presence, he stood there clad only in his shorts, tattered shirt with his red cross armband and his boots, and you could see the admiration and respect the men had for him – all men who could struggled to sit up – all eyes were focused on this man as he started his walk down the hut stopping at each man and chatting, giving them hope in what he said and in his very presence. There is a very fine line between hope and despair and many of these men had become so ill and despondent that they were very close to giving up altogether but the effect on them after Hunt had walked through and spoken to each one was dramatic – there was hope now and a determination to win out – you could feel the change in the atmosphere.

"After he had spoken with each one he made a short speech about how things were improving and that they were looking better and this all built them up a lot. Afterwards they all told me how glad they were that he had come across and how much they enjoyed having a talk with him and seeing him – and I was very glad that I had thought of it.

"I assisted Frank Cahill in the amputation of legs at Tanbaya. There must have been over 20 done there, to the best of my knowledge only four survived. What used to happen was that the arteries and blood vessels would be tied off but then they would slough away, they would not heal because of the poor quality of food, their bodies did not have the power to heal. The ends of the arteries would slough and they would spurt blood everywhere. They tried at first to nip a bit more off and re-do them, but the same thing happened, we had fellows in the hut walking round all the time with a tourniquet over their shoulder so that they were on the spot to dive on to these fellows.

"I remember Frank Cahill one night we called up to this fellow, he was bleeding so far up and his leg was so short that the only way we could stop it bleeding was to put digital pressure on the femoral artery, which is high up on the base of the stomach, which I did, and Frank Cahill did his best to tie off the blood vessels. It was of course hopeless. It was one of the most terrible things I've ever seen, this fellow lying back and he said to Frank Cahill, Am I going to die? and Frank Cahill said, I think so, and this fellow just looked at us and then started to recite the Lord's Prayer."

Bob Kelsey:

"The time came to move patients and all property from one side of the line to the other. One day I was told to help carry the heavy logs we had cut for fuel; staggering under my load I saw a Colonel sitting in the sun trimming his nails. I dared to ask, "Where do these logs go sir?" "DON'T ask me boy – do I look like a woodman?!" so I lurched along and found a likely dump. On my return for another log I was passed by George Clarke (30th) who was burdened with his log, and he asked, "Where do we put this Kels?" – I was inspired to reply, "Ask the Colonel, he's directing the traffic!" His scream of rage when George asked him brightened my day. I forgot to mention that it was Laurie Male who had first told me to ask the explosive Colonel where I was to place my log."

Gordon Nicholl:

"I slept in the Officers hut alongside Pat Wolfe. We used to work all day long every day from crack of dawn to dark and we would be in bed at night and all of a sudden he'd tap me – it could be midnight! – and he'd say, "You know that fellow so and so with the bad ulcer (or whatever) I'm worried about him, I want to go up and have a look at him, will you come with me?" and I would say "Yeah" – and we would go up in the middle of the night to see how this fellow was. I was talking to him one day, he was a Regular Indian Army with the rank of Master Gunner, which was like a super W.O.I. although he was a doctor. He was a very good pathologist also and I said to him, "With all your qualifications and experience in tropical disease why are you in the Army with the rank of Master Gunner, why aren't you in private practice in India?" and he said, "Gordon – in India – the same as at home in your Australia people are treated according to their means and if you got some rare disease that needed expensive treatment they may not be able to give it to you because you can't afford it – that happens more so in India – but as a medical officer in the Indian Army I do my rounds in the morning, I go into the officers hut and find the Lt.Colonel's such and such disease requires specialist treatment – without question of cost he gets it. When I finish my rounds there I go

Gordon Nicholl

W.O.1 Asst. Surgeon P. Wolfe, I.M.C.
Pic: Gordon Nicholl

into the ORs wards and I find the lowest private in the Indian Army with exactly the same disease but he gets exactly the same treatment because the cost does not come into it. This gives me satisfaction as a medical officer, which I would not get if I was in private life. So that is why I stay in the Army". Pat Wolfe was a wonderful man, fellows like that were needed on the Railway. Dr.Pat Wolfe, Assistant Surgeon, I.M.D.

"Captain Gwynne was a Ward Master, he came from Western Australia. I had a bit of a blue there with him at Tanbaya; he was absolutely non-medical, he had no knowledge of medicine at all and he interfered with a decision I had made about patients so I did my block and told him off. Major Hunt heard about it, he called us both in, sat us down and said, "What's this bloody argument I hear about? There's no bloody time for differences here – you two blokes got along until this happened now get back on the job and forget the whole bloody thing!" Gwynne did, and we got on alright after that. Hunt was like that – he had that sort of power to straighten things out and get things going."

Gordon Nicholl:

> Oct. 20 – Deaths now total 420. Increased air activity locally. Drying up of creek and subsequent removal of cook house on two occasions. Rumours of movement of entire force back to Changi. Corporal punishment for crimes. Desertion by one so punished, later captured. Purchase of canteen supplies

from native dealers. Issue of Jap cigarettes. Erection of Nip look-out tower. Movement of Wards 9,10,11 back across the line – move to Staff hut. Very leaky roof, sat up all night in rain.

Lieut. Bob Kelsey

George Castle:

Oct. 29 – Notified of move to another ward tomorrow. Have been getting fair meals and Japs have sent us more tasty stuff from their Mess. Lieut. Couch sent me 50 cts.

Nov. 3 '43 – Many happy returns Les be home before your next and have part. Beri beri is pretty bad, can't move out of bed now. Few eggs arrived today, I was still unlucky, never drew one. Mr. Couch presented me with 1 dollar to buy something but nothing available. No rations in for 2 days, food very light on. Can't sleep at night, gasping for breath, and bad headaches still.

Gordon Nicholl:

Nov. 7 – Very persistent rumours of move and appropriate steps taken in event of. Medical classification of patients and staff. Private Mess, Officers and WO's – batmen service by. Bags and bamboo poles used as stretchers. Amputation haemorrhages after tying off common femoral. Death of Cpl. Edgar.

George Castle:

Nov. 10 – Back in B.B. Ward again and very much worse. Spell in dysentery ward done me no good. Was notified last night of expected move back to Changi. Lot of fellows here won't make the trip. Canteen stuff expected today. I'll have to look on.

Nov. 19 – Marching orders came today, all bar 300 are going back to Singapore. Believed 4 of our unit with myself are to stop behind. Bananas, gula came in today. Mr. Couch gave me another 50 cts. so I was able to get some.

Gordon Nicholl:

Nov. 20 – Total deaths 667. First contingent of 200 move south by train.

200 daily for five days, including Major Hunt, Colonel Hutchinson, Alan Buttenshaw – 250 patients too ill to move left behind. Captain Cahill and myself remaining. Moved quarters back to Officers hut next to Pat Wolfe. Lectures by Padre Duckworth, late Cambridge University Rowing Eight. Indefinite length of stay in Burma. Numbers of men to truck 33 plus one Japanese guard and kitchen equipment. Sudden change in weather, very cold nights. Erection of huge air raid shelters by Japanese. Improvement in food and better treatment. Many haemorrhages from amputations during nights. Failure of any wound or incision to heal, many become fly-blown as do ulcers, removal by injection of chloroform water. 'Old Bill', our guard, gives generous treatment – very cold weather. Temperature 55° – develop pneumonia.

George Castle:

Nov. 21 – 200 men left on train yesterday, another 200 today. By Wednesday only 350 are to remain so food should be good after that. Has been very bad as men leaving are issued with the best of it. I am feeling better only M.O. said heart very swollen, get severe pain when moving about, tormented with scabies as well.

Bob Kelsey:

"I was searching in the rain forest for wild mushrooms to make soup for one of my men who could not eat rice, or would not, when I came into a small clearing. There I saw the camp surgeon Capt. Frank Cahill on his knees praying. I backed quietly away. His was a terrible job. Forced to decide whether to operate, or rather amputate while there was still a chance of recovery, or to wait until there was no alternative to amputating, which of course reduced the chance of survival. I believe that of 64 amputations only 4 survived the ordeal. It was sometimes my grim task to act as a runner between the Japanese carpenter and the operating 'table'. The primitive saw consisted of a blade beneath a stick of the same length, with two perpendicular sticks, one at each end, tied to the blade below the stick, and with a cord joining them above the horizontal stick. The cord was twisted to provide tension, rather like a hacksaw today. When the ghastly job was done I would run back with the saw. The Japanese would view the blood on it with a grunt of satisfaction."

Gordon Nicholl:

Dec.12: Deaths over 700 – pellagra and beri beri getting worse. Colossal oedema of patients bodies, eyes, stomach, penis and testicles. Amazing recovery of Sgt. Surtees from dysentery, cholera, cerebral malaria, beri beri, pneumonia, blackwater fever.

Gordon Nicholl:

"Bob Surtees, an Australian, was in my Ward. Major Hunt said to me that this fellow needs 24 hours a day constant vigil and attention and we'll have to find someone to do it. How we found this bloke I don't know – he was in Sigs. I think – but he volunteered to sit and sleep by Bob Surtees and tend to his wants 24 hours a day. He did this and Bob eventually recovered.

"Hunt was terribly busy because there were several huts in the area, he put me in charge of one which was across the railway line and it was there I came in contact with Major Phillips for the first time. We worked together and established a good relationship, so much so that when we eventually got back to Singapore he specifically asked for me to go and work with him in the Dysentery Ward. He was a very, very devoted man to his profession and his patients."

George Castle:

> Xmas Eve 1943 – Merry Xmas and Happy N.Y. to all at home. We look like having a bad Xmas, Japanese don't believe in Festivities. Our food has been bad and started malaria again on 21st. Buying party gone to village today so may buy something. Japanese inspect again tonight, only 240 left here now.
>
> Xmas Day 1943 – Feel well today, only circumstances against Xmas spirits. Bought 2 eggs today and 1 rotten – spoilt my vermicelli by breaking it on top, so bad luck continues. Finished day well with Concert in ward headed by Padre Duckworth, English.
>
> Dec.30 '43. Ward burnt out yesterday, all patients got out OK.

Les Parfrey ended up as an orderly at Tanbaya where trading was forbidden but those on cremation detail were able to meet natives while out collecting bamboo. Les would wear a shirt out to work and leave it hanging on a bush within sight until a native appeared. Negotiations would take place and after completing the deal in exchange for food, the native was allowed to remove the shirt which he would put on and then walk away.

A mate, also from the Riverina, Bill McKenzie, was in charge of cremation – some days they would have as many as 30/40 cremations and they were able to retain the odd blanket to barter with the natives.

Bruce Rayson died at Tanbaya in October from beri beri. Major Hunt did everything he could to save him. When the Force returned to Changi, the Japanese reviewing the deaths sent a signal to Kuching, Borneo, to inform his father, Major Hugh Rayson A.A.M.C., his son had died while working on the railway in Thailand.

CHAPTER SIX
LT.COL. POND'S PARTY

TAIMONTA – KONKOITA
MAY – NOVEMBER 1943

At Konkoita 700 A.I.F. of Parties Nos.1 and 2, under Lt.Col. S.A.F. Pond, OBE, 2/29 Bn., A.I.F. (a distinguished Infantry Commander) were halted and placed under the command of Lieut. Maruyama of the IJA Engineers. This party of 700 was subsequently detached from the IJA Administration of 'F' Force.

After a fortnight's marching, every party was quartered in immediate proximity to hundreds of coolies, who were suffering from some intestinal disease of which numbers died daily. The whole area was heavily fouled and infested with a plague of flies. The IJA pretended that the deaths were due to dysentery; it soon became certain that it was, in fact, cholera. Konkoita was the focal point of the infection which caused cholera to break out a few days later at all the working camps to which the force was dispersed.

Dr. Roy Mills recalled:

"At Takanun we had tents over bamboo floors, half slept on the bamboo and half slept underneath. The underneath was soft mud and I elected to sleep there because we used to get our shoulder blades buffetted by rifle butts and my shoulder blades were sore and the mud was soft.

"I vomited all one night and by morning I knew I couldn't do the Sick Parade at reveille. Colonel Pond and Capt. Ben Barnett came up and said, "Mills – there's a Sick Parade waiting! didn't you hear reveille?" and I said, "I can't do it –

Colonel Pond
Pic: 2/29 Bn. Assoc.

Captain R. Mills

can't walk". Now, not unkindly, but he said, "Mills you must!" meaning I could talk, I could think, I could write, and this is exactly what I would say to a man if he could walk, I'd say, "Son – you must!" – so they said to me, "Mills you must!" I was carried up and I did the Sick Parade, then warmed up a bit through the day and eventually I could walk. By afternoon I was round the tents and the hospital marquee, at night time I was still working. Now I had a temperature of 106° at reveille – that was very common – and I woke up to the fact that I had worked 18 hours today. I tell you that as an objective fact, but the men suffered that and had to work on the cutting, I did it in the comfort at RAP. It was grim, but you see Colonel Pond set, I think, a magnificent example; he saw that his officers had no better conditions than any of the men – food was the same. The thing that saved the officer was that when he was sick he didn't have to work, he had to do the cremations, the camp hygiene, getting wood for the fires, but at least he didn't have someone belting him if he faltered – and this saved the lives of the officers.

"I said to George Beecham, "George – if we only had some sulphur". Next day George came to me, straight-faced, "Sulphur ointment sir!" and he handed me sulphur ointment. He had a look in his eye which said Don't you ask me where it bloody well came from for I'm not going to tell you! You didn't ask – if you didn't know you didn't know – in case the Japanese asked questions and tortured a man. But I think George went to three 8 Div.Sigs fellows and they went a few kms up the line, away from our camp, scaled a telegraph pole, smashed the insulators and got sulphur for the Japanese had used molten sulphur over the bridge spoke holding the insulator on the cross bar.

"We had 102 cases that we labelled 'cholera', I am convinced that each one of them was cholera because the stool was absolutely voluminous; might be 2 litres at a time, just like rice water. The patients would get awfully dehydrated, their noses pinched, the whites of their eyes – their eyes would roll up and you would see the whites of their eyes and their fingers would be like a washerwoman's fingers. All would show what was typical signs in all the textbooks and the patient would have agonising cramps all over their body including the fingers. If you didn't do something about it they died. We managed to get through about 60%, but at the end of December, of patients who had been diagnosed as cholera which debilitated them, 50% of those were dead by December – either from cholera or having convalesced from cholera went down with other diseases, but there was about 60% we got through.

"There was a British camp about 3 kms north and more than half way through our cholera epidemic at Takanun, two British officers, Flt.Lieut. Willey and Flt.Lieut. Simpson, came down there and treated the cholera victims. They had managed to get a still somewhere and were making saline, prior to that we had to make our own solution from water gushing off the top of the tents and kitchen salt. This was boiled, filtered through charcoal into bottles and given through an ampule as a funnel – initially through my stethoscope rubber but later we got some rubber – and then through bamboo canulas. I taught the orderlies how to make them from bamboo like a long coarse needle, then we scorched them in flame. We had to make a little slice down in the vein then insert the canula and tie it in. Most patients would get four bottles of our saline and then a top up of another four bottles. A lot of the troops having lost their own water bottles had glass bottles, and they let us have those for the hospital."

In August, Colonel Pond summarised his plight in a letter to Colonel Banno to be forwarded to Japanese Administration:

> "The party under my command, originally 700, now consists of 523, of whom 37 are at Tamarumpat, and the balance are here. The party at Tamarumpat consists of men too sick to move and their number is decreasing by death every few days. They are without a medical officer and cannot obtain permission for nearby English and Australian doctors to visit them.
>
> "At Takanun there are 112 fit men, 19 light sick and 356 heavy sick men. Of the latter, 58 are isolated with cholera. There have been 20 deaths from cholera in this camp but the epidemic now appears to be under control. I should like to express appreciation of the efforts made by the Japanese medical authorities to assist in checking this epidemic – they have been most helpful.
>
> "We were recently permitted to send 70 men to a hospital down the river

but there at least another 185 men who should be evacuated to hospital as they will be unable to work for at least two months. At the present I am required to send 200 men to work every day and also have to provide 20 cooks and 24 nursing orderlies. As a result about 120 heavy sick men have to go to work on the railway even though suffering from beri beri, malaria and dysentery. The work party leaves camp about 0815 hours and returns usually about 2130 hours or later. The work is heavy, particularly in the almost constant rain and as a result sickness is increasing. I anticipate that if men with heavy malaria and dysentery are to continue going to work many of them will die.

"Of the men in this camp about 150 have no boots at all and over 150 have boots which are worn out beyond repair. The number of bootless men increases by about 30 per week. To provide boots for working men I took the boots of the men evacuated down river to hospital. I have made several applications for an issue of boots but without success. Most of the men without boots now have large septic sores on their feet through having to work in continual wet and often on rocky ground and they endure great hardships. We also have 117 men without a shirt and 54 men without a pair of shorts, while 256 men have only one shirt and 317 have only one pair of shorts, 134 men have no towel and 181 no ground sheets. Thanks to the issue by the IJA, all men now have a blanket. Food has improved somewhat during the past three weeks but there is a serious lack of meat and fish. We have had meat on only five occasions in the last five weeks and that at the rate of 40, 55, 70, 80 and 40 grammes per man only. There has been no fish or meat even for working men in the past week – vegetables only. In English camps in this vicinity meat is issued daily at the rate of 200 grammes per man as well as vegetables and fish. We also need tea and sugar.

"I have received orders that sick men in this camp are only to receive two meals a day and this order has been obeyed. I feel sure that as a result many of the sick men will not regain their health and strength and will not be able to work again. Some will no doubt die as a result.

"Accommodation has improved a little with the building of three double-decker stages and with the evacuation of the 60 men to hospital but nevertheless most men become wet at night in bed when it rains as it does every night. In consequence the deaths of a number of men have really been caused by exposure. I request that if this Force is required to move again some transport be provided for its baggage, tents, cooking utensils and rice, all of which have been required to be man-handled in the past. In my opinion, if this is not done, there will not be 100 men in the Force capable of doing any work after another move. Furthermore, most of the sick men need transport though some would be able to march if they carried no baggage.

"In conclusion, Sir, I trust that something may soon be done to improve the conditions of my men as I am very concerned at the number of deaths and the amount of sickness that have occurred."

"Bluey" Lee:

"Under the command of Lt.Col. Pond we had marched day and night from Banpong. A staging camp had not as yet been completed; malaria was rife, beri beri was affecting our health but we had not been as yet overly worked hard.

"Our biggest problem was shortage of good solid food such as meat. The cookhouse was close to the river below the camp, the guards were not giving us too hard a time; I was in the cookhouse team and one day was told by the Japanese Sergeant to take charge of the killing of a yak they had acquired – my special job was to arrange for the slaughter of the yak and I was told this only must take place in the presence of the Japanese Sergeant.

"I found one of our men who claimed he was an expert slaughterman – all he needed to do the job was one piece of neck rope and an axe. These were found easily as all men were looking forward to a feed of meat – after the guards had had first choice of course.

"The skinny yak, which was off-white in colour, had the rope placed around its neck and two men, one on either side, took the strain so as the yak would not move its head while 'expert' struck the yak between the horns. The first blow sent the yak to its knees and it got up shaking its head; the second blow put it down again but was up and started off pulling the rope holders with it. They had to let go and the yak, now free, galloped off into the bush. The Japanese Sergeant yelled out at us, no doubt in Japanese, calling us a stupid lot of bastards. Well! we thought there goes our meat ration, no way was that yak going to stop before it got to Burma – nevertheless as many men as could went looking for the off-white coloured yak.

"The 'slaughterman' was abused, the rope holders were abused, and I was responsible for the care and killing of the yak I received a few whacks around the head and the men complained about their meat now gone.

"Some hours had gone by when there was a yelling and calling and some of our men came into view leading a yak, brown and black in colour.

"When they arrived in front of me with the yak they said "Here's your yak, now kill the bastard and let's have cooked meat!" Blind Freddy could see it was a healthy looking yak but most different from the one that had run off.

"As the man put in charge of the killing of the yak, I had to go up to the Japanese Sergeant guard hut and tell him the yak had been caught and, as requested by himself, would he come down and watch the killing. He was most unpleasant about coming down but finally did so .

"In the meantime, two new rope holders had the yak ready and this time an expert slaughterman had the axe. The Japanese Sergeant took one look at the yak and in his English and Japanese language told me in no uncertain way that this was not the same yak, or in his words, "no suma suma" yak.

Ron Lee

"I went through quite a comical routine by counting the yak's ears = two, legs = 4, tail = 1, and to make sure he understood it was hopefully the same yak, I counted the yak's ribs in Japanese language. The Sergeant looked at me with a pitiful look, shook his head a couple of times and finally said "Okay-ga".

"With what the Japanese didn't want from the killed yak some hundreds of Lt.Col. Pond's men had meat broth for a couple of days.

"An incidental from this happening was that as a young man I learnt nothing was wasted from a killed yak. When the animal is stunned, you can cut a large neck artery and men would catch and fill their eating dixies with blood, wait until it congealed, then cook it up for afters. A new experience I shall never forget."

Jim Ling:

"Corporal Noel Chitty was with our group, he came from Melbourne and he used to tell us about it sometimes. He was a big man and a tower of strength, he worked like a slave on the line, apart from his own work he would always try and help some other man either with his work or carry his gear.

"About half way through when the monsoons hit and we were all working long hours, we came in one night about 10 pm – we were tired, cold, miserable, we were all hungry and this night we had our little bit of rice and were all lying down under our scanty shelter when Noel turned to me and Les Lowe and said, "Right! I've done all I can – I just feel now I've got nothing to worry about, no committments at home to worry about – I've decided not to go on!" We all sat until the early hours of the morning telling him how silly he was to talk like that, he was no different to the rest of us, and we needed him, but he was adamant, "No, I'm going to call it a day, I've had enough." We abused him for a while for we thought that might shock him out of the mood, but we all must have dropped

Captain B. Barnett
Pic: 8 Div. Sigs History

off to sleep eventually because when we woke to the yells the Japanese would give for reveille at 6 am, Noel was dead.

"Noel Chitty was a top bloke and one of the top heroes as far as our group were concerned, he was a real man in every way. We buried him that night along the line."

Dr. Roy Mills:

"Corporal Noel Chitty died at Upper Taimonta. He was jaundiced and had terrible pain in the muscles of his legs and it was clear he was suffering from what is called "Weil's disease" – in fact that was the only time I ever spoke to a Japanese medical officer who was of the same opinion as I and it was agreed that it was "Weil's disease". This really caused me great anxiety for it was something we could not have controlled – it is an infection from a rat and the virus is secreted in the urine of infected rats; we would not have been able to control it should the disease spread through the camp. We only had one other case and it did not get an epidemic.

"The men from Signals thought so much of Noel Chitty that instead of just burying him and take a map reference of the grave and keeping a record, they erected a wooden headstone, but afterwards it could not be located and it was probably swallowed up by the jungle.

"I had a man who was gravely ill and Padre Dolan sought my permission to administer what I thought were the Last Rites and I said, "Now look, Padre, no you don't – I don't want you pointing a bone at my patient!" Padre Dolan was a very gracious old man and he looked at me and gave me a talk as a father to a son and explained to me it was not the Last Rites but another important Unction – he was clearly a man of God and he made me feel very humble – apart from putting me in my place very nicely!

"Everyone who went into Pond's party had been able to march from Banpong to just near Konkoita – on average, we were fitter to start with than the remainder – we did have a hard time – when we marched we had to carry all our gear and were never able to stay at a stop long enough to get organised but we were able to send our worst sick down river from Takanun on two occasions.

“We were absolutely exhausted by the time we marched north to Upper Taimonta – we were all very thin – I remember I could wrap my fingers around my wrist and actually overlap them, I suppose I would have been about 7 stone then.

“The men were even worse – on some there was virtually no flesh just sinews – some men I could actually put my hand, thumb and middle finger, around their legs just above the knees.

“When we went north toward Taimonta we had to share huts with native Asians and at night they would come carrying bamboo flares and peer at you sleeping on the bamboo as part of their hut – it was weird, almost as if you were having nightmares all night long. After a couple of nights we put up barricades and that stopped them. We couldn’t communicate with them, they were having a terrible time but we could do nothing. As a result of having to share their huts we all got scabies and lice. We asked the cookhouse to give us enough boiling water and we dipped the clothes in and that fixed the lice. We had control of our own situation at Takanun under most terrible conditions but we got rid of the lice and scabies.”

Jim Ling:

“Padre Dolan, senior Roman Catholic Padre of the 8 Division, was a wonderful man, a bit of a larrikan, but he was good for the morale of the men. He was in our group on ‘F’ Force and he was always around with the men. When we were able to have a Church Service under a tree I sometimes acted as his altar boy – everybody who could would come too no matter what their religion. Paddy Dolan was wonderful like that in that he was the same to all the men.

“At Taimonta we all had dysentery and Paddy Dolan suffered along with us, I remember one night dragging myself out to the latrine to find Paddy Dolan next to me, swearing at the top of his voice about what he would do to the Japanese when he got back to Australia! He was a wonderful, outstanding man, Padre Paddy Dolan.”

Dr. Roy Mills:

“I had a book, “Medical Diseases of War’, and I would learn the page off by heart, tear it out, and on the back of it I would make notes, on the top of the page, between the lines, in the margins, one day I examined and made notes on 464 men. You could examine a fever patient in five minutes but with an ulcer – the orderly would say, 1½ inches, yesterday 1¼, and we would know it had got a bit bigger and we would have to cauterise it. We had been given a lot of bottles of disinfectant to put down the open pit latrines and amongst them was a bottle of pure carbolic acid phenyl which I had saved for I knew it might be very useful and it was. I had a Sigs man, Corporal Matthews, he had been a trained nurse, and he would just go round the edge of the ulcer with the carbolic. We knew from observation that an ulcer spread often two days before a patient had a malaria attack, so that when an ulcer spread, it would be cauterised and the patient go on to quinine even though we had very little quinine. When we had lentils, even just a very small supply, we would 'shoot' them wet under an old shirt, the shoots are a good source of Vitamin C, and we gave those to the people with ulcers and thus avoided having amputations. When the men's ulcers extended we carbolised them and gave them quinine and if we had lentils they got lentils that had been shot for Vitamin C."

Jim Ling:

"We moved up and down a bit but our area of operation was Koncoita, Takanun, Taimonta, Neike and Upper Neike. I remember Sig. Ken Davidson had an enormous ulcer on his shin, the doctors wanted to take his leg off but he didn't want that, so Roy Mills said, "Well, if you can look after him he will probably be alright". So Les Lowe organised it and there were six of us and we carried Ken with us wherever we went, and we got him over it.

"Takanun is very special in my memory for that is where my best mate, Terry O'Brien, died of cholera. We had been mates since we were boys together, we joined up together and we were in the Sigs. together right through – he was like a brother to me. I would have loved to have held Terry O'Brien's hand but he died of cholera – all I could do for him was to be part of the party to get the fire going – I'll never forget the cremation – "

Dr. Roy Mills:

"At Taimonta in October an extraordinary thing happened. We were moved into three brand new beautiful huts – they were clean, new, they leaked in the centre but didn't leak on to the bamboo platform, we wondered what was happening. The railway was moving down about 3 to 5 kms a day, it came through on 15th October – it was an amazing scene of human activity – pushing forward at that rate – sleepers brought forward stacked on rails supported on two bogies – unloaded carried in front by coolies then the rails are slid forward to the front track and laid – a new pair of rails goes down every 20 or 30 seconds with men pouncing on every rail – bolting them together – spacing them spiking them – terrific noise – a few hundred yards behind the motor trucks with flanged wheels and reversible gear following up with more sleeper rails – as soon as a pair of bogies are emptied of their load they are lifted off the track and the next one goes through – it was impressive.

"On 17th October the place swarmed with military police, high Japanese Generals, photographers, and there was a re-enactment of the joining of the line right beside these beautiful new huts. We were shunted into the jungle and were not allowed to watch, the only man who managed to have just a look was our Padre, he was peering through the bushes and had only managed to see a little of it before he was caught – he got a belting and a kick in the behind. But this was definitely a re-enactment because the line went past us two days before.

"That night we had a concert, there seemed to be a bit of levity in the Japanese lines, it was the only time we ever had a sing-song but it was abruptly halted, one man got a ruptured eardrum from it and we were back to cruelty that night. It was all make-believe.

"Colonel Pond believed he had an equal responsibility to get the Private soldier, as well as any Officcr, back to Australia; on the work party the Colonel had no control over what happened to the men, except to make continued protestations, he could not allocate the duties, but when we moved he decreed who should carry and the Officers were forced to work hard, harder and harder. Colonel Pond was almost ruthless in that if an officer could work then on these carries he had to work, he wanted to spare the men.

"Colonel Pond had had to have a toenail removed surgically and he was ordered not to march, but he did; when a man who was carrying faltered he joined in the carrying – the men respected him.

"When we were moving back to Taimonta from Takanun there was a carrying party with a sick man on a stretcher, the fellows up front kept getting stuck into the small man of the group on the back. When they halted, one turned round and said, "Get stuck into it!" – then "Sorry sir!" – Colonel Pond had stepped in when the original man had faltered, but he just said, "No offence – carry on!" He would do that quite unobtrusively, just hop in and help.

"We left Upper Taimonta on 6 November at 0930. We had to carry 26 stretcher cases, all our kitchen buckets and containers, five medical haversacks and one 50 lb. box of medical supplies. Many sick men, who should have been stretcher cases, were forced to walk. There were 19 of us, four of whom were sick, to carry four heavy beri beri cases. I waited near the half-way mark of the march to see how all the rear stretcher party was faring, the guard would not let me push ahead. One man, Pitches, 2/29, collapsed and had to be carried on an improvised stretcher. Eventually two A.A.M.C. men came back and we were able to press on and finally reach Neike after a horrific 14 kms march.

"No sooner were we there than a party of 107 had to march on to Sonkurai No.2 Camp, 12 kms further, where Captain Pete Hendry was. Captain Curlewis took the party with Capt. Weidersehn, Lloyd, Hardacre, Lieut. Gillies, May, Uren, Veitch. Pitches, 2/29, died."

During the fighting at the battle at Muar Max Benoit was awarded the Military Medal. Now, he and his mates decided they would escape first opportunity, conditions were so bad now was the time. Before he left, Max wrote this letter to his Mother, in part:

"Dear Mum,

If you receive this letter before hearing from me I shall not be coming home. At the time of writing I am somewhere in Northern Thailand, very close to the Burma border. We have recently been shifted from Singapore, where until about two months ago I have been held prisoner. Our food up to date has not been good, the main item of our diet being rice, very little else.

"Myself and two mates have decided to attempt an escape. We consider we have at least a 50-50 chance of getting through, and reckon on making the trip inside three months before the monsoons set in. We have roughly six or seven hundred miles to go. If we are caught we shall be shot, as that has been the policy of our hosts to date. The three of us are in fairly good physical condition and have decided to go whilst we still have our health. About eight men in ten are suffering from vitamin diseases and beri beri etc."

Nothing further was ever heard of him –

Max Benoit
Pic: L. Benoit

George Beecham

CHAPTER SEVEN
LOWER SONKURAI – SONKURAI
AUGUST – NOVEMBER 1943
NO. 2 CAMP

The first British arrived at Sonkurai on May 20 after a march at night of 315 kms. They found the accommodation was in unfinished huts which they occupied in the rain.

Next day they were put to work. Three days later 600 more men arrived, making a total 1600 men. Lt.Col. Pope was the Officer who believed they were going to the 'promised land' and who assumed command, but within a day he became ill and later died on 10 October 1943.

The British had marched through all the camps where cholera was reported to have broken out. On 23 May, the first cases were reported and by the end of May, 63 deaths had occurred. The huts were not yet roofed but the men were put to work on a bridge over a tributary of the Kwai Noi.

During June, Colonel Dillon requested me to endeavour to get into Sonkurai and find out if the rumours of up to 12 deaths a day there were true. Within a day I was able to walk into the camp; entering the first hut I asked for the Hut Leader – there was no one in charge – there was faeces over a wide area of ground and no one was concerned. I enquired if there were officers present, they were also ill at the next hut. Apparently a number of them were planning an escape (this attempt took place about the end of July). I reported back to Colonel Dillon what I had seen.

The Railway Station at Konkoita decorated for the re-enactment of the opening of the line joined together on October 17.
Pic: AWM.P406/40/1

Above: Malaya '41 - Noel Chitty and
Jim Ling Pic: Jim Ling

Left: Captain V. Brand, M.C., remained at Tamaranpat Hospital which collected about 200 stragglers who had become ill; later, many of these were sent down river by barge to Kanburi.
When they first arrived there all they had was an axe-head and a parang, nearby was a good stand of bamboo and they set about constructing a camp which became a working camp isolated from the rest of 'F' Force. At one stage Captain Brand walked to Neike so the Japanese had proof he really existed; with him on this walk was a 2/30 officer, Lieut. Kevin Donoghue, who was fluent in Japanese.
Pic: 2/29 Bn. Assoc.

Work continued on the bridge, by June 16 the last cholera death occurred, however dysentery, beri beri and ulcers were now endemic. The men were working on bridge construction under Lt. Abe, who had no regard for human life. He insisted on sick men being carried to work to operate hammer and tap.

On June 4, Lt.Col. Dillon requested Major Hunt, who was inspecting the Australian camp at Upper Sonkurai, to advise the Medical Officers at Changkaraya and Sonkurai concerning their medical problems, and in particular the handling of cholera.

Major Hunt reported:

"On 5th June I proceeded with Lieut. Fukuda to Upper Sonkurai where there were approx. 380 A.I.F. personnel. Capt. Allen, AASC, in charge of the camp, had been ill with beri beri, Major Gillies, RAMC, was attacked by malaria on the day of my arrival, cholera was just getting under way. I innoculated the camp and was able to initiate a cholera isolation hospital and to suggest certain other changes in medical and hygienic administration.

"Opportunity did not arise to visit Camp 5. I was able to interview Major Hanbury, RAMC, S.M.O. No.2 Camp, on my way back and discuss various problems with him; concerning a technical point on the treatment of dysentery under present circumstances we found ourselves unable to agree. Major Hanbury considered that he had both the cholera and the general medical situation well in hand, and did not require any assistance.

"As the men became weaker, caused by bad living conditions, totally inadequate rations, usually rice and onion water, their treatment by the IJA engineers became worse. Lt. Abe, the IJA engineer, insisted on so many men being found each day, that to obtain the desired number it was necessary to turn out large numbers of sick, frequently as many as 70% of the working party were sick men. The engineers made them shift logs, etc., far beyond strength and beat them when they failed. Representations were frequently made by me to Lt. Abe to reduce the number of men on working parties and also that their ill treatment by his men should be stopped, but nothing was ever done, and he refused to listen to all appeals. He stated that if the men were not produced his own men would go into the hospital and fetch them out. He admitted that these men were sick but insisted on the number required by him being found daily. An additional handicap was that in the camp there was only a 'Gunso' in charge of the IJA Admin. personnel, and although he was sympathetic towards the prisoners he was always over-ruled by the engineers, whose treatment of the prisoners at all times was callous and inhuman.

"Although officers were not forced to work on the bridge, so many were in hospital that it was impossible to organise them into works and hygiene squads as was done in the AIF camps. The proportion of sick in the camp was extremely high and the death rate was mounting."

In July the deaths were occurring in such a number that Captain Hendry at Neike was requested to send a working party to assist with the cremation duties.

"Ringer" Edwards, a Queenslander, and one of those sent said, "There were about 30 waiting to be cremated, the Poms were still drawing their rations. We set about cutting timber and in no time had the problem under control."

No sooner had the move of the advance party to the Burma Hospital started than an order was received to close Neike, Lower Sonkurai and Changaraya and to re-group at Sonkurai and Upper Sonkurai in such a way that each camp could provide approximately the same number of working men; a figure of 800 from each camp was mentioned.

Patients and staff for Burma were ordered to remain in the old camps until moved. The men who were so ill that they had not been selected for Burma were also to stay. Most of these were expected to die. This order was received at 1400 hours on 2 August and the move was ordered to be completed on the following day. It involved marching through rain, knee deep in mud, carrying all personal kit, cooking and medical gear, and with all patients other than those booked for the Burma Hospital or too ill to be sent there.

When Captain Peter Hendry reached Sonkurai in August he had with him Ted McGlynn, Harry Williams, Reg Jarman, Bob Wilson and a number of highly experienced 2/10 Field Ambulance staff of scroungers and found the British medical orderlies were senior to some of his top men who were Privates, so he promoted them – unknown to the British – and they then became Senior. Lt.Col. Dillon would have been aware of the promotions but nothing was said because he used some of these men to purchase goods from the Thai traders unknown to the Japanese.

Capt. Peter Hendry

The hospital was now a happier place than in the past with the Australians entirely involved in running the camp. Capt. Hendry livened the hospital up with a few concerts – there was "Benjo Pete and his Poopsters" singing western songs !

Captain Lloyd Cahill was left in charge at Lower Sonkurai to supervise the evacuation and transfer of those allocated to Sonkurai and Upper Sonkurai. This move effectively split Units and the highly successful junior officers who carried the administration of the camp were now surplus to less efficient officers.

As the movement of the Burma party commenced I was able to see the extent of the toll of seriously ill men. Many were not fit for travel however it was their only chance of survival to get to a place where they could at least rest and be under care of medical staff.

For Captain Cahill and Captain Taylor the pressure was easing; they were awaiting transfer to other camps and now were able to reflect on the epidemic days of May-June when there was so much depending on them. Now, Captain Lloyd Cahill took the opportunity of writing to Major Bruce Hunt on 26 August 1943:

"Dear Bruce,

> Some months ago when I was informed that I was to proceed up-country as one of the medical officers to 'F' Force I rather looked forward to the opportunity of seeing more of the East and escaping from the many pinpricks of Changi. However when I heard that no physician or surgeon was to accompany this body of 7000 men, I was astounded – so much so that I protested to Bruce Anderson. Bruce's hands were obviously tied. Then out of the blue, I heard you had volunteered to accompany this force. Like many others I was delighted, although I fully realised what a great sacrifice you were making. I will not say I was surprised, for such a sacrifice on your part was typical of what those who really knew you – and I have the temerity to include myself among those – felt certain you would make when the occasion arose. This has been an ill-fated force, but it was fortunate in having your leadership and judgement in the early dark days.
>
> "At Changi I thought I knew you rather well – your whims, likes and dislikes – but for the rest of my days my most vivid pictures of you will be your arrival – mud bespattered and grimed at the Staging Camp – your arrival at Lower Sonkurai in the early hours of morning, looking for a medical officer who was dying of cholera and the amazing energy and resource you displayed in overcoming the thousand and one obstacles you encountered after your arrival. John, Colin, Frank and myself are the few fortunates who have the privilege of living, knowing and working with you under such conditions.
>
> "One of the greatest disappointments of my life was Major Stevens' order that I was to remain in Thailand and not accompany you to Burma and now that the lads are beginning to move I feel it all the more. But such things are typical of the Army. My only hope is that soon we will all be united again in Changi or even more pleasant circumstances. It is impossible for me to express on paper, as it was in words before your departure, my debt of

gratitude to you for your teaching, advice and encouragement. It is indeed a pleasure to work for anyone who appreciates one's own efforts, no matter how humble they be. One of my greatest treasures will be a somewhat knocked about red covered book Rogers & Megaw – John and I will take it back to Australia no matter what else we leave behind.

"My sincerest good wishes for the success of the Burma Hospital – and one final word – look after yourself and do not work too hard. I have already heard our old friend the Beri Beri is about."

The following is an unsigned letter located in Major Hunt's Private Collection, obviously written by Captain John Taylor in similar vein to Capt. Lloyd Cahill.

"My Dear Bruce,

A few hurried lines, scribble during Col. Huston's flying visit to No.l Camp. Conditions here, at your old background, are now relatively pleasant; a small family of 266 of us, 200 being the Burma residue – no one at present dangerously ill or like to die – only one really bad ulcer, who, unfortunately may yet require amputation. The general health of the troops improving quite markedly – you would not recognise some of the men whom you worked as Burma C3 – they have filled out extraordinarily, on the life of ease and large amounts of rice. Lloyd and I are still here living quite a tranquil existence; our pleasant association however looks like coming to an end, for Col. Huston wants Lloyd to go to No.2 and self to No.3. At the latter camp things are pretty bloody if we can believe Major Stevens' last epistle. In any case I think the days of 'F' Force in Thailand are numbered as the railway track has reached No.5 in the north and Takanun in the south is proceeding apace.

"Lloyd has explained the situation ... instruments your personal books, papers and etc. I assure you Bruce, that until such time as these latter can be delivered into your hands, they will not pass out of Lloyd's and my sight.

"I want to thank you very sincerely for your splendid gift – my heart was just a bit too full at the time of your departure from here to express my feelings and gratitude adequately and in any case I always find such expressions easier to write than to say. It shall ever remain my most treasured possession – a souvenir – ".

The Asian labourers came to Lower Sonkurai in family groups, they did not seem to have any organisation, mothers with small children and teenagers – promised a better life and better conditions. The ones I saw I was told came from Malaya; one Tamil girl wearing a bright costume was hugging a tree in pain suffering from diarrhoea – they all had it – their clothing was in a foul condition. I drove past Lower Sonkurai and saw the piles of bodies – one black and one white – the wind was blowing their hair and gave them a life-like appearance.

Dr. Lloyd Cahill looking at the book, Rogers & Megaw, on Tropical Diseases which he had carried the 300 kms to Lower Sonkurai. This book was vital reference to all Doctors on tropical diseases. It was later presented to him with an inspection from Major Bruce Hunt.

Pic: Richard Wall

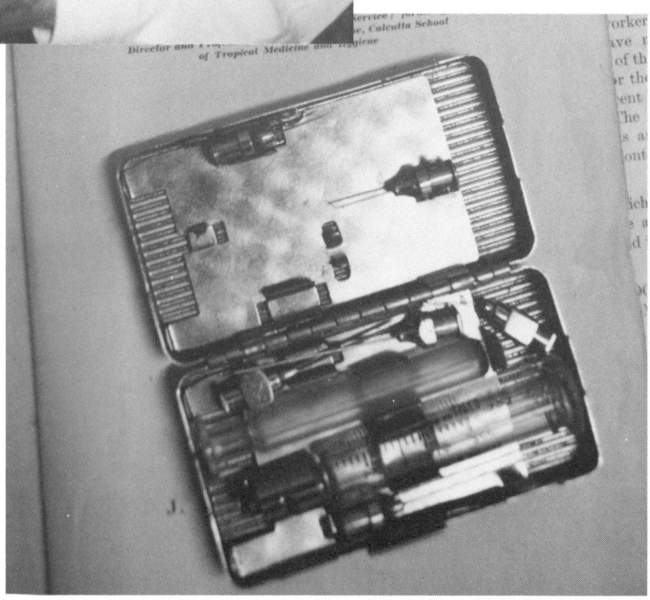

Hypodermic Syringe and case – Initially this was the only hypodermic syringe in the camp of 1800 men.

Pic: Richard Wall

David Oag farewelling his dog at Leeton, NSW, 1941.
NX.31462 W.D. Oag died 14.09.1943.

At this time Captain Lloyd Cahill was still in this camp and he recalls: "The Japanese had an area where the remaining sick or convalescents were and they put a bamboo slat across the hut and told me I could not go over it but eventually they let me go in and it was the most dreadful thing I had seen – babies were lying or crawling over their dead parents – the whole place completely fouled, vomitus, faeces, flies – and I could not convince the Japanese that there would be an outbreak of cholera before long. They were of the opinion that a bamboo slat would stop the infection spreading. Fortunately we still had a fire going and all I could do at that stage was to get the bodies out and cremate them."

Ken Crispin recorded:

> Thursday – Sept. 23: Definitely moving tomorrow No. 2 Camp. Cholera carriers, if any found, to stay here. Sick to be carried. Will necessitate two trips to carry all sick. Should be very difficult day. Carrying party taking up medical gear, bringing back sweet potatoes. IJA presents 6 bags rice, 22 bags beans, big fish and vermicelli to be eaten in two meals. Usually daily issue 12 bags rice and half bag beans, 1 bag whitebait. Railway pass through during night.

Frank McGovern, ex HMAS PERTH, 1942, became a POW in Java and was later moved to Burma in 'Williams Force'. Now on the plate laying party they worked round the clock. As they approached Sonkurai he remembers working the night shift – the sound of spikes being hammered in – the forward flat tops were loaded with sleepers or rails and pushed by a small diesel convertible rail/road six wheel drive vehicle. The work area was illuminated by burning pitchblend, which produced a lot of smoke, and bamboo flares and carbide lights. In the work parties were Dutch, Indonesian Dutch, British and Australian prisoners, sometimes natives; as the rail workers approached Sonkurai camp the sound the plate laying activities woke the men and they came out from their huts to watch the line going through.

Peter Rushforth:

"Of all the dramatic and heart-rending scenes that remain etched on my memory of the 'F' Force tragedy, the most traumatic occurred when we had completed the work at Sonkurai.

"Quite late at night the silence was broken by a distant rhythmic beating sound, then quite quickly out of the darkness came flaring lights, men carrying primitive looking torches and then before us was a scene of frenzied activity. Sleepers were laid, rails placed into position and hundreds of men, naked to the waist, their torsos glistening with sweat, worked in unison. Many of the workers were Asian working as slave labour with the European POWs.

"Over the chanting as workers drove spikes into the sleepers, Japanese guards yelled and gave orders, then as quickly as these men had appeared out of

Peter Rushforth

the darkness they disappeared out of sight and the sounds of machinery, hammering, chanting and guards yelling faded into the night."

Ken Crispin:

> Sept. 24: Tremendous breakfast. More hash (rice and pigeon peas) than could be eaten. No further meal till No. 2 Camp reached, so most took some for later in day. Excellent stew, with it, beans, vermicelli and fish. Issues made of salt – 1/4 lb per man and as much uncooked rice and beans as they could carry. It was the only way to use it, could not be cooked and eaten there. Moved to No. 2 Camp. Despite railway it was march and carry sick, medical and kitchen gear, everything. Road very muddy and treacherous. Trip very hard. Much gear, many sick, few fit men for carriers. Daily rain came 1/2 hour before end of march. March about 3.5 miles about 10.30 am to 4 pm. Very short owing to heavy burdens. Carriers also carried all their worldly possessions as PWs. September wettest month so far, has rained every day. No. 2 Camp Deaths reported a No. 3 Camp of Pte. D. Lace – 68 deaths 7 missing. L/Cpl. Jenkins had leg amputated. Camp somewhat mucky through so much rain. Latrines not covered. Showers installed water led through bamboo trough from higher up hillside, very good.
>
> Rations quite fair – good stews – browned rice for breakfast, issue one pint, one and a half pint. Half pint stew. When we settle down it is anticipated ration will be big improvement on Lower Sonkurai. Reclassification of old Camp No.1 personnel. Some to hospital, remainder rail/road work or camp duties according to fitness. Canteen operating. Soap, tobacco, toothpaste; when elephant comes, gula, peanuts, pig oil.

Bob Kelsey recalled:

"I have a vivid memory of my time in Sonkurai where I was sent with some 200 'fit' workers to help out the remnants of the Manchester Regiment slaving on the big bridge there. I asked a poor, skeletal man, "How is it that this camp, with seven Medical Officers, and a good supply of water and with the benefit of cholera vaccination before leaving Changi, should have lost so many men?"

"Sir", he answered, and I can see him still, "We died of brokin' 'arts".

"They were a city crowd with useless officers uninterested in their men,for example, where we, in Lower Sonkurai, soon learned to weave bamboo strips to form baskets to carry rice to several messing points, the men in Sonkurai had only one messing point at the cook house – necessitating a reveille some two hours before it was necessary. Also, it did not occur to them to have fires in their huts to make life more bearable, to dry their clothes and sterilise their dixies, as well as providing some light."

Ken Crispin:

> Sept.27: Camp divided into workers section and hospital, A.I.F. hospital and English hospital. All fed from one kitchen. More rice and better rations than at Lower Sonkurai but not so well cooked. Rumour of return to Changi as October. Railway runs right through centre of camp. Camp hygiene poor after Lower Sonkurai. Rations here expected to improve. Steamed pudding on for tea. Elephants in, practically every man has drawn half pint of gula malacca.

Captain Lloyd Cahill recalls:

"When I got up to Sonkurai it was almost as ghastly – I knew it consisted of almost British troops and some Australians – and the smell of tropical ulcers! I got it about a quarter of a mile away from the camp. A Warrant Officer was carrying the whole thing, the others did not seem to be doing very much about it all.

"The first day I went over the railway line to the Hospital section and I came across what I can only describe as "Golgotha" – there was a hill which had been used as a cremation point and there were skulls and bones and partly cremated bodies scattered all over the place; down behind that I found an Indian Army tent – I said What's this? and was told, "Oh this is the smallpox tent!" I looked in and there were about eight or ten virtual skeletons lying on the earth – nothing else nobody seemed to go near them – nobody wanted to go near them – poor devils – they were in a state of suspended animation. I organised and got a few volunteers to go over and clean them up and give them some food but they all died."

Popular English Chaplain Foster Haig, although ill himself, continued to talk to the sick and comfort as much as he could. When not so ill he would sing songs such as "Road to Mandalay" and at a more serious occasion, "The Holy City". He died at Sonkurai and was buried across the creek. Bob Wilson was one of the pall bearers. Captain Peter Hendry returned Foster Haig's Bible to his family in England.

Major Kevin Fagan, A.A.M.C. 'H' Force
Specialist Surgeon. Cared for many of the 'F' Force personnel sent down river to Kanburi for surgery.

CHAPTER EIGHT
RETURN TO KANBURI – SINGAPORE

By November, Neike had developed into a large base with several sidings, stacks of railway lines the Japanese had lifted from branch lines throughout Malaya – most of these rails were stamped "B.H.P." Many trains were now at the sidings to fuel up with firewood; the Japanese had removed the tree on which we had cut a Memorial plaque in September, we believed then that being teak it would last and be recovered after the war's end but the tree was close by and it represented valuable fuel.

At Sonkurai, Captain Lloyd Cahill was given a few minutes' notice to move: "They came along saying "Speedo Speedo! All men hurry!" so we packed up and marched to Neike – where the train arrived three weeks later! I got sick of sleeping in the mud at Neike so I crawled up on top of one of the stacks of rails, after a few nights I was joined by Captain "Curly" Curlewis who I hadn't seen for a couple of months. One night the Gonsu Sergeant came up and woke me up about ten o'clock, he was terribly excited and saying "Whoo whoo whoo!" and in came the train, but it was a brothel train and they opened the trucks and out popped these little girls in white uniforms, like nurses.

"The Japanese were given some tickets like you used to get at Luna Park and I woke 'Curly" and I said, "Curly! wake up! wake up!" he sat up saying, "What's the matter?!" and I said, "The brothel's arrived!" and he said "Where's my hat? where's my hat?" – a gentleman to the end was 'Curly'!

"And then the train did arrive and Col.Harris claimed me, he said "You are to come with me Cahill" and we went up to the front of the first flat top – you got all the dirt down the back – we travelled at night and it was cold. We got to a big railway centre down the line and Col. Harris said, "Come on Cahill, there is a friend of mine who is here" – this place was the first bit of civilisation I'd seen, there were a lot of lines and it was a big camp, and there was more food there than I had seen for a long time, eggs – it was all turned on, I kept reminding Col. Harris about the time and the fact that the train was due to go but he just kept on and of course we did miss the train and had to wait until the next one came down".

Earlier we loaded all the motor vehicles on to the flat tops, there were only a few serviceably sufficient to pull the wrecks on board and we climbed aboard.

The journey was frightening, when the train reached the Wampo Viaduct and the bridge along the cliff face above the Kwai Noi river the lines were tight and the wheels screamed as the train slowly crept along with every man looking at the river far below and knowing the many faults which had been covered up during the construction! We eventually arrived safely at Kanchanburi. Those who travelled at night did not have to suffer the agonising thought of Allied planes catching the train high above the river.

We reached Kanchanburi where, for the first time in eight months, we could enjoy eggs and fruit. It was here the men were classified for further duties. The Japanese gave notice and ordered 1000 fit men to be prepared to move in a matter of a week – ten days to Singapore.

Keith Meakin:

"The first party was to leave Upper Sonkurai for the journey south, there were 500 men. Lt.Col. Kappe, whom I hadn't seen during the whole time in camp, told me I was to go with him when the movement commenced. He also warned a senior W.O. officer to guard two large cases to be placed on the train. These cases were heavy, requiring two men to place them on the flat top truck, we eventually arrived at Kanburi and after some delay we were sent off to Bangkok where we were to be part of the 1000 so-called 'fit' men to return to Singapore.

"We remained there for some days, during that time the Japanese permitted purchases to be made through proper channels. Lt.Col. Kappe, who held the Force's funds, also placed orders together with anyone else who had money. By now Lt.Col. Kappe had several cases under his control, some of which were marked "Records". His batman, 'Snow' Dewsbury was present. Kappe had also been able to procure cartons of Virginia cigarettes.

"On December 10 the men were to board a barge for transportation to a ship, its destination Singapore. We were all standing around when Toyama appeared and said, "Kappe! Come with me". Kappe said to me to come too – and the cases were left with several carriers. They were placed on the barge but from that time on it was 'every man for himself' although some of the cases reached the ship."

'Bluey' Lee decided to investigate one case and found it contained an assortment of tinned food – the bulk of this particular case was Herrings and Tomato Sauce – food which should have been left for those at Sonkurai who were too ill to travel.

The ship was an old World War I vessel, coal burning, and of about 5000 tons; when it was underway Lt.Col. Kappe ordered officers to conduct a thorough search for his boxes – nothing was found. He ordered a parade and criticised the men for stealing the food. There are many versions of what he was reported to have said, the most common account was that he stood up on the Bridge, took off his shirt (displaying his good healthy condition) and offered to fight the culprits, he was jeered and 'booed' by the men who, by this time, were all smoking the Virginia cigarettes and the aroma was wafting past Kappe as he said, "You fools! It was your money I used to purchase that food for you to have on the voyage back to Singapore!" and he was given more 'booes'. He calmed down and effectively apologised to his own 8 Div.Signals for his own failure as a Commander ending, "I had to look after myself to tell the story."

The Captain found out there was a doctor on board – he sent for Captain Lloyd Cahill and explained to him by outlining the Sydney Harbour bridge that he had been to Sydney. He went away and came back with a large bottle labelled "Falk's Pharmacy George Street Sydney". It was a mixture for the treatment of venereal disease, the Captain wanted to know if he swallowed it, or rubbed it on!

The Japanese Captain was considerate and made the voyage as comfortable as possible, he stayed close to the coast all the way down.

During their voyage down the coast everyone was able to have frequent washes down with seawater. Despite that, Ed Bennett was told by his Changi mates, "You blokes stink!"

On 15th December the party arrived at Changi and was followed by other groups on successive days until 23rd December. One small party was diverted to Sime Road, Singapore, with 'H' Force.

When the Tanbaya survivors went by train to Kanburi, they picked up other sick from camps along the way. At Kanburi, one of Frank Smith's mates told him his brother Bob was on the train – he went off looking at all the stretcher cases and returned, telling his mate he couldn't see his brother anywhere. His mate replied, "That's him down there" and Frank looked at Bob who was about 6 stone and suffering severely from a tropical ulcer – "I didn't know my own brother" he said, "I gave him my bamboo water bottle and all the tobacco I had." Bob died at Kanburi.

Sid Musgrove:

"We came back in the last train, we had the worst of the sick, we had three blokes die in the truck and it was three days before the Japanese would let us get them out and bury them. Captain Taylor said to me 'They tell us we're going to have a bit of a stop Sid, if you can find something to get some water in will you wash these sick fellows? I've got my old blade razor and I'll shave them'. So I did that and we washed them and there was one fellow over in the corner and he hadn't moved for the whole trip and I got a bit short with him but I could have eaten my words for when we came to wash him and he dropped his shorts he had an enormous ulcer at the end of his spine – you could see the bone – it was pretty clean. I said to him 'What in the hell have your doctors been doing!? He was an Englishman and he said, "They would ask you how you are and before I could answer them they would be out the other end of the hut."

Austin Ellerman:

"I was in charge of the ulcer ward, we had 120 patients, 90 of whom could not walk.

"I was on the last train to depart for Kanburi as was Padre George Polain. At our first stop Padre Polain was to conduct a burial service at a small cemetery but he had sprained his ankle and was unable to walk; he asked me if I would go in his place and told me that as the train was due to pull out in 20 minutes the service would have to be cut short. At the cemetery I read the service at the grave then indicated to the guard that it was all finished, he turned to me and asked in halting English why I had not said "ashes to ashes dust to dust" and to save embarrassment I explained to him that this particular man's religion did not have those words, and we all went back to the train.

"Next day the train was struggling up an incline when the truck I was in was de-railed and started bumping over the sleepers. Lt. Bill McGeever, 2/26, hopped out of our truck and ran alongside soon catching up with the front of the engine and told them what had happened. The Japanese stopped the train, took a couple of heavy jacks from the front of the engine and jacked our truck back on the rails. Then they found the engine could not get a go on again, so an order was given "All men cut bamboo!" – we cut a supply and the engine soon got up enough heat and steam and we were on our way again, reaching Kanubri on 17 November 1943."

At Kanburi during the short stay everyone responded to extra food, the effect was quite incredible, many men putting on as much as a stone in weight and the sick men responded quickly. There was even the odd fight – or scuffle – broke out. While I was waiting my turn to use a fire another man was cooking up some food ahead of me in his dixie when a small Thai girl arrived – "You want sex?" He handed his dixie to me – "Don't burn it, back in ten minutes!"

The vultures greeted us back to the Camp site – where there were trees there were vultures -

When it was decided to clear the main body of the Force from Kanburi, Captain Barnett was selected by the IJA to remain in command of the sick.

Unfortunately, among the A.I.F. patients in this hospital was Major Bruce Hunt, who had developed acute cardiac beri beri. A considerable sum of money contributed from Officers' pay was left with the Senior Medical Officer, Lt.Col. Huston, for the purchase of extra food for the very ill.

Lieut. Wakabayashi, who adopted a humane attitude towards the sick in No.2 Camp, was left as the IJA Supervising Officer, and it was felt that he would at least not obstruct any action taken to restore the men to normal health.

Jim Ling:

"The Kanburi sick remained until April – Major Bruce Hunt examined every so-called 'fit' man, I was one of the lucky ones he examined for the next thing I was down on my back in one of the wards with cardiac beri beri. Now I didn't know I had cardiac beri beri till he told me – I didn't know he had it too. But from then until I was put on the train in April I was on my back; I was put on an improvised stretcher on to the train and then to Changi. You don't have any symptoms, I remember feeling I should be out working with the boys, but if I had not been examined by Hunt I wouldn't have made it. I remember seeing men in the hut alive one minute and then just drop dead with cardiac beri beri – they didn't know they had it."

On arriving back in Changi, after some rest, Padre Paddy Walsh reflected on the last eight months in Thailand: "The whole of the trip to Thailand and Burma was a good example of "Man's inhumanity to man". 'F' Force set off on the journey with high hopes but the train travel was but a foretaste of what lay ahead for the men; cramped into rice trucks, little or no food, no sanitation or water to bathe, the trip was a nightmare.

"The work of the Chaplains on the march was confined to trying to cheer up the men and help where they could but after the first 100 kms. it was all they could do to keep going themselves. Sunday, or any other day, as a day of rest was unknown.

"The IJA did not consider the need of at least an occasional visit to the men of their Chaplain was required, they found it hard to understand the need of one at all. Although there were five camps within easy reach of ours and I the only RC Chaplain within that area, only twice was I permitted to visit another camp. The first visit was to Upper Sonkurai, known as No.3 Camp, where there were 400 A.I.F. troops and no Chaplain. Later, when all the troops had been transferred from No.1 Camp to No.3 and No.2, an exchange of Chaplains was allowed.

"I stayed in No.2 Camp from 3rd October to 3rd November but it was in the beginning that there was a need of a visit because disease was more rife there than in other camps, deaths were averaging ten a day. Visiting other camps would not have caused any extra inconvenience for the IJA because I could have accompanied a ration party to and fro. When the transfer of troops was made from No.l to 2 and 3, I was stationed at No.3 and Padre Polain at No.2 where one of the Chaplains had died and the other gone to Burma.

"In No.3 Camp conditions were even more appalling than in No.l and difficulties greater. Supplies were running short here and services were reduced to one a week.

"Most of the cemetery work was under the care of Chaplains; at No.l we had the assistance of a good team and were able to make the cemetery look respectable, crosses with names and numbers carved and burnt on them placed over each grave and the site properly fenced. Here full credit must be given to Sgts. Crawford and Ambrose and Cpl. Nichol. The total deaths were 150.

"At No.3 Camp matter were worse, owing to the demand for road workers no men could be spared for permanent cemetery work and here I had to depend on the assistance of officers who were not required for other work. The cemetery was fenced but the graves marked only by numbers.

"There was no way we could ease the sick men, the best we could do was to supply smokes to some, when tobacco was available, or an occasional tin of milk. We arranged different lectures and concerts and for one period it was possible to have lecture in each hospital ward almost every night, but the supply of lectures soon ran out and we had spread them over a greater time. Earlier the Japanese had objected to the men singing but later we were able to arrange concerts for about once a week.

"Morale suffered under such terrible conditions; with men dying so rapidly each man would wonder if his turn would be next. Some of them even took to stealing from their mates, no article was safe if it had any saleable value among the natives. Strict measures were taken by our own Authorities but a certain amount of stealing still took place.

"But these actions were outweighed by the many cases of noble work and selflessness shown; I have seen many cases where men who themselves were sick and had to go to work each day would spend half the night looking after sick comrades, carrying them on their backs to the latrines, washing them and caring for them as best they could."

TRIBUTE BY LIEUT. NORM COUCH, PERSONAL ORDERLY OFFICER TO MAJOR BRUCE HUNT ON "F" FORCE. HE WAS KNOWN AS "KILLER" COUCH – OFFICER IN CHARGE OF 8 DIV. HEADQUARTERS DEFENCE AND DEPLOYMENT PLATOON. HE WAS NOT ONE TO TOLERATE SUSPECTED FIFTH COLUMNISTS WITHIN HIS AREA.

MAJOR BRUCE HUNT, A.A.M.C.

Bruce Attlee Hunt was a big and impressive man of incredible physical and mental endurance. He was highly astute, aggressive and had a deep understanding of human nature.

On the first night's march north from Kanburi Major Hunt was sorely tested and displayed the outstanding leadership qualities which were to make him a legendary benefactor on the Burma Line.

As Senior Medical Officer, Bruce Hunt stationed himself at the rear of the marching column and was directly involved with the sick and sore, the stragglers and the despondent. Conditions at the tail of the march were exhausting, pitiful and at times almost chaotic. During the marches the front of the column stopped for ten minutes every hour. Stages took longer than the night hours. At the rear the march never stopped. This was because the column merely reduced its length when forward troops stopped. It then stretched again when the men in front moved off. There was no respite for those at the tail where the need was greatest. It was under these most arduous conditions that Major Hunt first displayed his remarkable capacity as a leader, in seemingly impossible situations for the exercise of military discipline.

He carried his own and stragglers' gear in addition to medical supplies. Added to this he tended the sick and needy. He encouraged flagging men to greater efforts. And by sheer force of his unique personality did much in maintaining morale among ill, frail and dis-spirited men. This was but a foretaste of the almost unbelievable feats of man management Bruce Hunt reflected in the dangerous, horrifying and desperate period, soon to follow.

During the northward march Japanese guards flogged Bruce Hunt heavily with sticks, breaking his hand. He had demanded that sick men be rested. Bruce Hunt's spirit was never broken though he was totally immobilised by illness and exhaustion. He rejoined his party somewhere near Lower Sonkurai which shortly became a suburb of hell.

At Sonkurai, cholera struck the prisoners, adding greatly to their existing stresses and diseases. The troops were not innoculated against cholera until days after its onset. Death and fear of death overshadowed men already suffering the tortures of the damned with overwork, malnutrition, dysentery, malaria, typhus, ulcers and injuries inflicted by brutal guards, or caused by barbarous working conditions. Only the most trivial medical supplies were available. No hospital facilities existed. Despite strenuous efforts by POW Administration, hygiene was impossible. Filth, stench and horror omnipresent.

Maintenance of morale and survival-will was impossible at Lower Sonkurai among many men whose self-esteem and resistance to physical and mental stress had withered under starvation, disease and slave labour. For many, the burden of life outweighed the desire to live. Formerly staunch men soon reached the stage of hopelessness. However strong in body and mind an individual may be, he could be reduced to a darkened, gaunt, stinking skeleton in four hours, by cholera. It was in this terrifying situation where Bruce Hunt used the only two weapons available in his relentless fight to preserve life – pride and hope. Though himself a pessimist, he spread optimism. Where there was fear and despair, he strove to give hope and pride. Major Hunt had a messianic dimension. He was the dominant figure, the driving force, the metaphorical star to which men in peril looked for guidance. Without any doubt, many men, perhaps hundreds, survived the death-ridden Burma Line as the direct result of Major Hunt's fearless efforts. No words can portray how Bruce Hunt almost literally dragged demoralised men away from the funeral pyres by his skilled use of words, inspiration and encouragement.

At Tanbaya, South Burma, the POW Camp though ostensibly a "Hospital" was death-site for around 700 men in three to four months. At this camp, the Major was O.C. Hospital, Lt.Col. Hutchinson was Hospital Administrator and Major W.J.E. Phillips, R.A.M.C., Senior Medical Officer. The Major was the tireless evangelist of hope and self-esteem; he worked long, gruelling hours and, by example, produced great endeavours from his subordinates on all levels.

Australian and English prisoners came to Tanbaya by train from the south. Some were dead on arrival, some in extremis; all were diseased and weak; some were to have their legs amputated with a carpenter's hand saw. About half survived the "surgery"; septicaemia, haemorrhaging, inanition, or a combination of the latter coupled with world-weariness and loss of will to live, killing the others.

Morale maintenance was Bruce Hunt's forte and main objective, insofar as it was an instrument of survival. When thieving threatened discipline Major Hunt restored control with one application of corporal punishment. In retrospect the uninformed may deplore this courageous and desperate action. The perilous conditions demanded drastic action. And in that case it was successful in restoring the order and morale essential for the preservation of life.

Bruce Hunt saved countless Australian and English lives in Thailand and Burma. He did this in heroic fashion. Major Hunt's Burma Line leadership success stemmed from his personal attributes which made him a giant among all men in that soul-destroying environment. Bruce Hunt was a dynamic leader in indescribable circumstances because he was a dynamic man. He had self-esteem, intelligence, common-sense, aggression, empathy, sympathy and unusually high lucidity. But his greatest and most powerful tools were his personal presence and example; his giving hope to the hopeless; pride and courage to the weakened. He was a very bright star in an otherwise overcast and threatening sky.

No account, spoken or written, can paint an adequate picture of life and death on the Burma Line. No man has the command of words needed for conveying, in comprehensible terms, the courage and cowardice; the loyalty and treachery; the dedication and dereliction; the strengths and frailties; the kindness and brutality; the integrity and depravity; the magnificence and enormities of men, as revealed by and to those fated to pass through the entrails of hell, in Thailand Burma, during and after the Railway was built in 1943.

No verbal skills can create a fitting profile of a mighty man such as Bruce Hunt, Major, A.A.M.C., 8 Div. A.I.F. Bruce Attlee Hunt surmounted apparently impossible obstacles, in an environment which now defies even the imagination of witnesses to these events.

TRIBUTE TO MAJOR BRUCE HUNT BY LIEUT. RON EATON, MBE

Having refreshed my memory by reading my diary and other reports I am more than ever convinced that if it had not been for Bruce Hunt, John Taylor and Lloyd Cahill and Frank Cahill the large part of F Force I was associated with faced complete destruction.

If Bruce Hunt had not taken control at Lower Sonkurai when he did there would have been a greater disaster than it was. He took over when senior combatant officers were very ill.

With his medical skill, great physical strength and strong fearless personality he was able to impress on the Japanese his appreciation of the serious situation and his recommendations to save the whole force from disaster.

The tireless efforts of all the medical officers to combat the dreadful effects or the vicious tropical diseases with almost no resources and against terrific odds won the respect of all men. And also the respect of the Japanese.

How they had the physical strength to work in the awful conditions was little short of a miracle.

Bruce Hunt above all was a leader. He was up and down the line of camps advising everyone from Force HQ down and in the process getting much needed medical supplies. Mostly on foot he covered big distances in appalling conditions.

None of these Australian Medical Officers were experienced in tropical medicine including Cholera, Malaria, Cerebral Malaria, Encephalitis, Amoebic Dysentery, Beri Beri, Dengue Fever, Blackwater Fever, Scrub Typhus and Tropical Ulcers and Dermatitis.

But they quietly found out how to deal with it, saving countless lives.

And when all others had returned to Changi, Hunt and Taylor stayed a further four months at Kanburi with men too sick to travel.

I did not see the other doctors who did so much also.

I know they all performed magnificently.

It seemed to me that the conditions north of Neike up to The Three Pagoda Pass that is the area furthest from any signs of civilisation, an area of real wilderness, were the worst experienced on the whole railway project.

In the wet season the jungle tracks were virtually impassable, water was infected and every drop had to be boiled before use, nothing grew that could be eaten and in the dry season the water supply dried up.

The logistics of running hospitals of 1200/1500 patients all very sick with only 2/300 partially fit men to nurse and feed them and provide hygiene, cremation and burial services as well as walking long distances to manhandle the supply of rations such as they were, proved to be quite horrific.

This would be true even with access to medical supplies, surgical equipment, to operate with, uncontaminated water, proper buildings, light and heat, minimum basic food, none of which were available.

And not least without the fit men having to work in pouring tropical rain, often up to knees in mud, for 13 hours a day every day, this increasing the numbers of sick daily.

And this disregards the overall problem of the sadistic cruelty of many of the Japanese and Korean guards.

All these Australian doctors won the profound respect of every man who was there.

They performed far and away beyond the call of duty. Their magnificent efforts should be remembered forever and should be indelibly inscribed on the minds of every Australian child and adult.

Their unselfish efforts for their fellow men were a great example for all to follow and in particular the leadership and example of Hunt, supported by L. Cahill and J. Taylor, is without parallel.

LETTER WRITTEN BY MAJOR BRUCE HUNT TO DR. CAHILL RE HIS SON CAPT. FRANK CAHILL:

Now that our troubles are over, and a correspondence is likely to become a practical affair at an early date, I am taking a very early opportunity to write and tell you and Mrs. Cahill something of Frank's fine work in these hard years. I have had probably a rather better opportunity of seeing Frankie – to all his friends – on the job, than anybody else in this show, and the more I see of him, the more I think of his professional and personal qualities, and the more I value his friendship.

Our paths have lain together many times – sometimes in good places, more often in bad. I didn't know Frank before the campaign, but after it was over, I heard glowing reports of the excellent surgery he did at the Cathedral Dressing Station during the last days, and of his complete and selfless devotion to the job at that time. The first time I met him on more than nodding terms, was when he was admitted to my ward with a severe dengue in June, '42. He had a wretched week, and was so good about it, that I developed a fondness for him which has grown with the years.

Thereafter, for nine months or so, we were working in separate places, – he in Selerang, I in Roberts Hospital. We next came together when we were both appointed to "F" Force, that unlucky body of British and A.I.F. Troops which were sent up in April, 1943, to take part in the building of the Thailand-Burma Railway, and which lost 3000 of its 7000 members in the ensuing 12 months. It was a hard and desperate business – Frankie will tell you many of the grim details – and in both A.I.F. and British it made many reputations, and broke many others. If a man came out of the "F" Force show with an unblemished name, he can hold his head high for the rest of his life – it was the most searching test of essential character that I have seen in forty-six reasonably full years, which include eight years in the two A.I.F.'s.

On the road during the long march – in Lower Sonkurai camp, where I had the finest team of juniors any S.M.O. could possibly wish – and later in my hospital camp at Tanbaya Frank was always on the job. He did the big surgery when it came – did it cleanly and expeditiously, and satisfactorily with very few and poor tools, and in the most trying circumstances. But this was not the best nor the most important of his performances. Frank is a good doctor, he has a sound clinical judgement, a wide technical knowledge, and infinite kindness – all these qualities he devoted absolutely for the troops under his care. It was the instant daily little jobs that mattered more than the big stuff – jobs done in rain, in mud, in slush, in darkness – tired, hungry, and with men dying tragically all around one. Patching feet along the road, spotting cholera and early cerebral malaria in the middle of the night, with only a flickering bamboo torch for light – forcing desperately sick dysenteries to eat when their gorge revolted at the sight of food – improvising dressing and splints from the most unpromising materials – organising and training a team of skilled surgical dressers from crude volunteer labour from the combatant forces – these were the things that in the final reckoning made the difference between whether your man lived or died, and these were the things at which Frank and the "Gang" were supremely good. We got our A.I.F. out of the show with under half the mortality of our British Colleagues, and that is something for the M.O's who did the job, to be quietly proud of for the rest of their days.

At Tanbaya in Burma I was commanding a mixed British and Australian Hospital camp – Frank was the only other surgeon in the camp, and it was a great comfort and help to me to have somebody whom I could put on the job with the certain knowledge that the job would be done promptly, cleanly, and accurately, with no loose strings left to tie up after he had finished.

Very Sincerely yours,
(Signed) BRUCE HUNT
MAJOR. A.A.M.C.

EXTRACT FROM "PORTRAIT OF A MAN" BY R.H.S. KELSEY

Lt. Kelsey served in 2/26 Battalion.

"To this camp God sent Bruce Hunt with two junior medical officers, both Captains. He immediately persuaded two of the senior combatant officers to join him in a conference with the Jap Lieutenant nominally in charge. In fact, this camp was run by a sadistic Korean private.

"An immediate result of the conference was a 'promise' by the Japanese that palm leaf roofing would be provided, also shovels, and that all of the prisoners could work, for the first week, making the camp habitable.

"In the now constant downpour latrines were dug, roofs were wired to the walls, and the sleeping platforms, which were collapsing, were reinforced. And within three days the Japanese announced, "Enough, now you must leave your camp and work on the railway." This was to run along the nearby abandoned paddyfields. The whole area was uninhabited and devoid of wildlife, and we learnt that it was referred to by the Siamese as "The Valley of Death". With the exception of the senior officers, and those too sick to stand, every man in the camp was required to work on the railway, from before dawn, until after dark, seven days a week.

"Then, one never to be forgotten night, Bruce Hunt ordered a conference of all prisoner officers, to be held in the confined space at the end of a hut. We watched him fascinated, his face lit by the flickering flames of one of the hut's fires. "Gentlemen, things are grim." He had our attention! He went on, "I have diagnosed a disease of which I have had no experience. It does not occur in Australia. But I have read of it in text books, and I am sure it is Cholera."

"He continued, "I have conferred with the Japanese camp command and have learnt that they are, with good reason, terrified of the disease. They understand that without vaccination their prisoners could all die and they would lose their workforce and much 'face'. A supply of cholera vaccine has been requested from their main headquarters (some 15 miles down the track).

"In the meantime, work on the railway will temporarily cease." (Hunt seized on any excuse to stop his men working on the railway). "Fires will be kept alight at intervals in every hut. Before you use your eating utensils you will pass them through the flames, and you will see that your men do the same. Water must be boiled for at least seven minutes, no water will be drunk direct from the creek. Tomorrow we will scrape the surface filth from the camp area and it will be burnt or sterilised in the fires we will light over it. If a fly alights on the rice you are about to eat, the grains it lands on must be spooned out and burnt for, I assure you, if one contracts Cholera, one dies in great distress."

"And the next day the area was scraped of its surface mud and symbolically, if not successfully burnt. And the following day work resumed on the railway, while the deaths mounted. Ten, fifteen, and finally the terrible total of twenty died each day and were cremated with wet wood, in the pouring rain. And the cholera vaccine arrived! Never was a needle more eagerly awaited! Two weeks were required to pass before immunity was received, and never were days more anxiously passed, as friend after friend succumbed to the disease.

"But the days did pass, until cholera ceased to claim lives, yielding to the other killers – dysentery, malaria, tropical ulcers and utter exhaustion – and all the while the three doctors toiled through most of the hours of the day.

"To the fury of the Japanese command, Bruce Hunt would sometimes equip himself with three or four empty haversacks and stride down the track to the headquarters of Colonel Banno, a Japanese soldier who had some sense of honour. Hunt would play on this. He would hand him a written complaint to be forwarded by him to the Headquarters of the Red Cross in Switzerland. Then he would march back again, his haversacks bulging with anything he could beg, borrow or steal from the medical supplies under Banno's control. Once Banno gave Hunt a small bottle of Marmite with his apologies that he had nothing more to give, not knowing that Hunt had already used the Colonel's name to browbeat a Japanese medical orderly into giving him quinine and other useful medicines.

"One can still see him returning to Lower Sonkurai, haversacks slung from his huge hairy shoulders, mud from the waist down, and a grin on his face at the welcome which greeted him on all sides. Then, disposing of his booty, he would report to the camp command for the inevitable beating. And around the camp huts flashed the message of hope, "The Major's back!" No one had to ask, "Which Major?"

"Whenever he could he visited the sick and the dying in the huts reserved for them with a message of hope and encouragement – the falling death rate – the drugs he had scrounged from old Banno, his letter to the Red Cross, etc.

"The administration of the camp under men inspired by the Major went smoothly. Records were written in pencil on lengths of bamboo scraped of outer shine, baskets were woven from bamboo to contain rice which was carried hot from the 'cookhouse' to several messing points so that workers did not have to queue in the rain for an hour or more as they did in some other camps, and the dying were consoled and the ashes of the dead were blessed and a cross made and placed over them by the dedicated Padre "Paddy" Walsh.

"But the greatest benefit conferred on the men of Lower Sonkurai was the refusal of "The Major" to allow the very ill to work on the railway. Of course, it was impossible to protect them all, but by claiming dysentery sufferers or men with potentially fatal ulcers as having incipient cholera, and by putting them in what had been huts reserved for cholera patients, and then inviting the reluctant Japanese to "see for themselves" whether or not the men had cholera, he gained precious time for the very weak. His greatest success (proudly boasted on his visits to the sick) was the day when only 100 men were pronounced by him to be fit for work. His fearless sheltering of the sick and the exhausted from the slave gangs, and his medical skill was so energetically applied during those ten terrible months, that hundreds of Australian prisoners owed their lives to him.

"Of the scores of memories one has of this remarkable man, one stands out. It is a picture of him visiting the sick, himself exhausted and recently beaten, and pausing to place a hand gently on a feverish forehead, and murmuring in his beautiful accent, "Poor old boy". God rest his soul."

RECOLLECTION OF "F" FORCE – BY DAVID GRIFFIN, NX.69235

Few prisoners will ever forget the departure of 'F' Force and the tragic sequel of its return to Changi. Our captors had promoted 'F' Force as abundant food with the lure of exotic Siam and Burma as part almost of a tourist's package. Accordingly there was keen competiion to be a member of the party. Officers of the Indian Army even conducted a road race over 50 yards to determine who would be the lucky ones. When the first list came round, to my dismay, my name was on it. Having made no secret of my wish to remain in Changi, a Staff Sergeant from another Unit, who had not been chosen to go, asked me if he could take my place. His great friend with whom he had enlisted, was going and they both wanted to stay together. His success in having himself as a substitute for me, saved my life.

'F' Force was to leave at first light on 18 April, 1943 and many of us went to the barrack square before dawn to see them off. A convoy of Marmon-Harrington trucks manned by Japanese moved into the barrack square and the troops, carrying the clothes they wore and little else, clambered aboard. As dawn broke, the convoy under the watchful eye of Black Jack Galleghan and his faithful staff officer, Stewart Peach, in torrential rain rumbled off into the dawn of another Changi day. They vanished, as it were, without trace and were soon forgotten.

Months later, as Christmas was approaching, a rumour flashed round the prison camp, as rumours did, that 'F' Force was coming back. Unlike most rumours this one was true and we were about to face hideous fact. All prisoners of the Japanese wherever they were starved to the brink of death and thus we were not shocked by emaciated bodies. Without mirrors we could not see ourselves but we felt uncommonly thin; ribs and collar bones carving out an outline on gaunt frames was how we looked. Even so, we were totally unprepared for the human wreckage which returned to Changi as the survivors of 'F' Force. In the trucks sat slowly moving skeletons emaciated almost beyond belief, many with dreadful sores and peeling skin, some unable to move and others so light that a Changi prisoner had no difficulty in lifting them. This was the doleful return of 'F' Force – a living nightmare of degradation. By contrast the rest of us suddenly looked fit and strong, anxious to help but knowing now what to do.

Over the past year we had been hoarding odd scraps of food. Enough had been put aside – salt and red-palm oil and extra rice – even a little gula malacca – for our eagerly awaited Christmas dinner. Here was something we could do – not much, but something – 'F' Force could have our Christmas dinner, which was to have been our second in captivity. Without a moment's thought all this was given and given gladly to the remnants of 'F' Force. It was Changi's finest hour – a gesture of corporate unselfishness which has no parallel in my experience. It may not have one much to restore our comrades' health but it certainly helped their spirit. They felt, as many of them said, that they had come home to a warm welcome from their family. They joy was our reward: it was the best Christmas dinner any of us had never had.

Perhaps I should add for the record that both my Staff Sergeant and his companion came back and lived to tell the tale.

F FORCE

NUMBER	RANK	NAME	UNIT	PL. of DEATH	D.O.D.	AGE	ORIGIN
QX. 9725	Pte.	Adams, A.H.	2/26 Inf	Tanbaya	11.11.43.	33	Palmwood, Qld.
QX. 9936	Sgt.	Atkinson, E.S.	2/26 Inf	Upper Sonkurai	16.10.43.	38	Kelvin Grove, Qld
QX.10551	Cpl.	Atkins, F.L.	2/26 Inf	Tanbaya	12.12.43.	34	
QX.14494	Gnr.	Andrews, B.R.	2/10 RAA	Tanbaya	24.09.43.	24	Kedron, Qld.
QX.17041	Sgt.	Adams, E.V.	2/10 RAA	Lower Sonkurai	03.06.43.	28	Windsor, Qld.
NX.25808	Cpl.	Avard, G.	2/29 Inf	Upper Sonkurai	22.08.43.	22	Canterbury, NSW
NX.26523	Pte.	Archer, H.R.	H.Q.	Tanbaya	24.10.43.	40	Manly, NSW
NX.26721	Pte.	Angus, C.A.	27 Bde.	Takanoon	14.08.43.	32	Auburn, NSW
NX.26812	Pte.	Ayrton, H.R.	2/29 Inf	Takanoon	12.07.43.	22	Canowindra, NSW
NX.45594	L/Sgt.	Annand, C,	2/30 Inf	Kanburi	10.12.43.	32	Port Macquarie,NSW
VX.19506	Pte.	Allen,- R.R.	4 RMT	Tanbaya	05.11.43.	42	Swan Hill, Vic.
VX.25912	Pte.	Allder, S.T.	2/29 Inf	Tarsoa	06.08.43.	33	Ormond, Vic.
VX.38164	Pte.	Allan, G.M.	2/29 Inf	Takanoon	10.07.43.	23	Wonthaggi, Vic.
VX.40901	Pte.	Arbuthnot, M.	2/29 Inf	Neike	14.11.43.	25	Bonnie Doon, Vic
VX.45568	Spr.	Adams, W.	2/10 RAE	Sonkurai	19.08.43	30	Hawthorn, Vic.
VX.57090	Sgmn.	Albert, C.H.	8Dv.Sigs	Kanburi	23.09.43.	25	Boronia, Vic.
VX.61157	Pte.	Alford, E.G.	22Fd.Pk.	Changi	25.04.44.	28	Port Germain, SA
VX.62987	S/Sgt.	Appleby, H.A.	22Fd.Pk.	Upper Sonkurai	01.09.43.	25	East Malvern, Vic.
VX.65186	Pte.	Armit, W.F.G.	2/10 WS	Tanbaya	04.10.43.	28	Bindi, Vic.
SX.10964	Pte.	Atwill, J.E.D.	AASC	Prankalli	27.11.43	24	Glcrshre., UK
TX. 8281	Pte.	Absolom, G.	2/29 Inf	Takanoon	23.10.43.	21	Hobart, Tas.
QX. 8318	Pte.	Blackwell, J.L.	2/26 Inf	Lower Sonkurai	21.06.43.	42	Glebe Point, NSW
QX. 9412	Pte.	Berg, F.J.	2/26 Inf	Upper Sonkurai	09.10.43.	23	Cooroy, Qld.
QX. 9463	Gnr.	Bone, A.J.	2/10 RAA	Tanbaya	12.10.43.	37	Brisbane, Qld.
QX.10083	Pte.	Billsborough, H.W.	2/26 Inf	Kanburi	25.12.43.	43	Goondiwindi, Qld
QX.10686	Pte.	Blacow, W.	2/26 Inf	Lower Sonkurai	02.06.43.	33	Hawthorne, Qld.
QX.11502	Pte.	Benham, E.J.	2/26 Inf	Lower Sonkurai	29.05.43.	23	Ayr, Qld.
QX.13055	Pte.	Barkle, C.H.	27 Bde.	Chungkai	25.08.43.	31	
QX.13247	Pte.	Baker, R.G.	AASC	Tanbaya	01.10.43	23	Mackay, Qld.
QX.13275	Pte.	Brennan, J.T.	2/26 Inf	Kanburi	25.12.43	24	Mackay, Qld.
QX.13575	Pte.	Breen, P.	2/26 Inf	Sonkurai	23.08.43.	40	Ballykeeffe, Ire.
QX.13713	L/Cpl.	Brown, W.A.	2/26 Inf	Tanbaya	07.10.43.	39	Griffith, NSW
QX.14152	Pte.	Buchbach, R.	2/26 Inf	Tanbaya	19.10.43.	40	Shaw's Pocket, Qld.
QX.14828	Pte.	Burns, J.J.	2/26 Inf	Upper Sonkurai	10.09.43.	27	Goodna, Qld.
QX.14865	Pte.	Boon, J.C.	2/26 Inf	Lower Sonkurai	27.05.43.	42	
NX.14884	Sgt.	Browne, J.A.C.	2/10 RAA	Tanbaya	10.09.43.	32	Coorparoo, Qld.
QX.15291	Pte.	Bowers, J.E.	2/26 Inf	Lower Sonkurai	14.08.43.	21	Aloomba, Qld.
QX.16062	Sgt.	Bennett, A.E.	2/29 Inf	Lower Sonkurai	02.06.43.	26	Nundah, Qld.
QX.16287	Pte.	Beitz, G.V.	2/26 Inf	Upper Sonkurai	13.10.43.	21	Red Hill, Qld.
QX.16324	Pte.	Beresford, J.E.A.	2/26 Inf	Upper Sonkurai	22.08.43.	20	Cecil Plains, Qld
QX.16936	Pte.	Bidstrup, N.M.	2/26 Inf	Lower Sonkurai	27.05.43.	28	Clayfield, Qld.
QX.17362	Pte.	Brockhurst, A.W.	2/26 Inf	Lower Sonkurai	09.08.43.	32	
QX.18759	Gnr.	Buckley, L.	2/15 RAA	Tanbaya	21.11.43.	29	Sarina, Qld.
QX.19172	Pte.	Bazzo, J.V.	2/26 Inf	Lower Sonkurai	20.05.43.	27	Pomona, Qld.
QX.19361	Gnr.	Burns, F.E.	2/15 RAA	Tanbaya	02.10.43.	23	Annerley, Qld.
QX.19804	Cpl.	Brown, A.J.A.	10 WS	Lower Neike	03.06.43.	29	Boonah, Qld.
QX.20025	Pte.	Barwick, W.J.B.	2/26 Inf	Upper Sonkurai	24.06.43.	21	Woolloongabba, Qld.
QX.20461	Pte.	Bourke, W.J.	2/29 Inf	Kando	25.08.43.	22	Obi Obi, Qld.
QX.21870	Pte.	Brown, J.	2/19 Inf	Tanbaya	06.11.43.	41	

QX.21930	Pte.	Bignell, S.K.	2/30 Inf	Tanbaya	08.10.43.	23	Upper Coomera, Qld.
QX.23451	L/Cpl.	Benson, A.H.	2/26 Inf	Kanburi	10.12.43.	24	Charleville, Qld.
QX.23710	Pte.	Bradford, R.	2/26 Inf	Upper Sonkurai	03.10.43.	30	Tannymorel, Qld.
NX. 2123	Pte.	Bradley, B.W.	84 LAD	Kanburi	23.12.43.	33	Putney, NSW
NX. 2497	Pte.	Bee, R.J.F.	2/30 Inf	Upper Sonkurai	14.08.43.	31	Mascot, NSW
NX. 4392	Pte.	Bateman, S.H.	2/19 Inf	Lower Sonkurai	18.05.43.	23	Earlwood, NSW
NX.22787	Cpl.	Baker, D.P.	Provost	Kanburi	29.12.43.	22	Newtown, NSW
NX.26228	Pte.	Benson, J.B.	2/30 Inf	Kanburi	11.12.43.	36	Darlinghurst, NSW
NX.27234	Pte.	Bennett, J.J.	2/30 Inf	Tanbaya	29.11.43.	41	Glen Innes, NSW
NX.27836	Sgt.	Byrne, C.A.	2/15 RAA	Tanbaya	05.12.43.	42	
NX.29925	L/Cpl.	Bell, W.L.	2/30 Inf	Kanburi	15.12.43.	23	Narrabri, NSW
NX.30308	Pte.	Bancroft, I.	2/30 Inf	Neike	20.06.43.	27	Iluka, NSW
NX.31649	Cpl.	Baker, H.L.	2/30 Inf	Upper Sonkurai	07.11.43.	28	Annandale, NSW
NX.31809	Pte.	Bennett, A.H.	2/20 Inf	Kanburi	04.12.43.	27	Woodstock, NSW
NX.33134	L/Cpl.	Bricknell, J.M.	73 LAD	Upper Sonkurai	18.11.43.	34	Eastwood, NSW
NX.34273	Pte.	Bolt, R.	2/26 Inf	Upper Sonkurai	14.11.43.	29	Berry, NSW
NX.35234	Sgmn.	Bryce, W.	8DivSigs	Kanburi	20.10.43.	37	
NX.35612	Cpl.	Bertram, R.B.	Provost	Kanburi	04.12.43.	27	Wagga Wagga, NSW
NX.36242	Pte.	Bright, J. (S/A. Weston, J.)	2/30 Inf	Lower Sonkurai	07.09.43.	30	Geelong West, Vic.
NX.36616	Cpl.	Buswell, T.L.	Provost	Upper Sonkurai	13.09.43.	41	Dulwich Hill, NSW
NX.37065	Sgt.	Byrne, P.J.	GBD	Upper Sonkurai	26.09.43.	38	Kensington, NSW
NX.37310	Pte.	Blackstock, J.	2/30 Inf	Kando	29.08.43.	32	Parkes, NSW
NX.37559	Pte.	Bailey, H.A.	2/30 Inf	Kanburi	30.12.43.	41	Arncliffe, NSW
NX.37665	Pte.	Briggs, W.S.	MLFDU	Kanburi	15.02.44.	38	Oatley, NSW
NX.39714	Pte.	Bicket, W.S.	2/30 Inf	Upper Sonkurai	13.11.43.	23	Parkes, NSW
NX.39942	Pte.	Brent, S.	2/30 Inf	Tanbaya	20.12.43.	22	Wellington, NSW
NX.39965	L/Cpl.	Brindley, E.J.	GBD	Tanbaya	06.11.43.	26	Crows Nest, NSW
NX.40301	Cpl.	Buckham, J.H.	2/30 Inf	Upper Sonkurai	12.10.43.	29	Penshurst, NSW
NX.43474	Pte.	Boyd, J.	H.Q.	Lower Sonkurai	11.06.43.	28	Dungay, NSW
NX.44662	Spr.	Bishop, D.G.	2/12 RAE	Kanburi	09.12.43.	21	Narrabeen, NSW
NX.44917	Pte.	Betheras, C.B.	2/29 Inf	Changi	26.01.44.	31	Emmaville, NSW
NX.45104	Pte.	Butler, R.J.	2/29 Inf	Kanburi	10.01.44.	22	Black Swamp, NSW
NX.45186	Pte.	Beeston, D.D.	2/lOFAmb	Kanburi	16.10.43.	35	Newcastle, NSW
NX.46217	Gnr.	Bagley, N.	2/15 RAA	Lower Sonkurai	11.08.43.	28	Gloucester, NSW
NX.46624	Pte.	Bailey, W.J.	2/30 Inf	Changi	12.05.44.	35	Bellingen, NSW
NX.46914	Pte.	Brown, A.K.	2/30 Inf	Died on train	28.11.43.	27	Mascot, NSW
NX.46917	Pte.	Blackadder, C.J.	2/30 Inf	Upper Sonkurai	04.09.43.	30	Chambigne, NSW
NX.47279	Pte.	Breese, J.F.	2/30 Inf	Lower Sonkurai	25.06.43.	31	Bretti, NSW
NX.47335	Pte.	Brunsdon, A.G.	2/20 Inf	Tanbaya	16.09.43.	43	Macksville, NSW
NX.48846	Pte.	Bolton, L.H.	2/18 Inf	Tanbaya	01.10.43.	27	Berridale, NSW
NX.49330	Pte.	Bills, T.	2/19 Inf	Tanbaya	05.12.43.	34	Bankstown, NSW
NX.50505	W0.2	Blashki, V.S.	Div.HQ	Neike	26.11.43.	28	Bellevue Hill, NSW
NX.51727	Cpl.	Bates, H.J.	Div.HQ	Lower Sonkurai	05.06.43.	29	Bexley, NSW
NX.51798	Spr.	Biggs, A.G.	2/12 RAE	Tanbaya	18.10.43.	32	Merrylands, NSW
NX.52471	Cpl.	Borlase, A.W.R.	Provost	Lower Sonkurai	29.05.43.	25	Kondinen, WA
NX.54228	Pte.	Brownsmith, E.J.	2/30 Inf	Tanbaya	06.09.43.	22	Campsie, NSW
NX.54369	Pte.	Buttenshaw, E.	2/30 Inf	Kanburi	09.09.43.	25	Alexandria, NSW
NX.54980	Pte.	Bartlett, A.J.	2/30 Inf	Kanburi	02.12.43.	29	Waverley, NSW
NX.58187	L/Sgt.	Barns, V.	2/30 Inf	Lower Sonkurai	02.06.43.	23	Leichhardt, NSW
NX.58315	Pte.	Baxter, L.J.	2/30 Inf	Kanburi	14.01.44.	22	Picton, NSW

NX.58441	L/Cpl.	Badgery, B.C.	27BdeHQ	Takanoon	09.07.43.	25	Exeter, NSW
NX.59062	Cpl.	Butt, E.W.	2/30 Inf	Upper Sonkurai	16.11.43.	29	Waverley, NSW
NX.59485	L/Cpl.	Bayliss, W.C.	2/30 Inf	Lower Sonkurai	03.06.43.	35	Artarmon, NSW
NX.68307	W0.2	Baker, R.J.	Div.HQ	Upper Sonkurai	13.11.43.	27	Scone, NSW
NX.68414	Dvr.	Bourke, E.J.	2/3 MAC	Tanbaya	08.08.43.	41	Randwick, NSW
NX.77801	Pte.	Burton, F.W.	2/29 Inf	Tanbaya	07.10.43.	22	Annandale, NSW
VX.12356	Pte.	Bridgeford, H.M.	2/29 Inf	Lower Sonkurai	17.08.43.	36	Nth.Richmond,Vic.
VX.21384	Pte.	Bolton, D.G.	2/29 Inf	Kanburi	24.12.43.	27	Elwood, Vic.
VX.24682	Pte.	Burt, M.C.	2/29 Inf	Takanoon	20.07.43.	42	Hampton, Vic.
VX.26140	Spr.	Briggs, W.T.	2/10 RAE	Tamaranpat	08.07.43.	39	Malvern, Vic.
VX.27689	Pte.	Brun, H.L.	2/29 Inf	Tanbaya	24.09.43.	39	Nth. Fitzroy, Vic.
VX.28860	Sgmn.	Bedford, A.S.	8DivSigs	Lower Neike	27.07.43.	23	Camberwell, Vic.
VX.30221	Sgt.	Bezverkoff, C.C.	2/29 Inf	Takanoon	21.08.43.	31	
VX.32772	Sgmn.	Benoit, M.A.W. (MM)	8DivSigs	Taimonta	24.05.43.	23	Bayswater, Vic.
VX.36027	Pte.	Barry, L.G.	2/29 Inf	Taimonta	04.10.43.	24	Elliminyt, Vic.
VX.39326	Pte.	Bassett, H.	2/29 Inf	Kanburi	14.01.44.	24	Nth.Fitzroy, Vic
VX.40321	Pte.	Bloom, A.	2/29 Inf	Tamaranpat	18.07.43.	40	Richmond, Vic.
VX.40361	Cpl.	Barrow, A.I.	2/29 Inf	Kando	03.08.43.	28	Hampton, Vic.
VX.40630	Pte.	Burgess, F.H.	2/29 Inf	Upper Sonkurai	08.11.43.	35	South Yarra, Vic
VX.43936	Cpl.	Barker, F.R.	2/29 Inf	Kanburi	24.12.43.	26	Hawthorn, Vic.
VX.45274	Gnr.	Black, A.E.J.	4 A/Tk.	Changi	04.01.44.	30	East Geelong, Vic.
VX.47319	Pte.	Brownlie, A.J.C.	2/29 Inf	Lower Sonkurai	08.06.43.	28	Noorinbee Nth.Vic.
VX.48320	Cpl.	Braham, F.R.	Provost	Upper Sonkurai	30.09.43.	21	Ascot Vale, Vic.
VX.50087	Pte.	Bury, R.W.	4 RMT	Lower Sonkurai	15.07.43.	43	Mildura, Vic.
VX.53554	Pte.	Barg~sst R-.W.	13 AGH	Tanbaya	12.01.44.	38	South Yarra, Vic.
VX.53752	Spr.	Brennan, W.	Mob.B.	Upper Sonkurai	20.11.43.	40	Flemington, Vic.
VX.54586	Pte.	Britnell, E.J.	Fd.Bky.	Kanburi	22.12.43.	22	Bayswater, Vic.
VX.54759	Pte.	Briggs, J.	2/29 Inf	Upper Sonkurai	18.10.43.	37	Rutherglen, Vic.
VX.55835	Pte.	Baldwin, W.R.	2/29 Inf	Lower Sonkurai	27.05.43.	22	Bendigo, Vic.
VX.56456	Pte.	Bond, E.E.V.	2/29 Inf	Kanburi	21.01.44.	23	Carlton, Vic.
VX.61544	Pte.	Bignell, A.G.	2/29 Inf	Lower Sonkurai	01.06.43.	22	Preston, Vic.
VX.62325	Pte.	Beanland, I.J.	2/lOFdPk.	Upper Sonkurai	05.07.43.	41	Hopetoun, Vic.
VX.62860	Pte.	Barrett, R.S.	Postal	Kuie	21.09.43.	19	
VX.63525	Pte.	Bence, R.R.	2/29 Inf	Tanbaya	17.09.43.	29	Panmure, Vic.
VX.64644	Pte.	Bernal, J.	2/lOFdPk.	Upper Sonkurai	25.11.43.	32	Prahran, Vic.
SX. 7710	Pte.	Bayly, C.R.	AASC	Tanbaya	25.09.43.	29	East Moonta, SA
SX. 9682	Pte.	Bawden, J.S.	AASC	Tanbaya	08.09.43.	29	Col.Light Gdn, SA
SX.14541	Pte.	Barry, M.L.	AASC	Upper Sonkurai	12.01.43.	29	Solomontown, SA
TX. 5351	Pte.	Butler, V.R.	2/29 Inf	Tanbaya	11.11.43.	24	Launceston, Tas.
TX. 5627	Spr.	Berry, G.R.	2/10 RAE	Neike	22.08.43.	24	West Melbourne,Vic.
TX. 5788	Pte.	Broad, A.E.	2/26 Inf	Tanbaya	31.08.43.	38	Beaconsfield, Tas.
TX. 5866	Pte.	Billinghurst, G.M.	2/26 Inf	Lower Sonkurai	05.07.43.	20	Moonah, Tas.
TX. 8312	Pte.	Bannister, C.R.	2/29 Inf	Tanbaya	20.09.43.	21	Ranelagh, Tas.
WX. 6338	Spr.	Boyle, R.A.P.	2/6FPkRAE	Tamaranpat	01.07.43.	40	Boulder, W.A.
WX. 8165	Spr.	Bardsley, W.E.	2/6FPkRAE	Changi	22.04.44.	37	
WX.13113	Spr.	Boydell, A.L.	2/6FPkRAE	Takanoon	16.08.43.	37	North Collie, WA
QX. 9574	Pte.	Crooks, M.J.	2/26 Inf	Kanburi	16.01.44.	24	Mount Gravatt,Qld.
QX. 9803	Cpl.	Clough, R.W.	2/26 Inf	Kanburi	18.01.44.	27	Wellington Pt.,Qld.
QX. 9945	Pte.	Clark, A.E.	2/26 Inf	Tanbaya	06.10.43.	27	Ascot, Qld.
QX.10683	Pte.	Crowley, P.	2/26 Inf	Tanbaya	14.12.43.	24	Buranda, Qld.
QX.11113	Pte.	Cubby, G.E. (Abor.)	2/26 Inf	Kanburi	17.12.43.	30	Boggabilla, Qld.

QX.11138	Sgt.	Currie, S.C.	2/26 Inf	Tanbaya	30.10.43.	34	Kalbar, Qld.
QX.11417	L/Cpl.	Cameron, R.A.	2/26 Inf	Tanbaya	03.01.44.	30	Wynnum Central,Qld.
QX.11421	L/Cpl.	Cornell, E.J.	2/26 Inf	Kando	01.09.43.	35	Ipswich, Qld.
Qx~11481	Sgt.	Corcoran, T.J.M.	2/26 Inf	Lower Sonkurai	27.07.43.	27	Townsville, Qld.
QX.11787	Pte.	Christensen, P.A.	2/26 Inf	Sonkurai	30.08.43.	32	
QX.13555	Gnr.	Cuckson, G.H.	2/10 RAA	Upper Sonkurai	29.06.43.	42	Toowong, Qld.
QX.13696	Cpl.	Craft, G.H.	2/26 Inf	Sonkurai	03.10.43.	35	Nudgee Beach, Qld.
QX.15113	Cpl.	Curtis, E.J.	2/26 Inf	Changi	19.03.44	24	Ravenshoe, Qld.
QX.15292	Pte.	Coles, F.W.	2/26 Inf	Changi	09.05.44.	22	Ipswich, Qld.
QX.16442	Pte.	Cann, M.H.	2/26 Inf	Kanburi	24.12.43.	29	Singleton, NSW
QX.16514	Pte.	Chadwick, A.R.	2/26 Inf	Kanburi	15.12.43.	32	
QX.17117	Cpl.	Comerford, J.M.	2/26 Inf	Lower Sonkurai	25.05.43.	26	Paddington, Qld.
QX.18261	Pte.	Clifford, J.	2/30 Inf	Upper Sonkurai	10.11.43.	37	
QX.18395	Pte.	Campbell, C.J.	2/26 Inf	Tamaranpat	14.08.43.	32	Mitchell, Qld.
QX.20941	Pte.	Caine, F.	AAOC	Tanbaya	21.09.43.	38	Nottingham, UK
QX.21708	Gnr.	Crane, A.E.C.	2/10 RAA	Kanburi	23.12.43.	35	Nanango, Qld.
QX.21709	Gnr.	Crane, J.W.	2/10 RAA	Lower Sonkurai	29.05.43.	26	Nanango, Qld.
QX.22030	Pte.	Crawford, G.H.	10 AGH	Sonkurai	25.10.43.	22	
QX.23039	Pte.	Crust, C.	2/26 Inf	Upper Sonkurai	26.10.43.	22	Moonmera, Qld.
QX.23215	Pte.	Clifford, W.A.	2/29 Inf	Padang Besar	20.12.43.	28	Lowmead, Qld.
QX.23667	Pte.	Cannon, W.H.	AAOC	Tanbaya	17.10.43.	41	Oakey, Qld.
NX. 1161	Sgmn.	Carradice, T.	8DivSigs	Kuie	22.07.43.	36	Thirroul, NSW
NX. 2719	Pte.	Cotter, P.A.	2/30 Inf	Kanburi	06.12.43.	23	Murwillumbah, NSW
NX. 4208	Pte.	Culbert, P.A.	2/19 Inf	Tanbaya	02.10.43.	32	
NX. 4512	Pte.	Cumberland, W.A.	2/30 Inf	Upper Sonkurai	16.09.43.	24	Goulburn, NSW
NX.26414	Pte.	Cahill, R.E.	2/30 Inf	Upper Sonkurai	21.10.43.	27	Balgowlah, NSW
NX.27458	Pte.	Cook, J.A.	2/20 Inf	Kanburi	05.01.44.	32	Bungonia, NSW
NX.27884	Gnr.	Connelly, F.	2/15 RAA	Kanburi	14.01.44.	35	Bondi Jnctn., NSW
NX.30645	Gnr.	Cooper, B.T.K.	2/15 RAA	Tanbaya	15.11.43.	27	Cowra, NSW
NX.31694	Pte.	Cann, B.A.	2/30 Inf	Kanburi	14.12.43.	28	Essex, UK
NX.33271	Pte.	Chambers, D.R.N.	2/30 Inf	Upper Sonkurai	21.11.43.	22	Lakemba, NSW
NX.33710	Pte.	Casey, D.V.	2/29 Inf	Kanburi	12.12.43.	30	Bega, NSW
NX.34578	Pte.	Cox, A.S.	2/lOFAmb	Tanbaya	28.01.44.	26	Marrickville, NSW
NX.34579	L/Cpl.	Carew, J.J.	2/30 Inf	Upper Sonkurai	01.10.43.	38	Tempe, NSW
NX.35786	Pte.	Campbell, E.F.	2/30 Inf	Kanburi	03.12.43.	43	Bathurst, NSW
NX.35915	Pte.	Coady, K.J.	2/19 Inf	Lower Sonkurai	02.08.43.	28	Harden, NSW
NX.36510	Pte.	Cox, A.R.	2/30 Inf	Lower Sonkurai	07.06.43.	28	Hay, NSW
NX.41078	Pte.	Crossman, A.B.	2/30 Inf	Upper Sonkurai	16.10.43.	33	Armidale, NSW
NX.41583	Sgt.	Cope, C.T.	GBD	Tanbaya	25.11.43.	43	Crows Nest, NSW
NX.44812	Sigmn.	Carr, R.W.	8DivSigs	Sonkurai	01.09.43.	19	Granville, NSW
NX.44900	Pte.	Cameron, A.	2/29 Inf	Lower Sonkurai	28.05.43.	21	Bowraville, NSW
NX.46561	Pte.	Cook, M.	2/30 Inf	Upper Sonkurai	23.08.43.	24	Dorroughby, NSW
NX.47129	Pte.	Coote, G.B.	2/30 Inf	Lower Sonkurai	04.06.43.	34	Leura, NSW
NX.47355	Pte.	Carney, J.E.	2/30 Inf	Tanbaya	30.11.43.	25	Kempsey, NSW
NX.49433	Pte.	Croyle, A.R.	2/26 Inf	Kanburi	12.12.43.	34	West Maitland,NSW
NX.52055	Pte.	Chessell, A.B.	AASC	Tanbaya	02.09.43.	35	Marrickville, NSW
NX.54181	Cpl.	Crain, L.T.	Div.HQ	Upper Sonkurai	14.06.43.	25	Petersham, NSW
NX.55168	Pte.	Clark, K.W.	Div.HQ	Tanbaya	11.12.43.	24	Sydney, NSW
NX.55568	Pte.	Conen, S.G.	2/30 Inf	Upper Sonkurai	29.10.43.	37	Chatswood, NSW
NX.55941	Spr.	Clark, J.F.	2/12 RAE	Neike	20.06.43.	33	
NX.56964	Pte.	Colquhoun, P.H.	2/18 Inf	Tamaranpat	23.11.43.	28	Bondi, NSW

NX.58736	Sgt.	Cox, J.F.	AASC	Tanbaya	09.11.43.	32	Mosman, NSW
NX.71966	Pte.	Carroll, J.L.	2/30 Inf	Lower Sonkurai	22.06.43.	24	Murwillumbah, NSW
NX.73093	Sgmn.	Cotterill, H.S.	8DivSigs	Tanbaya	27.09.43.	27	Eastwood, NSW
VX.20746	Cpl.	Coutts, J.B.	2/29 Inf	Wanyai Hosp.	17.08.43.	37	Joyce's Creek, Vic.
VX.21715	Spr.	Covey, H.J.	2/10 RAE	Kanburi	30.11.43.	30	Ringwood, Vic
VX.22930	Spr.	Castles, P.	2/10 RAE	Lower Sonkurai	07.06.43.	27	Richmond, Vic.
VX.28074	Gnr.	Case, L.F.	4 A/Tk.	Sonkurai	25.08.43.	29	Irymple, Vic.
VX.39293	S/Sgt.	Carter, E.H.	AAOC	Tanbaya	08.10.43.	33	Yarram, Vic.
VX.40956	Pte.	Clayton, V.E.	2/29 Inf	Upper Sonkurai	17.11.43.	26	Cohuna, Vic.
VX.40971	Spr.	Carson, J.	2/10 RAE	Tamaranpat	17.07.43.	29	Brunswick, Vic.
VX.44417	Pte.	Curtin, N.W.	2/4 Wksp.	Kanburi	11.12.43.	27	West Preston, Vic.
VX.45618	Pte.	Carter, P.J.	2/29 Inf	Upper Sonkurai	01.11.43.	29	Balmoral, Vic.
VX.45692	Pte.	Cawley, M.V.	AAOC	Upper Sonkurai	22.08.43.	28	Balaclava, Vic.
VX.45776	Dvr.	Conroy, J.C.	2/2 MAC	Kanburi	22.12.43.	37	Stawell, Vic.
VX.45954	L/Cpl.	Chitty, G.N.	8DivSigs	Taimonta	21.09.43.	34	East Malvern, Vic.
VX.46207	Pte.	Cowell, F.J.	2/29 Inf	Changi	18.05.43.	23	
VX.46481	Pte.	Cattanach, K.A.	2/29 Inf	Taimonta	27.05.43.	30	Armadale, Vic.
VX.48402	Pte.	Carr, L.M.	2/29 Inf	Tanbaya	01.12.43.	25	
VX.50727	Gnr.	Cahill, T.R.	4 A/Tk.	Lower Sonkurai	26.05.43.	28	East Brunswick, Vic.
VX.55996	Pte.	Cofield, W.C.	27BdeHQ	Upper Sonkurai	03.10.43.	22	Wahgunyah, Vic.
VX.57195	Sgmn.	Cruickshank, W.H.L.	8DivSigs	Kuie	26.07.43.	46	
VX.58281	Pte.	Coles, L.E.G.	13 AGH	Changi	14.01.44.	35	Milford, Vic.
VX.60257	Pte.	Cousins, N.R.C.	2/29 Inf	Chungkai	29.08.43.	22	Thornbury, Vic.
VX.60460	Pte.	Collins, H.G.A.	2/29 Inf	Prankalli	28.11.43.	22	Port Campbell, Vic.
VX.60691	Pte.	Church, J.R.L.	2/29 Inf	Sonkurai	20.08.43.	29	Kyabram, Vic.
VX.62543	Cpl.	Callahan, D.J.	Admn.HQ	Tanbaya	28.09 43.	24	Ballarat, Vic
VX.65523	Pte.	Campbell, R.W.	2/26 Inf	Tanbaya	02.10.43.	23	Sandringham, Vic.
SX. 8912	Sgt.	Colgan, H.K.	AASC	Prankalli	24.11.43.	32	Cowandilla, SA
SX.10167	Cpl.	Clark, C.M.	AASC	Tanbaya	02.10.43.	26	Joslin, SA
TX. 4447	Pte.	Crawford, K.L.	2/29 Inf	Tanbaya	16.01.44.	23	Ridgley, Tas.
TX. 5609	Spr.	Cohen, R.J.	2/10 RAE	Taimonta	31.05.43.	37	Devonport, Tas.
WX. 6853	Sgmn.	Cole, F.H.	8DivSigs	Tanbaya	27.08.43.	23	Narrogin, WA
WX. 9770	Dvr.	Croxford, F.H.J.	4 RMT	Upper Sonkurai	04.11.43.	37	Mt.Hawthorn, WA
WX. 9889	Spr.	Campbell, N.D.	2/6 FdPk	Kanburi	19.09.43.	34	Perth, WA
WX. 9918	Pte.	Chandler, H.J.	4 RMT	Lower Sonkurai	19.05.43.	37	Latham, WA
WX.10384	Spr.	Constantine, L.N.	2/6 FdPk	Lower Sonkurai	24.08.43.	32	Yalgoo, WA
WX.10595	Spr.	Cox, R.J.	2/6 FdPk	Kanburi	21.09.43.	22	Victoria Park, WA
QX. 9888	Pte.	Duncan, T.P.	2/26 Inf	Sonkurai	26.08.43.	38	Caboolture, Qld.
QX.14907	Gnr.	Dow, R.McA.	2/10 RAA	Lower Neike	28.05.43.	39	Brisbane, Qld.
QX.15050	Pte.	Dunne, D.P.	2/26 Inf	Kanburi	06.12.43.	33	
QX.17158	Pte.	Dwyer, J.F.	2/26 Inf	Upper Sonkurai	19.08.43.	26	New Farm, Qld.
QX.17541	Gnr.	DeVries, J.W.	2/10 RAA	Tanbaya	20.09.43.	33	Highgate Hill, Qld.
QX.21267	Gnr.	Dossel, V.W.	2/15 RAA	Sonkurai	17.08.43.	37	Memerami, Qld.
QX.22349	Pte.	DeCourcey, R.L.	2/26 Inf	Kanburi	15.12.43.	22	Townsville, Qld.
NX. 5699	Gnr.	Dobell, G.C.	2/15 RAA	Kanburi	28.12.43.	37	Kogarah, NSW
NX. 7046	Pte.	Dunn, A.A.	Provost	Tanbaya	25.09.43.	30	Rylstone, NSW
NX.10474	Spr.	Davis, L.	2/12 RAE	Kanburi	05.01.44.	24	Carlingford, NSW
NX.16090	Pte.	Denton, C.R.	2/30 Inf	Upper Sonkurai	10.09.43.	28	Tamworth, NSW
NX.21813	Pte.	Dorse, H.J.	2/30 Inf	Tanbaya	24.01.44.	24	Cessnock, NSW
NX.32626	Sgt.	Donnelly, R.	8Div.HQ	Lower Sonkurai	27.05.43.	31	Tempe, NSW
NX.32628	Pte.	Dunn, R.	HQ AASC	Tarsoa	30.11.43 4	2	Homebush, NSW

NX.36597	Sgt.	Doolan, A.A.	2/30 Inf	Upper Sonkurai	09.11.43.	35	Stawell, Vic.
NX.36748	Pte.	Durnan, W.J.	27Bde.HQ	Kanburi	06.09.43.	39	Kamarah, NSW
NX.37699	Pte.	Dean, J.B.	2/30 Inf	Upper Sonkurai	27.11.43.	21	North Perth, WA
NX.43247	Spr.	Dennis, L.A.	2/12 RAE	Upper Sonkurai	15.11.43.	30	West Ryde, NSW
NX.43486	Pte.	Dear, R.J.	2/29 Inf	Takanoon	04.08.43.	27	Cootamundra, NSW
NX.46196	Pte.	Davison, R.	2/30 Inf	Kanburi	04.12.43.	29	Nth.Lismore, NSW
NX.47140	Pte.	Dalton, R.	2/30 Inf	Upper Sonkurai	22.11.43.	21	Waratah, NSW
NX.53639	Pte.	Davidson, E.L.	2/30 Inf	Kanburi	08.12.43.	26	Maroubra, NSW
NX.55136	Pte.	Dickson, H.R.	AASC	Kanburi	08.03.44.	41	Campsie, NSW
NX.55686	Sgmn.	Denneen, W.E.	8 DivSigs	Upper Sonkurai	16.06.43.	28	Sydney, NSW
NX.58739	Pte.	Dale, A.B.	HQ AASC	Upper Sonkurai	25.08.43.	37	Jerilderie, NSW
NX.59645	Pte.	Donovan, J.S.	2/30 Inf	Changi	07.02.44.	29	Hurstville, NSW
NX.71234	Pte.	Doust, R.J.	HQ AASC	Upper Sonkurai	07.06.43.	25	Manly, NSW
VX.17368	Spr.	Drummond, F.G.	2/10 RAE	Tarsoa	07.08.43.	30	Daylesford, Vic.
VX.23975	Pte.	Davey, W.J.	4 RMT	Sonkurai	28.10.43.	39	Yarraville, Vic.
VX.33184	Spr.	Deveson, L.C.	2/10 RAE	Lower Sonkurai	31.05.43.	32	Stanmore, NSW
VX.34391	Spr.	Dawson, J.W.	2/10 RAE	Tanbaya	24.11.43.	24	Beaconsfield, Vi
VX.34486	Pte.	Dawson, A.H.	2/29 Inf	Kanburi	13.01.44.	37	Bendigo, Vic.
VX.39407	Chpln.	Dean, A.R.	AACD	Kinsayok	09.07.43.	39	Mildura, Vic.
VX.43543	Pte.	Dempster, J.M.	2/29 Inf	Upper Sonkurai	21.10.43.	25	Burnley, Vic.
VX.45595	Lieut.	Dobbie, F.A.	2/10 RAE	Takanoon	16.08.43.	35	Camberwell, Vic.
VX.48503	Pte.	Duthie, S.C.	2/29 Inf	Kanburi	22.09.43.	28	Hamilton, Vic.
VX.55158	Pte.	Devereaux, R.E.	2/29 Inf	Upper Sonkurai	20.11.43.	22	Hampton, Vic.
VX.56699	Pte.	Downie, J.T.	2/29 Inf	Lower Neilc~	16.05.43.	28	Shepparton, Vic.
VX.61666	Pte.	Dalton, A.W.	2/10 ORD	Changi	23.04.44.	31	Kensington, Vic.
SX. 8981	Pte.	Downing, J.A.	AASC	Lower Sonkurai	10.08.43.	41	
SX.13848	Pte.	Daly, G.M.	2/26 Inf	Lower Neike	10.06.43.	24	Jamestown, SA
TX. 5843	Pte.	Dick, M.	2/26 Inf	Sonkurai	25.08.43.	21	Devonport, Tas.
TX. 8040	Spr.	Dixon, A.W.	2/10 RAE	Changi	22.12.43.	24	Hobart, Tas.
~X. 8276	Pte.	Dudfield, A.E.	2/26 Inf	Tanbaya	17.10.43.	26	Forth, Tas.
WX.10143	Pte.	Dunn, H.R.	4 RMT	Upper Sonkurai	14.11.43.	38	Ayr, Scotland
WX.10989	Pte.	Dawson, D.J.	27 AADC	Kanburi	09.12.43.	38	Midland Jnctn.,WA
WX.11159	Lieut.	Downes, H.W.	2/6 RAE	Neike	23.07.43.	25	Nedlands, WA
WX.12440	Spr.	Dempster, G.V.	2/6 RAE	Tanbaya	03.10.43.	34	Cowaramup, WA
QX.14699	Sgt.	Evans, M.	2/26 Inf	Kanburi	02.12.43.	27	Eulimba, Qld.
NX.31534	Pte.	Emanuel, R.E.	27Bde.HQ	Takanoon	26.07.43.	26	Hamilton, NSW
NX.35905	Cpl.	Edwards, J.T.	2/19 Inf	Tanbaya	21.09.43.	40	Bringagee, NSW
NX.36839	Pte.	Edmondstone, B.J.	2/30 Inf	Lower Sonkurai	29.08.43.	41	Wagga Wagga, NSW
NX.41634	Cpl.	Edgar, E.S.B.	GBD	Tanbaya	13.09.43.	42	Armidale, NSW
NX.45847	L/Sgt.	Everingham, A.C.	2/30 Inf	Lower Sonkurai	26.05.43.	28	Malabar, NSW
NX.47295	L/Cpl.	Earea, H.J.M.	2/30 Inf	Kanburi	26.01.44.	25	Lorne, NSW
NX.55177	Pte.	Elmhirst, H.W.F.	2/lOFAmb	Kanburi	30.11.43.	35	
NX.57402	Dvr.	Evans, H.S.	Provost	Sonkurai	15.11.43.	24	Enfield, NSW
NX.65917	Pte.	Edwards, C.	H.Q.	Lower Sonkurai	28.05.43.	29	Coogee, NSW
NX.68286	Pte.	English, A.C.	2/30 Inf	Lower Neike	16.05.43.	23	Kogarah, NSW
VX.16791	Spr.	Evans, J.F.	2/10 RAE	Lower Neike	16.07.43.	22	Abbotsford, Vic.
VX.22574	Pte.	Edmonds, G.H.	2/29 Inf	Chungkai	29.09.43.	35	Armadale, Vic.
VX.56482	Cpl.	Emus, J.F.	2 EchHQ	Takanoon	08.08.43.	39	
VX.64382	Pte.	Easterbrook, J.	2/29 Inf	Takanoon	25.07.43.	35	Warrnambool,Vic.
TX. 5733	Pte.	Eley, A.A.	2/29 Inf	Tamaranpat	06.08.43.	38	Karoola, Tas.
WX. 8504	Pte.	Elder, F.F.	86 LAD	Upper Sonkurai	11.06.43.	38	Mt.Hawthorn, WA

QX. 1722	Pte.	Fraser, H.D.	2/26 Inf	Kanburi	05.02.44.	36	Townsville, Qld.
QX. 9387	Pte.	Ford, G.A.	2/26 Inf	Kanburi	16.12.43.	26	Banyo, Qld.
QX. 9406	Pte.	Finney, A.E.	2/26 Inf	Upper Sonkurai	19.09.43.	29	Eumundi, Qld.
QX.10086	Pte.	Fuller, S.V.	2/26 Inf	Tanbaya	05.09.43.	29	Crows Nest,Qld.
QX.10204	Pte.	Freier, F.W.	2/26 Inf	Tanbaya	10.12.43.	39	Toowoomba, Qld.
QX.12288	Pte.	Fitzpatrick, R.	2/26 Inf	Lower Sonkurai	28.05.43.	32	Liverpool, UK
QX.13634	Bdr.	Freeman, W.	2/10 RAA	Changi	12.01.44.	39	Brisbane, Qld.
QX.14350	L/Cpl.	Ferguson, R.P.	AASC	Kanburi	25.12.43.	28	Clayfield, Qld.
QX.14776	Pte.	Flynn, C.F.	2/26 Inf	Lower Sonkurai	27.05.43.	37	Manly, Qld.
QX.14809	Gnr.	Foreman, J.N.	2/10 RAA	Upper Sonkurai	25.11.43.	23	Wilston, Qld.
QX.15552	Pte.	Fitzgerald, T.E.	2/30 Inf	Sonkurai	15.11.43.	28	Cairns, Qld.
NX.27286	Sgt.	Fowler, J.J.	2/15 RAA	Upper Sonkurai	04.10.43.	26	Quirindi, NSW
NX.30117	Cpl.	Fishburn, W.G.	Provost	Lower Sonkurai	31.05.43.	24	
NX.30732	Pte.	Fletcher, J.	2/30 Inf	Koncoita	28.11.43.	35	Bangor,Nthn.Ire.
NX.31135	Pte.	Forsyth, J.A.	2/20 Inf	Neike	15.08.43.	23	Coogee, NSW
NX.37323	Pte.	Franks, J.T.	2/30 Inf	Upper Sonkurai	27.10.43.	32	Jugiong, NSW
NX.37917	Pte.	Fordham, R.G.	MLFDU	Upper Sonkurai	21.08.43.	34	Marrickville, NSW
NX.45730	Pte.	Freeman, R.M.T.	2/30 Inf	Kanburi	11.12.43.	24	Wallsend, NSW
NX.45759	L/Cpl.	Flanagan, F.W.	2/30 Inf	Upper Sonkurai	28.09.43.	35	Blandford, NSW
NX.46200	Pte.	Fletcher, R.C.	2/30 Inf	Upper Sonkurai	27.10.43.	29	Sth.Lismore, NSW
NX.49892	Pte.	Faulks, E.H.	2/29 Inf	Sonkurai	01.11.43.	26	Alstonville, NSW
NX.51805	Pte.	Farr, D.B.	2/30 Inf	Tanbaya	27.10.43.	28	Wyoming, NSW
NX.51986	Pte.	Farley, M.J.	2/30 Inf	Changi	22.12.43.	22	Nevertire, NSW
NX.58730	Sgmn.	Flint, S.	8DivSigs	Neike	06.08.43.	26	Narrabeen, NSW
NX.69880	Pte.	Franklin, J.A.	2/30 Inf	Lower Sonkurai	31.05.43.	29	Mackay, Qld.
VX.40990	Pte.	Flanagan, S.W.	2/29 Inf	Lower Sonkurai	10.06.43.	36	Creswick, Vic.
VX.43166	Pte.	Fullarton, E.L.	2/29 Inf	Tanbaya	31.10.43.	41	St. Kilda, Vic.
VX.44160	Spr.	Fry, C.	2/10 RAE	Tamaranpat	11.08.43.	26	Warragul, Vic.
VX.44939	Pte.	Forster, G.P.	2/29 Inf	Tarsoa	27.07.43.	24	Edenhope, Vic.
VX.45204	Pte.	Freeman, E.J.N.	2/29 Inf	Tanbaya	18.10.43.	27	Bentleigh, Vic.
VX.50292	Pte.	Farrell, J.P.	4 RMT	Lower Neike	04.06.43.	31	Ripplebrook, Vic
VX.56037	Pte.	Frost, H.R.J.	2/29 Inf	Kanburi	11.12.43.	24	Milltown, Vic.
VX.56340	Pte.	Forrester, A.W.	2/29 Inf	Kanburi	17.10.43.	33	West Preston, Vic.
VX.58998	Pte.	Fagan, J.E.	2/29 Inf	Tanbaya	14.10.43.	22	Hampton, Vic.
VX.59001	Sgmn.	Ferguson, G.H.	8DivSigs	Tanbaya	11.10.43.	21	Essendon, Vic.
VX.60101	Pte.	Fitridge, M.H.	2/29 Inf	Kanburi	11.12 43.	28	Northcote, Vic.
VX.64081	Pte.	Finn, E.N.	2/29 Inf	Kraw Krie	26.06.43.	24	Oakleigh, Vic.
VX.64972	Pte.	Fuller, B.R.	2/29 Inf	Takanoon	10.08.43.	22	Richmond, Vic.
TX. 5648	Pte.	Findlay, D.R.	2/29 Inf	Changi	10.07.44.	25	Wesley Vale,Tas
TX. 5795	Pte.	Fulton, J.M.	2/26 Inf	Tanbaya	09.09.43.	22	Legana, Tas.
TX. 5873	Pte.	Fenton, M.W.	2/29 Inf	Tanbaya	08.11.43.	32	Smithton, Tas.
WX.10965	Pte.	French, E.L.	4 RMT	Kanburi	03.12.43.	43	East Fremantle, WA
QX. 1839	L/Bdr.	Gartside, F.F.	2/10 RAA	Sonkurai	04.11.43.	42	
QX. 8399	Pte.	Grant, G.A.	2/26 Inf	Tanbaya	25.09.43.	32	Glenella, Qld.
QX. 8702	Pte.	Greisbach, S.	2/26 Inf	Tanbaya	17.10.43.	23	Blackstone, Qld
QX.10898	Pte.	Gilchrist, R.J.	2/26 Inf	Lower Sonkurai	31.07.43.	40	Pialba, Qld.
QX.10945	Pte.	Gibbards, T.F.D.	2/26 Inf	Lower Sonkurai	07.06.43.	23	Wynnum, Qld.
QX.14688	Pte.	Grant, E.R.	2/26 Inf	Lower Sonkurai	31.05.43.	24	Hamilton, Qld.
QX.14789	Pte.	Gagen, A.H.	2/26 Inf	Sonkurai	18.08.43.	37	Sandgate, Qld.
QX.16517	Sgt.	Gibbs, F.O.	2/26 Inf	Lower Sonkurai	31.05.43.	27	Toowoomba, Qld.
QX.16632	Pte.	Gillott, S.R.B.	2/26 Inf	Tanbaya	27.09.43.	24	Warwick, Qld.

QX.17538	Gnr.	Graham, F.H.	2/10 RAA	Lower Neike	17.06.43.	26	Windsor, Qld.
QX.17934	S/Sgt.	Gibson, A.E.L.H.	2/26 Inf	Tanbaya	26.10.43.	41	Clayfield, Qld.
QX.18586	Pte.	Graham, W.A.	2/26 Inf	Tanbaya	13.09.43.	34	Mackay, Qld.
QX.19446	Pte.	Gallagher, D.	27Bde.HQ	Upper Sonkurai	08.06.43.	31	Liverpool, UK
QX.23022	Pte.	Galvin, F.J.	2/26 Inf	Changi	26.03.44.	25	
QX.23161	Pte.	Graham, G.A.T.	2/30 Inf	Upper Sonkurai	20.09.43.	25	Mount Larcom,Qld.
QX.23949	Pte.	Gunthorpe, R.G.	2/26 Inf	Tanbaya	12.11.43.	41	Casino, NSW
NX.25780	Pte.	Godley, D.	2/30 Inf	Upper Sonkurai	30.08.43.	32	Stocksbridge,UK
NX.25931	Cpl.	Gore, T.J.	2/18 Inf	Lower Sonkurai	28.05.43.	30	Rylstone, NSW
NX.27444	Pte.	Gottaas, E.L.	2/30 Inf	Upper Sonkurai	18.10.43.	24	Bemboka, NSW
NX.34399	Cpl.	Graham, G.	HQ AASC	Tanbaya	06.09.43.	33	Sth.Melbourne,Vic.
NX.36474	Pte.	Galvin, M.M.	2/30 Inf	Upper Sonkurai	21.10.43.	30	West Wyalong,NSW
NX.37364	Pte.	Guy, V.G.	2/30 Inf	Upper Sonkurai	01.09.43.	21	Kingston, NSW
NX.37715	Pte.	Gardner, S.L.	2/30 Inf	Upper Sonkurai	25.11.43.	25	Mullumbimby, NSW
NX.42596	Pte.	Golding, J.B. (See Rash, J.G.)	2/30 Inf	Lower Sonkurai	03.06.43.	23	Kogarah Bay, NSW
NX.47320	Pte.	Godbolt, H.	2/30 Inf	Lower Neike	17.05.43.	30	Taree, NSW
NX.47779	Pte.	Giggins, S.E.	2/30 Inf	Kanburi	16.12.43.	23	Broadwater, NSW
NX.51043	Pte.	Gaffney, W.O.	AASC	Tanbaya	21.11.43.	.29	Ryde, NSW
NX.51747	Pte.	Guest, W.C.	8Div.HQ	Tanbaya	19.12.43.	23	Rockdale, NSW
NX.58219	L/Cpl.	Glover, L.C.	2/30 Inf	Tanbaya	07.10.43.	25	Cowra, NSW
NX.71854	Pte.	Gylpin, L.A.	8Div.HQ	Lower Sonkurai	15.06.43.	30	
VX.25131	Pte.	Gleeson, T.E.	2/29 Inf	Tanbaya	30.10.43.	43	
VX.26860	Cpl.	Gorey, F.H.D.	8Div.Sigs	Upper Sonkurai	14.08.43.	28	Caulfield, Vic.
VX.28086	Sgmn.	Giddings, A.R.	8Div.Sigs	Kranji	05.06.44.	32	Sandringham,Vic
VX.35361	Sgmn.	Grundy, A.G.	8Div.Sigs	Tanbaya	03.10.43.	27	
VX.36669	Cpl.	Gardiner, C.I.	2/29 Inf	Tanbaya	27.10.43.	37	Dovercourt, UK
VX.41657	Sgt.	Galvin, E.A.	AASC	Tanbaya	13.10.43.	31	East Malvern,Vic.
VX.41755	Pte.	Griffin, H.	2/29 Inf	Kanburi	09.12.43.	29	Nth.Melbourne, Vic.
VX.43183	Cpl.	Grosvenor, H.C.	2/29 Inf	Kanburi	20.10.43.	40	Burwood, NSW
VX.43988	Pte.	Glew, L.K.	2/29 Inf	Lower Sonkurai	16.06.43.	27	Malvern, Vic.
VX.44013	Pte.	Grafton, E.W.	2/29 Inf	Upper Sonkurai	19.07.43.	39	
VX.45764	Pte.	Graham, A.L.R.	2/29 Inf	Kanburi	03.12.43.	35	Stawell, Vic.
VX.46098	Pte.	Granger, W.	2/29 Inf	Sonkurai	20.08.43.	28	Clydebank, Vic.
VX.46139	Cpl.	Graham, C.P.	4 RMT	Kanburi	05.01.44.	25	Traralgon, Vic.
VX.50017	Pte.	Glover, H.A.	4 RMT	Lower Sonkurai	22.08.43.	29	Newbury, Vic.
VX.50956	Pte.	Gray, J.	2/29 Inf	Takanoon	12.07.43.	29	
VX.53638	Sgmn.	Gorey, T.	8Div.Sigs	Kanburi	07.12.43.	25	Caulfield, Vic.
VX.56005	Pte.	Greenhill, W.R.	2/29 Inf	Takanoon	10.07.43.	32	Beechworth, Vic
VX.60700	Spr.	Gowans, T.	2/10 RAE	Bangkok	05.12.43.	30	Oakleigh, Vic.
VX.60713	Pte.	Gilbert, C.C.	2/29 Inf	Takanoon	19.07.43.	22	Wangaratta, Vic
VX.65214	Cpl.	Gardiner, G.A.	2/29 Inf	Tanbaya	21.11.43.	26	Preston, Vic.
SX. 8821	Sgmn.	Griffits, J.T.	8Div.Sigs	Kanburi	28.05.43.	30	Hilton, S.A.
SX. 9877	L/Cpl.	Gordon, C.L.	AASC	Kanburi	07.01.44.	32	Wolseley, SA
TX. 5745	Pte.	Gardam, C.W.	2/29 Inf	Takanoon	27.07.43.	21	Takone, Tas.
WX. 8674	Pte.	Gregory, J.E.J.	2/4 MG	Lower Sonkurai	01.06.43.	39	Kalgoorlie, WA
WX. 9131	Pte.	Goodwin, R.	2/4 MG	Tanbaya	06.11.43.	27	
WX.10628	Pte.	Guilfoyle, F.W.	4 RMT	Upper Sonkurai	15.10.43.	42	Perth, WA
QX. 4940	Sgmn.	Hart, F.H.	8DivSigs	Neike	21.11.43.	34	Kangaroo Pt.,Qld
QX. 9401	Pte.	Hodgson, M.P.	2/26 Inf	Tanbaya	18.09.43.	34	Southport, Qld.
QX. 9647	Gnr.	Harvey, G.	2/10 RAA	Kanburi	14.12.43.	23	Annerley, Qld.

QX.10825	Pte.	Hoffman, A.R.	AASC	Kanburi	21.01.44.	43	Tiaro, Qld.
QX.10948	Cpl.	Hudson, H.	2/26 Inf	Upper Sonkurai	06.11.43.	27	Gayndah, Qld.
QX.12331	Pte.	Hollyman, W.H.	2/26 Inf	Lower Sonkurai	28.05.43.	27	Runcorn, Qld.
QX.13699	Gnr.	Horton, E.F.C.	2/10 RAA	Kanburi	30.11.43.	23	Paddington, Qld.
QX.14681	Gnr.	Hutton, G.D.	2/10 RAA	Sonkurai	24.08.43.	23	Clayfield, Qld.
QX.15279	Pte.	Hansen, W.D.	2/26 Inf	Lower Sonkurai	31.05.43.	27	
QX.17249	Sgt.	Hoar, V.P.	2/26 Inf	Upper Sonkurai	26.10.43.	33	Fairfield, Qld.
QX.19297	Pte.	Hayes, A.S.	2/26 Inf	Tanbaya	14.12.43.	41	Chinderah, NSW
QX.21544	Pte.	Hoelscher, A.	2/26 Inf	Tanbaya	13.10.43.	22	
NX. 2721	Pte.	Hadley, J.M.	2/30 Inf	Upper Sonkurai	04.11.43.	22	Castle Hill, NSW
NX. 2835	Pte.	Heasman, O.H.J.	2/30 Inf	Takanoon	14.05.43.	29	Granville, NSW
NX. 4406	Pte.	Hughes, A.M.	27Bde.HQ	Kanburi	05.10.43.	21	Lindfield, NSW
NX.17252	Pte.	Hooper, P.V.	2/30 Inf	Kanburi	26.11.43.	27	Bondi, NSW
NX.19506	Cpl.	Hardie, M.J.	2/19 Inf	Kuie	29.08.43.	22	Seaforth, NSW
NX.25775	Sgmn.	Hobbs, J.E.	8DivSigs	Tanbaya	03.11.43.	36	Pitt Town, NSW
NX.27100	Gnr.	Hammond, T.P.	2/15 RAA	Kanburi	01.02.44.	26	Burwood, NSW
NX.27191	Pte.	Hudson, W.M.C.	2/30 Inf	Ipoh	19.12.43.	42	Chadwell Hth.,UK
NX.27516	Gnr.	Hopkins, S.J.	2/15 RAA	Kanburi	23.11.43.	26	Undercliffe, NSW
NX.27941	Gnr.	Hawkins, C.	2/15 RAA	Tanbaya	23.10.43.	27	Rappville, NSW
NX.29052	Gnr.	Holme, G.	2/15 RAA	Upper Sonkurai	05.09.43.	40	Mangrove Mtn.,NSW
NX.31491	L/Cpl.	Heuston, S.C.	2/30 Inf	Kanburi	02.12.43.	37	Punchbowl, NSW
NX.33906	Sgt.	Hood, R.	2/30 Inf	Tanbaya	10.10.43.	37	Candelo, NSW
NX.36493	Cpl.	Hanna, R.C.	2/30 Inf	Kanburi	15.02.44.	37	Hay, NSW
NX.36556	Cpl.	Hoskinson, J.C.	2/30 Inf	Upper Sonkurai	30.09.43.	37	Wagga Wagga, NSW
NX.37334	Pte.	Hurry, E.E.	2/30 Inf	Upper Sonkurai	03.09.43.	22	Avondale, NSW
NX.37680	Pte.	Holman, T.I.	2/30 Inf	Upper Sonkurai	07.10.43.	21	Woollahra, NSW
NX.41262	Cpl.	Hickson, B.M.P.	2/30 Inf	Upper Sonkurai	07.11.43.	36	Manly, NSW
NX.43642	Pte.	Hunter, K.J.	2/18 Inf	Tanbaya	07.11.43.	20	Ashbury, NSW
NX.47485	Pte.	Haiser, G.F.	AASC	Kanburi	07.02.44.	22	Dunoon, NSW
NX.47681	Pte.	Hudson, H.F.	2/30 Inf	Upper Sonkurai	25.08.43.	25	
NX.48796	Cpl.	Hoggett, N.V.	2/29 Inf	Chungkai	06.09.43.	23	West Ryde, NSW
NX.50622	Cpl.	Heriot, W.E.	GBD	Takanoon	05.07.43.	42	Deniliquin, NSW
NX.52607	Spr.	Hutchings, G.J.	2/12 RAE	Kanburi	20.12.43.	25	Cootamundra, NSW
NX.55430	Pte.	Harding, G.N.	2/19 Inf	Kanburi	05.10.43.	34	Victoria Park,WA
NX.55820	Pte.	Hendrie, R.N.A.	2/18 Inf	Lower Sonkurai	19.06.43.	22	Bowral, NSW
NX.56747	Cpl.	Higgins, T.H.	2/30 Inf	Lower Sonkurai	27.05.43.	37	Sans Souci, NSW
NX.56912	Sgmn.	Hunter, R.M.	8DivSigs	Kanburi	30.11.43.	32	Crows Nest, NSW
NX.58216	Pte.	Harvey, C.	2/30 Inf	Kanburi	16.12.43.	24	Canowindra, NSW
NX.58311	Pte.	Hewitt, R.D.	2/30 Inf	Upper Sonkurai	25.09.43.	39	Northbridge, NSW
NX.59073	Pte.	Hopkins, F.L.	2/29 Inf	Tanbaya	05.10.43.	35	Mortlake, NSW
NX.68186	Pte.	Hodges, A.W.J.	2/30 Inf	Upper Sonkurai	16.10.43.	25	Tamworth, NSW
NX.68212	Sgmn.	Holloway, R.F.	8DivSigs	Neike	27.11.43.	25	Ashfield, NSW
VX.12982	Pte.	Hamilton, N.	2/29 Inf	Taimonta	31.05.43.	31	Chelsea, Vic.
VX.13711	Pte.	Holmes, S.A.B.	2/29 Inf	Changi	14.01.44.	29	Skipton, Vic.
VX.27856	Sgt.	Hutchings, W.L.	8DivSigs	Prankalli	28.11.43.	26	Sandringham, Vic
VX.33906	Pte.	Harvey, A.J.	2/29 Inf	Takanoon	10.07.43.	30	Nyah, Vic.
VX.34720	Sgt.	Haden, J.	2/29 Inf	Tanbaya	08.10~43.	34	Sunshine, Vic
VX.37174	Spr.	Heywood, R.A.	2/10 RAE	Taimonta	29.05.43.	40	
VX.43322	Pte.	Hamilton, A.M.	2/29 Inf	Tarsoa	07.08.43.	31	Wonthaggi, Vic.
VX.44748	Pte.	Howell, J.J.	2/29 Inf	Takanoon	20.07.43.	42	Benalla, Vic.
VX.51244	Sgt.	Hodge, A.H.	Provost	Changi	08.03.44.	41	Chelsea, Vic.

VX.55087	Cpl.	Hollier, A.N.	27BdeHQ	Tarsoa	02.09.43.	23	Cheltenham, Vic.
VX.55386	Pte.	Hart, E.	2/29 Inf	Tanbaya	19.09.43.	38	Holbeach, U.K.
VX.56388	Pte.	Hales, F.C.	2/29 Inf	Kinsiouk	01.11.43.	26	Horsham, Vic.
VX.56421	Pte.	Harper, W.A.	2/29 Inf	Takanoon	10.08.43.	41	
VX.60687	Pte.	Higgs, G.M.	2/29 Inf	Upper Sonkurai	21.10.43.	38	Arnold, Vic.
VX.63617	Pte.	Halpin, G.H.L.	2/26 Inf	Upper Sonkurai	23.10.43.	25	Forbes, NSW
VX.63626	Pte.	Hardy, H.J.	2/29 Inf	Kanburi	04.12.43.	33	Benalla, Vic.
SX. 8389	Pte.	Hunter, S.L.	AASC	Kanburi	08.12.43.	29	Evandale, SA
SX. 8588	Pte.	Hammond, W.J.	AASC	Tanbaya	13.10.43.	29	Taplan, SA
SX. 9197	Pte.	Hardingham, M.P.	AASC	Kanburi	20.12.43.	22	Hay, NSW
TX. 8112	Pte.	Holloway, B.H.	2/29~Inf	Tanbaya	23.10.43.	23	Police Pt., Tas.
WX. 7079	Spr.	Hawcroft, N.	2/6FPkRAE	Kraw Krie	27.06.43.	36	Subiaco, WA
WX. 7801	Pte.	Hackshaw, A.	2/4 MG	Tanbaya	02.11.43.	38	Cannington, WA
WX. 8250	Pte.	Halbert, F.	2/4 MG	Lower Sonkurai	04.06.43.	35	Yunndaga, WA
WX. 8638	Spr.	Hellmrich, L.C.	2/6FPkRAE	Kanburi	22.12.43.	33	West Midland,WA
WX. 9320	Pte.	Heal, H.W.	2/4 MG	Tanbaya	22.12.43.	33	Scarborough, WA
WX.18022	Pte.	Heinz-Smith, F.J.	2/4 MG	Upper Sonkurai	23.10.43.	40	Claremont, WA
QX. 8329	Pte.	Ings, W.J.	2/26 Inf	Tanbaya	10.11.43.	33	Campsie, NSW
QX.13934	Pte.	Irwin, R.J.	2/26 Inf	Lower Sonkurai	06.06.43.	33	
QX.21449	Pte.	Ireland, G.A.	2/26 Inf	Upper Sonkurai	23.10.43.	27	Nambour, Qld.
NX.72972	Pte.	Ives, A.S.	2/30 Inf	Lower Sonkurai	18.09.43.	35	Megalong, NSW
NX.73089	Pte.	Irwin, H.G.	2/18 Inf	Upper Sonkurai	16.10.43.	29	Bourke, NSW
VX.62839	Pte.	Ireland, F.S.	2/26 Inf	Takanoon	16.07.43.	39	Malvern, Vic.
QX. 9294	Pte.	Jones, C.J.	2/26 Inf	Kanburi	01.01.44.	41	Deagon, Qld.
QX.11728	L/Cpl.	Jamieson, A.	2/29 Inf	Changi	21.01.44.	23	Esk, Qld.
QX.11742	Pte.	Jurgens, V.	2/29 Inf	Kanburi	27.11.43.	29	Merinda, Qld.
NX. 2529	Pte.	Johnson, H.T.	2/30 Inf	Kanburi	30.12.43.	40	Mosman, NSW
NX.26604	Bdr.	Johnstone, S.	2/15 RAA	Kanburi	03.12.43.	35	Bredbo, NSW
NX.29189	Pte.	James, R.T.	2/30 Inf	Lower Sonkurai	31.05.43.	24	Channon, NSW
NX.30490	Pte.	Jones, R.	2/30 Inf	Tanbaya	14.10.43.	40	Muswellbrook, NSW
NX.33063	Cpl.	Jenkins, F.B.	Div.HQ	Tanbaya	26.09.43.	29	Arncliffe, NSW
NX.36604	Pte.	Jones, C.C.	27BdeHQ	Tanbaya	26.10.43.	26	Boree Creek, NSW
NX.37335	L/Cpl.	Jenkins, E.R.M.	2/30 Inf	Tanbaya	22.09.43.	27	Mosman, NSW
NX.40566	Pte.	Jarrett, A.P.	2/18 Inf	Lower Sonkurai	03.08.43.	36	Inverell, NSW
NX.48194	Pte.	Jones, G.P.	2/29 Inf	Kanburi	26.11.43.	25	Kyogle, NSW
NX.54838	Cpl.	Jarrett, G.H.	2/20 Inf	Lower Sonkurai	28.05.43.	32	Barrengarry, NSW
NX.57774	Pte.	Johnson, T.	2/30 Inf	Upper Sonkurai	10.08.43.	28	Marrickville, NSW
NX.67449	Cpl.	Johnson, R.W.	2/30 Inf	Lower Sonkurai	02.09.43.	23	Kogarah, NSW
NX.70137	Sgmn.	Johnstone, R.M.	8DivSigs	Kanburi	11.09.43.	26	Neutral Bay, NSW
NX.72924	Pte.	Jones, W.H.	2/20 Inf	Upper Sonkurai	11.10.43.	39	Newtown, NSW
NX.77857	Pte.	Jackson, R.G. (S/A. Patterson, J.J.)	2/30 Inf	Kanburi	11.12.43.	25	Port Kembla, NSW
VX.37894	Gnr.	James, S.E.	4 A/Tk	Sonkurai	18.08.43.	23	Mathoura, NSW
VX.38346	Cpl.	Jeans, W.G.	2/29 Inf	Tanbaya	06.10.43.	33	Nyah, Vic.
VX.41164	Pte.	Johnson, R.	2/29 Inf	Tamaranpat	29.06.43.	26	Yarrawonga, Vic.
VX.44357	Cpl.	Johnston, F.H.	2/29 Inf	Takanoon	18.08.43.	25	East Brunswick,Vic.
VX.44460	Pte.	Johnson, R.M.	2/29 Inf	Changi	27.12.43.	36	Northcote, Vic.
VX.45376	Cpl.	Jacobs, D.T.	2/29 Inf	Kanburi	24.12.43.	25	Frankston, Vic.
VX.56452	Spr.	Johnston, K.R.	2/10 RAE	Changi	22.12.43.	24	Northcote, Vic.
VX.64101	Pte.	Jackson, W.H.	2/29 Inf	Kanburi	22.11.43.	41	West Melbourne,Vic.
VX.64406	Pte.	Johnson, F.T.	2/10 ORD	Upper Sonkurai	30.10.43.	21	Carnegie, Vic.

SX. 8857	Pte.	Johnson, G.A.	8DivSalv	Upper Sonkurai	11.10.43.	31	Plympton, SA
TX. 4838	Pte.	Jones, M.J.A.	2/26 Inf	Upper Sonkurai	30.05.43.	22	Hobart, Tas.
WX. 7234	Pte.	Jones, I.W.	2/4 MG	Upper Sonkurai	14.11.43.	43	
WX.10160	Pte.	Jones, A.J.	4 RMT	Tanbaya	24.11.43.	38	Abergavenny, UK
QX.10178	Pte.	Kirkbride, C.A.E.	2/26 Inf	Kanburi	08.12.43.	24	Bymount, Qld.
QX.10585	Pte.	Kerr, G.D.A.	2/26 Inf	Lower Sonkurai	20.06.43.	24	Bundaberg, Qld.
QX.11122	Pte.	Kliendienst, A.R.	2/26 Inf	Lower Sonkurai	16.06.43.	33	Armidale, NSW
QX.15108	Pte.	Keeling, J.W.	2/26 Inf	Lower Sonkurai	01.06.43.	28	Cairns, Qld.
QX.16949	Pte.	King, E.H.	2/26 Inf	Kanburi	15.01.44.	38	Toowoomba, Qld.
QX.18667	Pte.	King, H.G.	13 AGH	Kanburi	05.12.43.	22	Homebush, Qld.
QX.18804	Pte.	Keen, C.	10 AGH	Lower Sonkurai	03.06.43.	34	
QX.23528	Pte.	Kelly, L.	2/29 Inf	Tanbaya	29.09.43.	35	Redcliffe, Qld.
NX.26199	Cpl.	Knowles, F.H.	Provost	Lower Sonkurai	30.07.43.	44	Georgetown,NSW
NX.32761	Pte.	Knox, H.G.	Div.HQ	Neike	07.08.43.	38	Glebe, NSW
NX.37583	Pte.	Kiely, T.J.	27BdeHQ	Tamaranpat	19.07.43.	26	Nth.Melbourne, Vic.
NX.37603	Pte.	Keighley, W.W.	2/30 Inf	Lower Sonkurai	26.05.43.	24	Sylvania, NSW
NX.45972	Pte.	Kime, K.G.	2/30 Inf	Upper Sonkurai	13.11.43.	23	Newcastle, NSW
NX.47104	Pte.	Kitchener, I.J~	2/30 Inf	Kanburi	07.12.43.	35	Murdunna, Tas.
NX.49754	Pte.	Kacergis, J.	2/29 Inf	Kanburi	09.02.44.	38	Clapton, U.K.
NX.58376	Pte.	Kay, D.H.	AASC	Upper Sonkurai	12.11.43.	27	Magill, SA
VX.27924	Sgmn.	Kirk, W.S.	8DivSigs	Kanburi	01.04.44.	23	
VX.35771	Spr.	Kingsland, L.	2/10 RAE	Kraw Krie	04.07.43.	27	Coburg, Vic.
VX.36079	Pte.	Kennedy, B.	2/29 Inf	Kanburi	20.09.43.	26	West Melbourne, Vic.
VX.36132	Pte.	Kneale, V.J.	2/29 Inf	Lower Sonkurai	31.08.43.	42	Richmond, Vic.
SX. 8940	Pte.	Kelly, W.J.	8DivSalv	Upper Sonkurai	10.09.43.	42	Elliston, SA
SX.14931	Pte.	Kennett, M.	2/lOFdPk	Upper Sonkurai	29.08.43.	21	Sandalwood, SA
WX.14465	L/Sgt.	Kennedy, L.J.	2/1 HBty	Kanburi	11.12.43.	33	South Perth, WA
QX. 9869	Gnr.	Leslie, R.S.	2/10 RAA	Sonkurai	26.08.43.	33	Dutton Park, Qld.
QX. 9970	Sgt.	Little, C.K.	2/26 Inf	Kanburi	06.12.43.	28	Gympie, Qld.
QX.11215	Sgt.	Lang, J.	2/26 Inf	Sonkurai	23.08.43.	39	Toowoomba, Qld.
QX.12296	Pte.	Lawson, W.	2/26 Inf	Upper Sonkurai	28.09.43.	32	New Farm, Qld.
QX.13653	Cpl.	Lawson, N.	2/26 Inf	Lower Sonkurai	21.05.43.	26	
QX.14746	Pte.	Long, J.G.	2/26 Inf	Lower Sonkurai	27.05.43.	26	South Brisbane, Qld.
QX.15812	Pte.	Langton, D.W.	2/29 Inf	Kanburi	26.10.43.	26	Mareeba, Qld.
QX.18309	Pte.	Lucht, N.	2/29 Inf	Taimonta	31.10.43.	21	Toowoomba, Qld.
QX.18668	Pte.	Long, E.	2/26 Inf	Sonkurai	31.08.43.	24	Mackay, Qld.
QX.18670	Cpl.	Lemberg, R.E.	2/26 Inf	Sonkurai	30.08.43.	33	Mackay, Qld.
NX. 1653	L/Cpl.	Levitt, L.C.	2/30 Inf	Kanburi	04.12.43.	20	Baulkham Hills,NSW
NX.10443	Gnr.	Lane, H.J.	2/15 RAA	Lower Sonkurai	20.06.43.	43	Sydney, NSW
NX.24140	Pte.	Love, R.J.	2/20 Inf	Tanbaya	17.10.43.	38	Mortlake, NSW
NX.27010	Pte.	Landow, M.L.	2/30 Inf	Lower Sonkurai	31.05.43.	25	Manly, NSW
NX.37499	Pte.	Lusby, R.L.	2/30 Inf	Tanbaya	20.09.43.	25	Roseville, NSW
NX.37653	Pte.	Lacey, D.C.	2/30 Inf	Upper Sonkurai	14.09.43.	22	Waverley, NSW
NX.41145	Pte.	Love, S.G.	2/30 Inf	Tanbaya	03.10.43.	22	Woolomin, NSW
NX.46265	Pte.	Lee, T.	2/30 Inf	Upper Sonkurai	18.11.43.	35	Woogoolga, NSW
NX.48249	Pte.	Lewis, R.	2/29 Inf	Kanburi	10.12.43.	21	Silverdale, NSW
NX.51324	Pte.	Lambert, A.S.	74 LAD	Upper Sonkurai	22.09.43.	26	Mosman, NSW
NX.51867	S/Sgt.	Lobb, F.T.	2/19 Inf	Upper Sonkurai	13.08.43.	34	Willoughby, NSW
NX.54736	Pte.	Lumby, D.R.	2/30 Inf	Lower Sonkurai	29.05.43.	30	Boggabri, NSW
NX.57103	Pte.	Lee, G.	27BdeHQ	Kanburi	25.12.43.	24	Petersham, NSW
NX.66478	Pte.	Luckie, L.M.	2/3 MAC	Upper Sonkurai	01.09.43.	29	

NX.67340	Pte.	Lee, V.G.	AASC	Tanbaya	25.09.43.	28	
NX.70123	Pte.	Lyon, W.R.B.	2/30 Inf	Upper Sonkurai	25.11.43.	34	Bellbrook, NSW
NX.70260	Lieut.	Lusk, F.G.	2/20 Inf	Upper Sonkurai	07.06.43.	36	Newcastle, NSW
NX.72166	Spr.	Lee, I.E.	HQ RAE	Upper Sonkurai	28.07.43.	21	Beranghi Cr.Hd,NSW
VX.25798	S/Sgt	Lovell, B.	22BdeWks	Lower Sonkurai	03.06.43.	23	Northcote, Vic.
VX.27855	Pte.	Lee, C.	2/26 Inf	Tanbaya	19.11.43.	24	
VX.28736	Dvr.	LeBas, F.	2/2 MAC	Upper Sonkurai	15.07.43.	36	Oakleigh, Vic.
VX.29916	Pte.	Lewis, J.L.	27BdeHQ	Kanburi	14.09.43.	35	Maidstone, Vic.
VX.32670	Pte.	Lyall, D.R.	2/9FdAmb	Neike	18.08.43.	23	Box Hill, Vic.
VX.37384	Cpl.	Lawson, R.C.	2/29 Inf	Kuie	09.09.43.	35	Parkdale, Vic.
VX.39630	Cpl.	Lark, J.W.	Postal	Tanbaya	24.09.43.	42	
VX.42268	Pte.	Lonsdale, I.O.	2.29 Inf	Kanburi	25.11.43.	42	Cheltenham, Vic.
VX.44532	Cpl.	Lambert, C.J.	2/2 MAC	Upper Sonkurai	04.06.43.	37	Albury, NSW
VX.44963	Pte.	Lane, N.J.	4 RMT	Upper Sonkurai	20.09.43.	35	North Shore, Vic
VX.46037	Pte.	Lambert, W.H.	2/29 Inf	Upper Sonkurai	24.09.43.	34	Hawthorn, Vic.
VX.47515	Pte.	Larkin, F.M.	22BdeWk.	Tanbaya	22.10.43.	35	Ascot Vale, Vic.
VX.56603	Pte.	Lamb, R.	2/29 Inf	Takanoon	20.07.43.	32	Cootamundra, NSW
VX.56712	Pte.	Letwin, G.	13 AGH	Sonkurai	07.10.43.	23	Elwood, Vic.
VX.61472	Pte.	Lampard, H.J.	2/29 Inf	Kanburi	28.02.44.	21	Hamilton, Vic.
VX.64569	Pte.	Lacey, J.F.	2/29 Inf	Tanbaya	14.11.43.	24	Nth.Carlton, Vic
TX. 2953	Sgmn.	Ledger, E.B.	8DivSigs	Sonkurai	15.08.43.	23	
TX. 3227	Sgt.	Lloyd, J.H.G.	27BdeHQ	Takanoon	21.07.43.	40	Hawkes Bay, NZ
QX.10793	Cpl.	McMurtrie, M.S.	2/26 Inf	Neike	14.11.43.	27	Bundaberg, Qld
QX.13451	Pte.	McLean, H.J.	2/26 Inf	Kanburi	16.12.43.	37	Hendra, Qld.
QX.13657	Gnr.	McCreary, A.B.	2/10 RAA	Lower Sonkurai	21.05.43.	35	Annerly, Qld.
QX.14588	Bdr.	McMillan, W.	2/10 RAA	Kanburi	31.12.43.	24	Nundah, Qld.
QX.17489	Pte.	MacLeod, J.D.	2/26 Inf	Lower Sonkurai	03.06.43.	34	Logan Vllge,Qld.
QX.17150	L/Cpl.	McDonald, I.H.	2/26 Inf	Tarbaya	08.10.43.	28	Maclagan, Qld.
QX.17636	Pte.	McKay, A.	2/26 Inf	Chungkai	14.09.43.	37	Chermside, Qld.
QX.19996	Pte.	McDowell, W.A.	2/26 Inf	Lower Sonkurai	05.06.43.	32	
NX. 4643	Cpl.	McCormick, H.R.	2/30 Inf	Lower Sonkurai	15.06.43.	31	Taree, NSW
NX.15405	W0.2	McAlister, A.J.	2/30 Inf	Kanburi	12.12.43.	28	Hurstville, NSW
NX.26339	Pte.	McCallum, E.R.	2/30 Inf	Upper Sonkurai	19.08.43.	23	Lidcombe, NSW
NX.31365	Pte.	McHugh, M.J.	2/30 Inf	Kanburi	01.02.44.	38	Sydney, NSW
NX.35609	Pte.	McGlynn, W.A.	2/19 Inf	Lower Sonkurai	08.06.43.	24	Young, NSW
NX.37443	Pte.	McGee, T.C.P.	2/30 Inf	Upper Sonkurai	09.09.43.	23	Springdale, NSW
NX.37456	Pte.	McNamara, W.P.	2/30 Inf	Changi	29.12.43.	35	Mascot, NSW
NX.42271	Sgmn.	McMahon, L.G.	8DivSigs	Changi	31.12.43.	31	Ungarie, NSW
NX.43106	Pte.	McCullagh, H.V.	GBD	Upper Sonkurai	22.11.43.	39	Wingham, NSW
NX.45514	Spr.	McPhee, J.	2/12 RAE	Lower Sonkurai	29.08.43.	40	Millers Point,NSW
NX.51931	S/Sgt.	McGregor, A.G.	2/30 Inf	Lower Sonkurai	31.05.43.	41	Leichhardt, NSW
NX.53849	Pte.	MacDonald, M.J.	8Div.HQ	Upper Sonkurai	17.11.43.	30	Canterbury, NSW
NX.57668	Dvr.	McArthur, E.A.	8Div.HQ	Tanbaya	11.11.43.	31	Condobolin, NSW
NX.65377	Pte.	McBurney, E.H.	73 LAD	Upper Sonkurai	17.09.43.	26	Marrickville, NSW
NX.69146	Sgmn.	McCartney, R.A.	8DivSigs	Tanbaya	16.10.43.	23	Taree, NSW
VX.25830	Pte.	McIntosh, M.K.	2/29 Inf	Takanoon	04.08.43.	39	Doncaster, Vic.
VX.31956	Spr.	McPhail, A.R.	2/10 RAE	Upper Sonkurai	15.06.43.	23	Kerang, Vic.
VX.33121	Dvr.	McLeod, D.	2/2 MAC	Upper Sonkurai	19.09.43.	42	Tighnabruaich, Scot.
VX.35635	L/Cpl.	McKechnie, A.N.	2/10 RAE	Upper Sonkurai	14.10.43.	36	Harcourt, Vic.
VX.40839	Cpl.	McPherson, A.	2/10 RAE	Tanbaya	25.10.43.	33	Alphington, Vic
VX.42413	Sgt.	McCalman, I.F.	2/29 Inf	Tamaranpat	12.07.43.	24	Sandford, Vic.

VX.46693	L/Cpl.	McDonald, A.G.	8DivSigs	Upper Sonkurai	08.08.43.	26	Ballarat, Vic.
VX.48022	Pte.	McIntyre, R.	2/29 Inf	Sonkurai	20.08.43.	31	Weatherboard,Vic.
VX.55993	Pte.	McMillan, C.J.	2/29 Inf	Neike	19.11.43.	20	Corowa, NSW
VX.57245	Spr.	McBride, R.W.	AAMC	Neike	26.11.43.	23	Barham, NSW
VX.61250	Pte.	McFadyen, J.A.	2/26 Inf	Lower Sonkurai	04.06.43.	27	Kalimna, Vic.
VX.63564	Pte.	McEvoy, A.	2/26 Inf	Lower Sonkurai	27.08.43.	43	Tarraville, Vic
SX. 6506	Pte.	MacIvor, D.	AASC	Tarsoa	02.08.43.	30	Rosewater, SA
SX. 9357	Cpl.	McDonald, D.J.	AASC	Tanbaya	11.12.43.	29	Corny Point, SA
SX.12235	Sgt.	McCulloch, D.	27BdeWks	Tanbaya	03.09.43.	41	
WX. 6973	Spr.	McIntosh, W.L.	2/6FPkRAE	Kanburi	30.10.43.	40	Cannington, WA
WX. 8435	Pte.	McCann, R.	2/4 MG	Upper Sonkurai	23.11.43.	35	
WX. 9849	Pte.	MacIntosh, A.J.L.	2/4 MG	Tanbaya	10.11.43.	23	Bassendean, WA
WX. 9928	Pte.	McLeod, L.D.	4 RMT	Tanbaya	11.09.43.	42	Albany, WA
QX. 9571	Sgt.	Matthews, L.J.	2/26 Inf	Upper Sonkurai	10.09.43.	23	Mayne, Qld.
QX. 9776	Pte.	Mussing, E.	2/26 Inf	Lower Sonkurai	07.07.43.	34	Murwillumbah, NSW
QX. 9824	Pte.	Marshall, S.I.	2/26 Inf	Tanbaya	04.11.43.	35	Holland Park, Qld.
QX.10239	Sgt.	Mulvena, W.H.	2/26 Inf	Lower Sonkurai	28.05.43.	45	Toowoomba, Qld.
QX.12048	Pte.	Mallory, W.J.	2/26 Inf	Lower Sonkurai	01.06.43.	31	Barcaldine, Qld.
QX.15103	Cpl.	Mills, A.	2/26 Inf	Kanburi	11.01.44.	41	Innisfail, Qld.
QX.16411	Sgt.	Mooney, J.	2/26 Inf	Lower Sonkurai	13.08.43.	37	Toowoomba, Qld.
QX.16456	Pte.	Mapleston, K.N.	2/26 Inf	Tanbaya	12.10.43.	39	Toowoomba, Qld.
QX.16587	Pte.	Manteit, E.A.	2/26 Inf	Upper Sonkurai	04.10.43.	24	Chinchilla, Qld.
QX.16925	Gnr.	Moore, P.H.	2/10 RAA	Kanburi	16.12.43.	32	
QX.18065	Pte.	Martin, S.D.	2/26 Inf	Tanbaya	01.09.43.	22	Stanthorpe, Qld.
QX.21824	Pte.	Middleton, D.H.	2/29 Inf	Tanbaya	24.11.43.	22	Mundubbera, Qld.
QX.23466	Pte.	Maurer, L.C.	2/29 Inf	Upper Sonkurai	24.11.43.	37	Paddington, Qld.
NX. 2713	Sgmn.	Mullens, E.G.W.	8DivSigs	Takanoon	29.08.43.	25	Abbotsford, NSW
NX. 2732	Pte.	Maudsley, M.J.	2/30 Inf	Lower Sonkurai	31.05.43.	28	Potts Point, NSW
NX. 4396	Pte.	Murray, R.S.	2/30 Inf	Lower Sonkurai	13.08.43.	23	Blackheath, NSW
NX.20449	Pte.	Mudford, C.H.	2/30 Inf	Kanburi	06.01.44.	25	Petersham, NSW
NX.26934	Pte.	Marshall, L.R.	2/30 Inf	Changi	28.04.44.	26	
NX.29725	Pte.	Mahony, J.	2/30 Inf	Kanburi	17.12.43.	41	Newcastle, NSW
NX.31563	Pte.	Moseley, H.J.	2/30 Inf	Lower Sonkurai	25.05.43.	29	Manly, NSW
NX.31689	L/Cpl.	Mason, W.C.	2/30 Inf	Changi	12.03.44.	24	Boorowa, NSW
NX.32285	Pte.	Marchbank, W.G.	10 AGH	Tanbaya	03.10.43.	42	Rozelle, NSW
NX.32510	Sgmn.	Mackie, H.	8DivSigs	Tanbaya	04.10.43.	24	Wallsend, NSW
NX.33604	Pte.	Musgrave, R.S.S.	2/30 Inf	Sonkurai	31.10.43.	25	Seaforth, NSW
NX.35185	Pte.	Muir, R.J.	10 AGH	Tanbaya	05.12.43.	29	Ladysmith, NSW
NX.36248	Pte.	Murphy, P.J.	2/30 Inf	Upper Sonkurai	18.10.43.	32	Rankins Sprngs.NSW
NX.37330	Gnr.	Magee, D.J.	2/15 RAA	Tanbaya	22.11.43.	24	Lane Cove, NSW
NX.37575	Cpl.	Mitchell, B.	2/30 Inf	Kanburi	04.12.43.	21	Roseville, NSW
NX.37636	Pte.	Marsh, D.H.	2/30 Inf	Sonkurai	10.11.43.	35	Campsie, NSW
NX.37685	Pte.	Mansfield, C.R.	2/30 Inf	Upper Sonkurai	05.10.43.	23	Adaminaby, NSW
NX.38303	Pte.	Mulholland, D.C.	2/29 Inf	Sonkurai	21.08.43.	22	Nth.Portland,Vic
NX.39209	Pte.	Moseley, J.T.	2/29 Inf	Upper Sonkurai	09.11.43.	29	Port Kembla,NSW
NX.46510	Pte.	May, L.C.	2/30 Inf	Kuie	07.08.43.	32	Nth.Lismore, NSW
NX.47154	Pte.	Macourt, L.L.	2/30 Inf	Kanburi	08.12.43.	30	Hamilton, NSW
NX.47760	Pte.	Marsh, S.F.	2/30 Inf	Lower Sonkurai	30.05.43.	31	East Sydney, NSW
NX.48554	Pte.	Miller, W.J.	Postal	Upper Sonkurai	28.09.43.	20	Kentucky, NSW
NX.51375	Sgmn.	Morrison, L.	8DivSigs	Tamaranpat	03.08.43.	29	Nth.Auburn, NSW
NX.51495	Pte.	Mercer, J.W.J.	4 RMT	Upper Sonkurai	29.07.43.	38	St.Peters, NSW

NX.52253	Pte.	Muffett, D.	2/30 Inf	Upper Sonkurai	24.09.43.	29	Bondi, NSW
NX.53427	Spr.	Muller, R.F.	2/12 RAE	Lower Sonkurai	07.06.43.	25	BrightonLeSands,NSW
NX.57169	Pte.	Mead, W.D.	2/26 Inf	Kanburi	31.01.44.	24	Willoughby, NSW
NX.59175	Pte.	Mansfield, L.N.	2/30 Inf	Upper Sonkurai	04.09.43.	23	Dulwich Hill, NSW
NX.65616	Sgt.	Murray, I.	Provost	Tanbaya	11.09.43.	35	Enmore, NSW
NX.67195	Cpl.	Machin, R.H.	2/29 Inf	Lower Sonkurai	03.06.43.	38	Nyngan, NSW
NX.68425	Cpl.	Maitland, J.T.J.	13 AGH	Tamaranpat	04.08.43.	41	Coogee, NSW
NX.71450	Pte.	Miners, J.W.	2/26 Inf	Tanbaya	16.10.43.	25	Holts Flat, NSW
NX.71952	Pte.	Mahoney, J.B.	2/19 Inf	Takanoon	01.08.43.	23	Woodenbong, NSW
VX.24317	Cpl.	Main, L.J.	2/10 RAE	Kraw Krie	10.07.43.	35	Caulfield, Vic.
VX.25757	Pte.	Murchison, K.W.	2/29 Inf	Tanbaya	26.10.43.	36	
VX.32066	Pte.	Morton, C.H.L.	AASC	Tanbaya	09.11.43.	26	Toorak, Vic.
VX.40692	Pte.	Martin, A.A.	2/29 Inf	Kanburi	13.12.43.	49	St.Kilda, Vic.
VX.43346	Pte.	Martin, A.C.L.	4 RMT	Upper Sonkurai	13.08.43.	34	Sth.Caulfield, Vic.
VX.43916	Sgmn.	Miller, M.J.	8DivSigs	Taimonta	12.06.43.	23	Hawthorn, Vic.
VX.45714	Pte.	Martin, E.	2/29 Inf	Lower Sonkurai	29.05.43.	27	Ballarat, Vic.
VX.45951	Pte.	Martin, L.R.A.	2/29 Inf	Kanburi	12.12.43.	20	Parkdale, Vic.
VX.46584	Pte.	Mattingley, C.R.	2/29 Inf	Upper Sonkurai	23.09.43.	38	Geelong, Vic.
VX.50224	Pte.	Middleton, R.A.B.	2/29 Inf	Tanbaya	20.09.43.	23	Camperdown, Vic
VX.63457	Pte.	Meikle, H.J.	27FPkAAOC	Upper Sonkurai	18.08.43.	24	Coburg, Vic.
SX. 7592	Sgmn.	Miller, C.G.	8DivSigs	Taimonta	24.05.43.	25	Sturt, SA
SX. 9953	Pte.	Mulvihill, F.E.	AASC	Tamaranpat	24.11.43.	24	Col.Light Gdns., SA
TX. 4343	Sgt.	Martin, J.W.	2/29 Inf	Lower Sonkurai	01.06.43.	34	Sandy Bay, Tas.
TX. 5799	Pte.	Miller, S.	2/26 Inf	Kanburi	18.12.43.	23	Glengarry, Tas.
QX. 7861	Pte.	Needham, J.R.W.	2/26 Inf	Tanbaya	27.10.43.	30	Cardwell, Qld.
QX. 9633	Gnr.	Newman, J.	2/10 RAA	Kanburi	29.11.43.	25	Old Maroon, Qld.
QX.10955	L/Cpl.	Ninnes, C.F.	2/26 Inf	Kanburi	19.12.43.	24	Gympie, Qld.
QX.15916	Pte.	Newman, H.	2/30 Inf.	Upper Sonkurai	28.09.43.	39	
QX.16927	Gnr.	Neill, W.B.	2/10 RAA	Kanburi	14.01.44.	39	Mosman, NSW
QX.21573	Cpl.	Neill, H.J.	2/30 Inf	Upper Sonkurai	03.11.43.	32	Kangaroo Point, Qld.
QX.23057	Pte.	Nichols, F.A.	2/29 Inf	Taimonta	28.09.43.	34	Goondiwindi, Qld
NX.23337	Pte.	Needs, C.W.E.	8Div.HQ	Tanbaya	01.12.43.	37	Redfern, NSW
NX.45781	Pte.	Nosworthy, N.W.	8DivHQ	Lower Sonkurai	02.08.43.	36	Sydney, NSW
NX.47385	Pte.	Nyberg, W.L.	2/30 Inf	Tanbaya	09.11.43.	34	Wauchope, NSW
NX.47548	Pte.	Nowlan, F.V.	2/30 Inf	Lower Neike	23.05.43.	26	Casino, NSW
NX.48083	Sgmn.	Newberry, F.	8DivSigs	Kanburi	21.10.43.	21	Bondi Junction, NSW
NX.60583	Pte.	Noakes, E.F.	2/30 Inf	Lower Sonkurai	01.06.43.	30	Rye Park, NSW
NX.68356	Pte.	Neale, J.G.	87 LAD	Kanburi	13.12.43.	27	Penrith, NSW
VX.16789	Spr.	Nathan, C.A.	2/10 RAE	Tanbaya	09.09.43.	25	Nth.Richmond,Vic
VX.32355	Pte.	Nestor, C.M.	2/29 Inf	Changi	04.04.44.	38	Ballarat, Vic.
VX.39503	Pte.	Nicholas, E.D,B.	10 AGH	Tanbaya	11.12.43.	26	Camberwell, Vic.
VX.40960	Pte.	Nancarrow, L.J.	2/29 Inf	Sonkurai	05.09.43.	41	
VX.43263	Pte.	Nagle, L.	2/29 Inf	Kanburi	25.12.43.	32	Melbourne, Vic.
VX.46150	Pte.	Nicholls, W.J.	2/29 Inf	Sonkurai	29.10.43.	39	Newry, Vic.
VX.47885	Pte.	Nowlan, J.A.	4 RMT	Tanbaya	29.08.43.	43	Bass, Vic.
VX.56171	Pte.	Newell, C.A.R.	2/29 Inf	Kanburi	05.01.44.	23	Carlton, Vic.
VX.59785	Pte.	Nash, T.H.	2/29 Inf	Lower Sonkurai	25.05.43.	21	Rushworth, Vic.
TX. 8179	Pte.	Newman, L.C.	2/29 Inf	Kuie	13.08.43.	22	Hobart, Tas.
QX.12341	Pte.	O'Connor, R.W.	2/26 Inf	Lower Sonkurai	27.05.43.	26	Longreach, Qld.
QX.21351	Pte.	Ostrofski, D.E.	2/26 Inf	Lower Sonkurai	11.06.43.	26	Toogoolawah, Qld
QX.21894	Pte.	Ogilvy, J.D.	2/29 Inf	Kanburi	24.12.43.	26	Maryborough, Qld

QX.23695	Pte.	Owens, J.	2/29 Inf	Upper Sonkurai	07.11.43.	29	Gympie, Qld.
NX.31462	Cpl.	Oag, W.D.	2/19 Inf	Kanburi	14.09.43.	31	Leeton, NSW
NX.43418	Pte.	O'Shaughnessy, T.C.	2/19 Inf	Tanbaya	14.09.43.	22	Marrickville, NSW
NX.47155	Pte.	O'Connor, E.R.	AASC	Upper Sonkurai	23.10.43.	34	Newcastle, NSW
NX.57292	Pte.	Owen, C.D.	2/30 Inf	Lower Sonkurai	19.07.43.	27	Petersham, NSW
NX.60147	Sgmn.	O'Brien, T.R.W.P.	8DivSigs	Takanoon	24.07.43.	26	Willoughby, NSW
NX.68733	Sgmn.	O'Donoghue, P.C.	8DivSigs	Kanburi	15.12.43.	22	Zetland, NSW
NX.68977	Pte.	Orr, J.E.	2/30 Inf	Tanbaya	18.10.43.	36	NcstleOnTyne, UK
NX.72107	Pte.	O'Driscoll, G.E.	8DivSigs	Tamaranpat	29.07.43.	21	Tabulam, NSW
VX.28730	Pte.	Ogden, J.D.W.	2/29 Inf	Upper Sonkurai	20.08.43.	31	Oakleigh, Vic.
VX.39167	Pte.	O'Shea, R.J.	2/29 Inf	Taimonta	26.05.43.	22	Sth.Melbourne, Vic.
VX.47004	Cpl.	O'Loughlin, L.A.	2/29 Inf	Kanburi	20.12.43.	23	DurhamLead, Vic.
VX.59918	Pte.	Oughtred, W.M.	2/29 Inf	Tanbaya	05.10.43.	27	Wycheproof, Vic.
SX. 2319	Sgt.	Owen, R.G.	AASC	Lower Sonkurai	01.06.43.	32	Elliston, SA
WX. 8174	L/Sgt.	O'Leary, D.M.	2/4 MG	Upper Sonkurai	14.11.43.	33	Narrogin, WA
WX. 9287	Pte.	Osborne, J.R.	2/4 MG	Upper Sonkurai	27.09.43.	28	Korbel, WA
QX. 8378	Pte.	Park, E.H.	2/26 Inf	Lower Neike	30.07.43.	41	Caloundra, Qld.
QX. 9431	Pte.	Pearman, G.S.	2/26 Inf	Tanbaya	14.10.43.	22	Palmwoods, Qld.
QX. 9626	Pte.	Paull, S.J.	2/26 Inf	Kanburi	05.12.43.	40	Buranda, Qld.
QX. 9933	Pte.	Pascoe, W.H.	2/26 Inf	Tanbaya	04.10.43.	35	Valley, Qld.
QX.10619	Cpl.	Pedelty, J.W.	2/26 Inf	Lower Sonkurai	26.05.43.	38	Maryborough, Qld
QX.10907	Pte.	Payne, T.R.	2/26 Inf	Lower Sonkurai	13.06.43.	30	Sth.Grafton, NSW
QX.10958	Pte.	Petty, L.J.	2/26 Inf	Tanbaya	08.10.43.	25	Gladstone, Qld.
QX.11301	Pte.	Philipson,H.J.	2/26 Inf	Upper Sonkurai	08.11 43.	26	Proserpine, Qld
QX.12092	Cpl.	Pusch, J.	2/26 Inf	Sonkurai	22.08.43.	27	Mackay, Qld
QX.12305	Pte.	Paull, F.J.	2/26 Inf	Upper Sonkurai	23.11.43.	25	Paddington Qld
QX.13096	Pte.	Powell, G.	2/30 Inf	Upper Sonkurai	13.09.43.	34	Tirroan, Qld.
QX.13747	Pte.	Pye, S.S.L.	2/26 Inf	Tanbaya	09.12.43.	31	
QX.14771	Pte.	Pearse, E.B.	AASC	Tanbaya	04.09.43.	35	
QX.14968	Cpl.	Porter, S.	2/30 Inf	Lower Sonkurai	16.09.43.	48	
QX.17207	Bdr.	Porter, E.S.	2/10 RAA	Lower Sonkurai	27.05.43.	34	Brisbane, Qld.
NX. 6940	Pte.	Percy, A.B.	8DivHQ	Kanburi	20.12.43.	24	Gladesville, NSW
NX.25939	Pte.	Power, A.J.R.	2/29 Inf	Tamaranpat	02.08.43.	30	Candelo, NSW
NX.30194	L/Bdr.	Price, N.J.W.	2/15 RAA	Tanbaya	03.11.43.	22	Warnervale, NSW
	(S/A Thompson, G.J.)						
NX.32913	Spr.	Playford, E.S.	2/12 RAE	Kanburi	08.12.43.	41	
NX.35683	Pte.	Phillips, I.C.	2/30 Inf	Tanbaya	28.09.43.	42	
NX.36501	Pte.	Pratt, J.	2/30 Inf	Upper Sonkurai	23.09.43.	36	Peak Hill, NSW
NX.39739	Pte.	Paice, G.D.	2/29 Inf	Tanbaya	02.11.43.	28	Lithgow, NSW
NX.41146	Pte.	Phillips, C.O.	2/29 Inf	Neike	02.08.43.	20	Bendemeer, NSW
NX.41394	Pte.	Parsons, J.T.	2/30 Inf	Tanbaya	02.11.43.	38	Glen Innes, NSW
NX.46640	Pte.	Philp, S.P.	2/30 Inf	Lower Sonkurai	29.05.43.	28	Ballina, NSW
NX.47015	Pte.	Palmer, E.J.	2/30 Inf	Kranji	25.07.44.	26	Evans Head, NSW
NX.47846	Pte.	Prichard, K.D.	2/30 Inf	Upper Sonkurai	29.10.43.	28	Goulburn, NSW
NX.48427	Pte.	Pike, C.C.	2/30 Inf	Kensayo	29.11.43.	34	Chatswood, NSW
NX.54762	Pte.	Phillips, J.E.	2/20 Inf	Upper Sonkurai	04.10.43.	24	Llanelly, Wales
NX.57128	Cpl.	Payne, J.R.	Provost	Upper Sonkurai	09.10.43.	24	Wellington, NSW
NX.57356	Sgt.	Petty, H.G.	2/30 Inf	Upper Sonkurai	21.11.43.	41	Canberra, ACT
NX.58692	Pte.	Paradise, A.J.	74 LAD	Changi	06.02.44.	32	Canterbury, NSW
NX.73584	Pte.	Parker, R.E.	2/29 Inf	Kanburi	16.12.43.	24	

NX.77857	Pte.	Patterson, J.J. (See Jackson, R.J.)	2/30 Inf	Kanburi	11.12.43.	25	Port Kembla, NSW
NX.78657	Pte.	Polglase, J.C.	2/29 Inf	Kanburi	26.11.43.	28	Willoughby, NSW
VX.29559	Pte.	Palmer, E.	2/29 Inf	Changi	07.01.44.	28	VioletTown, Vic.
VX.30909	Pte.	Paton, R.	AAOC	Upper Sonkurai	10.10.43.	23	Moonie Ponds, Vic
VX.34794	Pte.	Pauwels, A.J.	2/29 Inf	Tanbaya	16.11.43.	20	Belmont, Vic.
VX.35534	Spr.	Price, D.L.	2/10 RAE	Taimonta	06.06.43.	25	Wandin Yallock,Vic.
VX.35753	L/Cpl.	Patullo, J.D.H.	2/29 Inf	Tanbaya	21.09.43.	44	Collingwood, Vic
VX.36522	Cpl.	Pryke, A.B.	2/29 Inf	Takanoon	12.08.43.	26	Springvale, Vic.
VX.36943	Spr.	Phelan, B.	2/10 RAE	Kanburi	26.12.43.	22	Clayton, Vic.
VX.40338	Pte.	Post, W.L.A.	2/29 Inf	Takanoon	27.07.43.	31	Richmond, Vic.
VX.43895	Pte.	Pattinson, L.W.	2/29 Inf	Kanburi	18.10.43.	31	Oakleigh, Vic.
VX.44382	Pte.	Pope, L.F.	AASC	Upper Sonkurai	10.11.43.	26	Coburg, Vic.
VX.45727	Pte.	Page, A.E.	2/29 Inf	Tanbaya	13.11.43.	35	Ballarat, Vic.
VX.46799	Pte.	Pitches, I.H.	2/29 Inf	Neike	07.11.43.	37	Deepdene, Vic.
VX.48751	Pte.	Priest, R.	2/29 Inf	Lower Sonkurai	20.08.43.	25	Hawthorn, Vic.
VX.55507	Pte.	Pippard, E.	2/29 Inf	Sonkurai	15.08.43.	30	Mentone, Vic.
VX.55827	Pte.	Phillips, D.C.B.	2/lOFWk.	Upper Sonkurai	25.10.43.	21	Sandringham, Vic.
VX.59535	Pte.	Pledger, F.C.	27BdeAAOC	Upper Sonkurai	05.06.43.	23	West Geelong, Vic
VX.59967	Pte.	Parker, M.G.	4 A/Tk.	Tanbaya	09.09.43.	21	Gardenvale, Vic.
VX.60977	Pte.	Pratt, R.F.	2/29 Inf	Kanburi	10.09.43.	19	Regent, Vic.
SX.11593	Pte.	Pettman, L.E.K.	4 RMT	Kanburi	05.12.43.	43	Henley Beach, SA
TX. 5134	Pte.	Pennington, L.J.	AASC	Kanburi	01.10.43.	29	Derby, Tas.
TX. 5281	Pte.	Panton, T.R.	2/29 Inf	Taimonta	09.06.43.	20	Launceston, Tas.
TX. 8313	Pte.	Peachey, L.G.	2/29 Inf	Kanburi	08.12.43.	21	Perth, Tas.
WX. 6384	Spr.	Pettigrove, S.V.	2/6FPk.	Upper Sonkurai	11.11.43.	42	Shenton Park, WA
WX. 9073	Cpl.	Paterson, W.J.	2/4 MG	Lower Neike	25.07.43.	27	MorningtonMills,WA
NX.47009	Pte.	Quirk, W.G.	2/30 Inf	Tanbaya	24.10.43.	35	Cudgen, NSW
NX.57104	Pte.	Quinn, T.A.	10 AGH	Tanbaya	26.09.43.	30	Petersham, NSW
NX.65486	Pte.	Quintal, L.P.	2/30 Inf	Tanbaya	16.10.43.	23	Norfolk Island
VX.45924	Pte.	Quin, F.V.	27BdeHQ	Kanburi	06.11.43.	35	
WX.10957	Pte.	Quilter, G.T.	4 RMT	Lower Sonkurai	03.06.43.	40	
QX. 1690	Sgt.	Rogers, J.	2/26 Inf	Kanburi	16.12.43.	42	Lindfield, NSW
QX.10594	Pte.	Row, C.	2/26 Inf	Lower Sonkurai	30.08.43.	30	Goodwood, Qld.
QX.10814	Sgt.	Roselt, E.C.	2/26 Inf	Tanbaya	10.11.43.	42	Bundaberg, Qld.
QX.11025	Pte.	Reid, C.	2/26 Inf	Tanbaya	14.09.43.	24	Richmond, Vic.
QX.15211	Pte.	Rowntree, A.N.	2/26 Inf	Tanbaya	25.10.43.	33	Cardross, Vic.
QX.20320	Pte.	Rickards, J.N.	2/26 Inf	Lower Sonkurai	05.06.43.	23	Rosalie, Qld.
QX.22309	Pte.	Richards, G.C.	2/26 Inf	Tanbaya	17.11.43.	42	Semaphore, SA
QX.23778	Pte.	Rowe, H.V.	2/26 Inf	Lower Sonkurai	09.08.43.	25	Nambour, Qld.
NX. 8768	Pte.	Ralph, C.	2/30 Inf	Upper Sonkurai	15.11.43.	24	Birchgrove, NSW
NX.20865	Pte.	Rydiard, J.F.	27BdeHQ	Takanoon	10.08.43.	26	Manly, NSW
NX.23803	Gnr.	Rosenberg, A.	2/15 RAA	Kanburi	26.12.43.	41	Double Bay, NSW
NX.26070	Gnr.	Robinson, R.S.	2/15 RAA	Kanburi	04.01.44.	26	Vaucluse, NSW
NX.30912	Sgt.	Roberts, B.S.	2/18 Inf	Tanbaya	10.12.43.	25	Chatswood, NSW
NX.31816	Cpl.	Rogers, F.A.	2/29 Inf	Tanbaya	25.09.43.	24	Bondi Junction,NS
NX.33038	Pte.	Reinhard, L.J.	2/30 Inf	Upper Sonkurai	25.10.43.	30	Coonamble, NSW
NX.33145	Pte.	Roberts, K.H.	2/18 Inf	Kanburi	22.02.44.	23	Hornsby, NSW
NX.34316	Pte.	Russell, C.J.	2/30 Inf	Kanburi	24.12.43.	26	Mayfield, NSW
NX.40236	Pte.	Roberts, G.G.	Provost	Neike	05.08.43.	42	
NX.40387	Pte.	Reeves, M.	2/18 Inf	Tanbaya	22.10.43.	27	Warialda, NSW

NX.42596	Pte.	Rash, J.G. (S/A. Golding, J.B.)	2/30 Inf	Lower Sonkurai	03.06.43.	23	Kogarah Bay, NSW
NX.43526	Cpl.	Rodda, N.	Admn.HQ	Tanbaya	20.09.43.	23	Enfield, NSW
NX.43916	Pte.	Robinson, A.J.	2/19 Inf	Kanburi	28.10.43.	34	Botany, NSW
NX.47456	Cpl.	Rowe, A.N.	2/30 Inf	Sonkurai	14.11.43.	46	East Kempsey, NSW
NX.47466	Pte.	Reilly, A.W.	2/30 Inf	Kanburi	05.12.43.	35	Alstonville, NSW
NX.48273	Sgmn.	Rees, P.D.	8DivSigs	Tanbaya	11.01.44.	21	Canberra, ACT
NX.50113	Pte.	Reed, J.	2/30 Inf	Kanburi	25.12.43.	21	Kyogle, NSW
NX.50207	Pte.	Reid, K.S.	2/30 Inf	Upper Sonkurai	30.09.43.	21	Croydon, NSW
NX.51181	Pte.	Reeves, W.R.	2/30 Inf	Lower Sonkurai	23.07.43.	27	Dubbo, NSW
NX.59083	Sgmn.	Roberts, C.D.	8DivSigs	Upper Sonkurai	03.07.43.	34	Lindfield, NSW
NX.70021	Pte.	Riddell, A.M.	84 LAD	Prankalli	28.11.43.	36	Berala, NSW
NX.73009	Pte.	Rayson, B.H.	2/30 Inf	Tanbaya	24.10.43.	23	Arakoon, NSW
VX.39273	S/Sgt.	Rossiter, W.J.	13 AGH	Tamaranpat	09.08.43.	27	Yarram, Vic.
VX.41142	Pte.	Riley, W.G.	2/29 Inf	Kanburi	19.09.43.	26	Carlton, Vic.
VX.41495	Pte.	Rogers, A.A.	22BdeWks	Upper Sonkurai	22.10.43.	22	Thornbury, Vic.
VX.41694	Pte.	Redden, J.S.	2/29 Inf	Tanbaya	29.09.43.	27	Malvern, Vic.
VX.41992	Gnr.	Reed, W.R.	4 A/Tk.	Kanburi	02.12.43.	31	Carlton, Vic.
VX.43216	Pte.	Rawson, D.N.	2/29 Inf	Upper Sonkurai	31.10.43.	25	Burnley, Vic.
VX.47157	Pte.	Rankin, C.	2/29 Inf	Kanburi	10.12.43.	34	Kooyong, Vic.
VX.50250	Pte.	Rider, E.V.	4 RMT	Kanburi	09.12.43.	24	Blackburn, Vic.
VX.55502	Pte.	Roberts, H.E.	2/2 MAC	Upper Sonkurai	07.10.43.	29	Caulfield, Vic.
VX.55924	Pte.	Rose, M.J.	2/29 Inf	Taimonta	04.11.43.	24	Sydney, NSW
VX.59511	Pte.	Rotheram, J.E.	2/29 Inf	Lower Sonkurai	30.05.43.	41	North Fitzroy, Vic.
VX.63566	Pte.	Robertson, M.	2/29 Inf	Kanburi	08.04.44.	22	
VX.64289	Pte.	Rose, K.L.	2/26 Inf	Tanbaya	06.09.43.	23	Cobram, Vic.
VX.65088	Cpl.	Ralph, A.F.	2/29 Inf	Takanoon	27.07.43.	19	Ararat, Vic.
SX. 8112	Pte.	Robinson, B.N.	27BdeWks	Upper Sonkurai	04.10.43.	40	Inman Valley, SA
SX.11047	Cpl.	Ryan, L.J.	AASC	Sonkurai	03.11.43.	41	Adelaide, S.A.
SX. 5172	Pte.	Riggs, R.W.	2/3 MAC	Kanburi	29.09.43.	24	Burnie, Tas.
TX. 5850	Pte.	Radford, N.	2/29 Inf	Kanburi	15.09.43.	37	Romaine, Tas.
TX. 6286	Spr.	Ryan, H.W.	2/6FdPk	Lower Sonkurai	01.06.43.	38	Perth, WA
QX. 8449	Pte.	Sands, E.	2/26 Inf	Lower Sonkurai	30.05.43.	23	Sth.Townsville, Qld.
QX. 9322	Gnr.	Savage, J.A.	2/10 RAA	Kanburi	13.12.43.	29	Windsor, Qld.
QX.11338	Pte.	Small, F.C.L.	2/26 Inf	Upper Sonkurai	22.10.43.	25	Proserpine, Qld.
QX.12347	Pte.	Stickley, S.A.	2/26 Inf	Upper Sonkurai	05.10.43.	26	Rockhampton,Qld
QX.12934	Pte.	Sellick, M.E.	2/26 Inf	Lower Sonkurai	06.06.43.	21	Condong, NSW
QX.14071	Pte.	Slater, R.R.	2/26 Inf	Sonkurai	18.11.43.	32	Sth.Kensington,NSW
QX.14116	Sgt.	Sutton, E.J.H.	2/26 Inf	Upper Sonkurai	11.10.43.	32	
QX.14762	Pte.	Shirley, E.J.	2/26 Inf	Upper Sonkurai	22.08.43	26	Norman Park, Qld.
QX.15586	Gnr.	Simmonds, G.E.C.	2/10 RAA	Tanbaya	03.10.43	40	Sandgate, Qld.
QX.17199	Pte.	Schofield, J.F.	2/26 Inf	Tanbaya	11.10.43.	29	Bulimba, Qld.
QX.19199	Pte.	Soutter, R.J.	2/26 Inf	Tanbaya	08.10.43.	28	Red Hill, Qld
QX.19544	Pte.	Stanberg, G.E.	2/26 Inf	Sonkurai	13.08.43.	26	
QX.21350	Pte.	Spletter, J.J.	2/26 Inf	Lower Sonkurai	21.08.43.	38	Boonah, Qld.
QX.22099	Pte.	Sweatman, K.T.	2/29 Inf	Tamaranpat	23.11.43.	22	Auchenflower, Qld.
QX.22393	Pte.	Scriven, E.J.	2/30 Inf	Lower Sonkurai	28.05.43.	28	Windsor, Qld.
QX.23332	Pte.	Smith, R.	2/26 Inf	Kanburi	03.12.43.	30	Appletree Ck.,Qld.
QX.23345	Pte.	Simpson, T.	2/26 Inf	Upper Sonkurai	29.09.43.	26	Gympie, Qld.
QX.25478	Pte.	Sullivan, B.A.	33Dntl.	Tamaranpat	04.07.43.	28	Greenslopes, Qld
NX. 2495	Pte.	Sinclair, G.W.	2/30 Inf	Upper Sonkurai	22.10.43.	22	Balmain, NSW

NX. 2573	Pte.	Smith, C.J.	2/30 Inf	Upper Sonkurai	01.11.43.	28	Byron Bay, NSW
NX. 4647	Spr.	Stenlund, S.V.	2/12 RAE	Changi	24.02.44.	27	Aberdeen, NSW
NX.19965	W0.2	Shaw, W.A.	2/15 RAA	Tanbaya	25.10.43.	21	Guildford, NSW
NX.20386	Pte.	Smith, J.S.C.	2/20 Inf	Lower Sonkurai	14.06.43.	25	Ourimbah, NSW
NX.22913	Cpl.	Sawyers, A.G.	Provost	Kanburi	29.11.43.	29	Greigs Flat, NSW
NX.26513	Pte.	Stone, J.E.	H.Q.	Lower Sonkurai	31.05.43.	26	Marrickville, NSW
NX.27045	Sgmn.	Stewart, J.C.	8DivSigs	Takanoon	23.09.43.	34	Gladesville, NSW
NX.27452	Pte.	Smith, W.T.	2/30 Inf	Upper Sonkurai	20.11.43.	24	Bega, NSW
NX.27586	Pte.	Spurway, M.F.	2/20 Inf	Upper Sonkurai	12.11.43.	22	West Ryde, NSW
NX.27601	Pte.	Smith, A.J.	2/30 Inf	Upper Sonkurai	01.06.43.	39	Bristol, UK
NX.29700	Sgmn.	Smith, M.D.	8DivSigs	Chungkai	07.10.43.	25	
NX.31671	Pte.	Somerville, J.	2/30 Inf	Upper Sonkurai	28.10.43.	38	Tweed Heads, NSW
NX.32505	Pte.	Starr, W.E.	2/30 Inf	Upper Sonkurai	04.11.43.	29	Alexandria, NSW
NX.32900	Pte.	Smith, R.	2/30 Inf	Kanburi	02.12.43.	29	Lewisham, NSW
NX.35447	Pte.	Sayers, L.R.T.	2/26 Inf	Kanburi	04.01.44.	24	Darlington Pt., NSW
NX.35491	Pte.	Simpson, D.G.	2/19 Inf	Kanburi	17.12.43.	27	Chatswood, NSW
NX.36573	Cpl.	Symes, W.A.	8DivSigs	Tanbaya	20.01.44.	27	Lewisham, NSW
NX.40704	Cpl.	Smith, F.B.	Provost	Upper Sonkurai	13.10.43.	42	Glen Innes, NSW
NX.42308	Pte.	Sarginson, F.G.	2/30 Inf	Lower Sonkurai	11.06.43.	36	Exeter, NSW
NX.44541	Pte.	Stokes, F.C.	Postal	Neike	08.08.43.	28	Canterbury, NSW
NX.45539	Pte.	Supple, V.T.	2/lOFdAmb	Lower Sonkurai	31.05.43.	35	Comara, NSW
NX.47591	Pte.	Standing, E.G.	2/30 Inf	Kanburi	07.02.44.	39	Sth. Lismore, NSW
NX.47651	Pte.	Staader, A.E.	2/30 Inf	Upper Sonkurai	22.08.43.	26	
NX.48055	Pte.	Standfield, C.W.	2/29 Inf	Koncoita	23.11.43.	22	Kyogle, NSW
NX.52574	Pte.	Salmon, J.A.	2/29 Inf	Tanbaya	17.10.43.	31	Mosman, NSW
NX.53037	Spr.	Smith, L.E.	2/12 RAE	Tamaranpat	07.07.43.	25	Fairfield, NSW
NX.53042	Pte.	Simpson, J.T.	2/30 Inf	Upper Sonkurai	20.10.43.	30	Waratah, NSW
NX.53747	Pte.	Shaw, M.D.	2/30 Inf	Lower Sonkurai	29.05.43.	35	North Bondi, NSW
NX.54466	Pte.	Stone, A.E.	2/30 Inf	Lower Sonkurai	27.05.43.	25	Paddington, NSW
NX.55717	Pte.	Smyth, P.T.	2/30 Inf	Neike	22.11.43.	21	Coogee, NSW
NX.57017	Sgt.	Steer, V.J.	AdmnHQ	Sonkurai	26.08.43.	38	Manly, NSW
NX.58605	Cpl.	Shore, G.R.	HQ.AAOC	Upper Sonkurai	13.11.43.	47	Strathfield, NSW
NX.60553	Sgmn.	Solomon, J.C.	8DivSigs	Upper Sonkurai	16.09.43.	24	Hurlstone Park, NSW
NX.66852	Pte.	Small, R.H.	2/lOFdAmb	Lower Sonkurai	29.06.43.	22	Mortdale, NSW
NX.67819	Spr.	Scutts, F.	2/12 RAE	Upper Sonkurai	23.10.43.	36	Hurlstone Pk., NSW
NX.69022	Pte.	Seidel, C.F.	2/30 Inf	Lower Sonkurai	25.05.43.	29	Mongarlowe, NSW
NX.71853	Pte.	Smith, R.E.	2/20 Inf	Kanburi	20.12.43.	24	Narromine, NSW
NX.73105	Pte.	Starling, W.J.	2/30 Inf	Kanburi	15.02.44.	35	Parramatta, NSW
NX.73332	Pte.	Starr, J.H.	2/19 Inf	Kanburi	03.12.43.	25	Kingsford, NSW
VX.22310	Pte.	Smilie, W.E.	2/29 Inf	Tanbaya	20.11.43.	42	Camberwell, Vic.
VX.29430	Pte.	Schofield, W.H.	2/29 Inf	Kraw Krie	25.06.43.	34	Northcote, Vic.
VX.33459	Pte.	Siemers, A.A.	2/29 Inf	Neike	28.11.43.	27	Kincumber, NSW
VX.36982	Pte.	Spokes, C.W.B.	2/29 Inf	Changi	06.02.44.	31	Colac, Vic.
VX.37297	Cpl.	Smith, E.C.D.	2/29 Inf	Lower Sonkurai	28.05.43.	24	Swan Hill, Vic.
VX.38378	Pte.	Staples, A.R.	2/29 Inf	Upper Sonkurai	29.08.43.	27	Bendigo, Vic.
VX.39795	Pte.	Sullivan, L.W.	27BdeWks	Lower Sonkurai	09.06.43.	22	Hawthorn, Vic.
VX.40110	Dvr.	Scott, E.A.L.	2/2 MAC	Upper Sonkurai	11.08.43.	41	Glen Thompson, Vic.
VX.40201	W0.2	Stiles, L.V.	2/29 Inf	Takanoon	14.07.~3.	33	Mt.Gambier, SA
VX.42467	Pte.	Sephton, P.H.	2/29 Inf	Takanoon	24.07.43.	23	Oakleigh, Vic.
VX.42811	Pte.	Sandell, E.A.	2/9FdAmb	Tanbaya	26.11.43.	25	
VX.43772	Cpl.	Slater, M.	2/29 Inf	Kanburi	13.10.43.	25	

VX.45590	Pte.	Saunders, G.F.	2/29 Inf	Tarsoa	28.07.43.	37	Kyabram, Vic.
VX.45783	Pte.	Shimmin, R.S.	2/29 Inf	Neike	13.08.43.	24	
VX.46155	Pte.	Saunders, A.A.	2/9FdAmb	Kanburi	05.12.43.	36	Glengarry, Vic.
VX.48316	Pte.	Simpson, R.W.	4 RMT	Tanbaya	26.10.43.	38	Cobram, Vic.
VX.55567	Pte.	Sjursen, A.J.	2/29 Inf	Kanburi	06.12.43.	37	
VX.58643	Pte.	Sampson, H.J.	2/29 Inf	Tanbaya	04.12.43.	41	West Brunswick, Vic.
VX.59146	Pte.	Smith, J.B.	2/9FdAmb	Upper Sonkurai	26.10.43.	24	St. Kilda, Vic.
VX.59176	Pte.	Simpfendorfer, A.O.	13 AGH	Tanbaya	20.10.43.	32	Albury, NSW
VX.60324	Pte.	Small, R.G.	13 AGH	Kanburi	15.12.43.	22	Albert Park, Vic
VX.61236	Pte.	Sweatman, A.E.	13 AGH	Tanbaya	05.11.43.	24	Ballarat, Vic.
VX.61561	Pte.	Schneider, R,S.	2/29 Inf	Tanbaya	14.12.43.	20	South Yarra, Vic
VX.65556	Pte.	Salkeld, A.W.	2/26 Inf	Tanbaya	05.09.43.	28	Hopetoun, Vic.
SX. 7039	Sgmn.	Sexton, J.	8DivSigs	Takanoon	19.07.43.	24	Mitcham, SA
SX. 7220	Sgmn.	Symons, E.	8DivSigs	Taimonta	24.05.43.	25	Exeter, SA
SX. 8053	Sgt.	Sawyers, S.W.	AASC	Lower Sonkurai	29.05.43.	38	Glen Osmond, SA
SX.10636	Pte.	Slater, K.E.	AASC	Lower Sonkurai	08.06.43.	25	Kilroo, SA
TX. 4423	Pte.	Shaw, W.T.	2/3 MAC	Sonkurai	23.10.43.	23	Hobart, Tas.
WX. 6532	Spr.	Sparke, A.H.	2/6FdPk	Tanbaya	26.01.44.	30	Victoria Park, WA
WX. 9143	Pte.	Smith, M.J.	2/4 MG	Tanbaya	13.11.43.	27	Mukinbudin, WA
WX.14644	Sgt.	Smith, C.V.	2/4 MG	Upper Sonkurai	22.10.43.	38	East Rockingham, WA
QX.11394	Sgt.	Tippett, H.E.	2/26 Inf	Upper Sonkurai	08.11.43.	23	Townsville, Qld.
QX.13946	Cpl.	Taylor, R.B.	2/26 Inf	Sonkurai	19.09.43.	23	Sth.Brisbane, Qld
QX.14706	Pte.	Townsend, J.H.	2/26 Inf	Kanburi	13.09.43.	26	Camp Hill, Qld.
QX.17300	Pte.	Trotter, R.F.	AASC	Kranji	15.07.44.	35	
NX. 633	Pte.	Turner, R.	2/30 Inf	Kanburi	24.12.43.	21	Mudgee, NSW
NX. 7937	Pte.	Turner, G.	2/26 Inf	Padang Besar	18.12.43.	37	
NX. 8271	Spr.	Turley, W.H.	2/12 RAE	Kanburi	12.12.43.	36	Ilford, NSW
NX.25015	Gnr.	Tindal, R.T.	2/15 RAA	Upper Sonkurai	10.11.43.	23	Killara, NSW
NX.27784	Gnr.	Thew, W.A.	2/15 RAA	Lower Sonkurai	30.05.43.	35	Surry Hills, NSW
NX.30547	Pte.	Tucker, S.E.	2/30 Inf	Upper Sonkurai	03.09.43.	31	Dubbo, NSW
NX.30642	Pte.	Tait, F.E.	2/30 Inf	Upper Sonkurai	23.11.43.	23	Bellingen, NSW
NX.31451	Spr.	Thompson, A.J.	2/12 RAE	Kanburi	11.12.43.	38	Lismore, NSW
NX.32857	Spr.	Turner, A.S.	2/12 RAE	Upper Sonkurai	06.06.43.	36	Petersham, NSW
NX.33519	Pte.	Trapnell, R.A.	2/30 Inf	Sonkurai	05.10.43.	31	Katoomba, NSW
NX.34552	Pte.	Toussard, L.J.	2/30 Inf	Lower Sonkurai	22.06.43.	32	Rozelle, NSW
NX.41117	Pte.	Tickle, E.A.	27BdeHQ	Tarsoa	18.08.43.	33	Wollun, NSW
NX.41485	Sgmn.	Tasker, D.H.	8DivSigs	Tamaranpat	01.07.43.	34	Parkes, NSW
NX.49211	Gnr.	Turner, R.A.	2/15 RAA	Tanbaya	09.10.43.	25	Coffs Harbour, NSW
NX.51216	Pte.	Turner, T.M.	2/19 Inf	Upper Sonkurai	05.11.43.	20	Mt.Victoria, NSW
NX.51270	Pte.	Tunbridge, T.A.	2/30 Inf	Upper Sonkurai	11.11.43.	41	Hill End, NSW
NX.54739	Pte.	Tapp, D.S.	2/30 Inf	Singapore	22.12.43.	35	Tamworth, NSW
NX.55026	Pte.	Thomas, A.J.S.	10 AGH	Kanburi	23.02.44.	42	Redfern, NSW
NX.56826	Pte.	Tuckey, F.H.	2/30 Inf	Changi	11.01.44.	40	North Sydney, NSW
NX.57645	Cpl.	Tyson, J.S.	2/30 Inf	Lower Sonkurai	04.06.43.	34	
NX.57665	Pte.	Thornberry, E.	AASC	Sonkurai	04.11.43.	35	Cudal, NSW
NX.58941	Pte.	Thomas, S.W.	10 AGH	Lower Sonkurai	01.06.43.	27	Darlinghurst, NSW
NX.68499	Pte.	Trotter, L.H.	2/20 Inf	Tanbaya	12.09.43.	23	Hallidays Point, NSW
NX.69247	Dvr.	Thomson, W.C.	4 RMT	Tanbaya	20.09.43.	24	Granville, NSW
VX.23554	Spr.	Thomas, F.E.	2/10 RAE	Lower Sonkurai	21.07.43.	22	Fairfield, Vic.
VX.40927	Pte.	Taylor, M.T.	2/29 Inf	Changi	12.01.44.	26	Ascot Vale, Vic.
VX.42029	Cpl.	Thompson, H.V.	2/10 RAE	Kanburi	08.12.43.	37	Wandin North, Vic.

VX.46263	Pte.	Thompson, W.	2/29 Inf	Takanoon	16.07.43.	39	Wodonga, Vic.
VX.46778	Spr.	Tulloch, N.L.	2/10 RAE	Upper Sonkurai	11.11.43.	29	Ascot Vale, Vic.
VX.48277	Dvr.	Tremellen, W.E.	2/2 MAC	Upper Sonkurai	07.11.43.	28	Tallygaroopna,Vic.
VX.55047	Pte.	Thornell, L.T.	2/29 Inf	Kanburi	28.10.43.	24	Somerville, Vic.
VX.59112	Cpl.	Tschampion, K.J.	2/29 Inf	Upper Sonkurai	11.09.43.	27	Cockatoo, Vic.
VX.60104	Pte.	Tierney, C.	2/2 MAC	Upper Sonkurai	27.06.43.	30	
VX.61372	Pte.	Tennant, W.B.	27FPk.	Tanbaya	24.10.43.	24	
VX.62654	Pte.	Twyford, G.	2/26 Inf	Lower Sonkurai	03.06.43.	20	St. Kilda, Vic.
VX.63037	Sgt.	Tippett, A.W.	2/29 Inf	Tanbaya	19.11.43.	24	Coloraine, Vic.
VX.64135	Pte.	Taylor, R.N.	2/29 Inf	Kanburi	25.10.43.	24	Merbein, Vic.
TX. 4532	Cpl.	Thurley, E.R.	Provost	Kanburi	03.12.43.	24	Eugenana, Tas.
TX. 5825	Pte.	Turner, H.W.	2/26 Inf	Lower Sonkurai	11.06.43.	32	Moonah, Tas.
WX. 4921	Sgt.	Taylor, J.T.	2/4 MG	Upper Sonkurai	11.07.43.	37	Dunkeld, Scot.
WX. 7183	Sgt.	Thompson, R.S.	2/6FdPk	Takanoon	13.07.43.	31	Perth, WA
WX. 8699	Pte.	Thackrah, C.B.	2/4 MG	Tanbaya	19.09.43.	40	Reading, U.K.
VX.63651	Pte.	Underwood, C.W.	2/26 Inf	Lower Sonkurai	29.05.43.	28	Barham, NSW
QX.19575	Pte.	Vines, J.T.	2/26 Inf	Tanbaya	28.09.43.	23	Nanango, Qld.
NX.15563	Pte.	Vincent, H.R.W.	2/30 Inf	Neike	12.08.43.	25	Narrabri, NSW
NX.34624	Pte.	Verrender, G.D.	AASC	Upper Sonkurai	15.10.43.	26	Earlwood, NSW
NX.43665	Pte.	Vellacott, G.W.	13 AGH	Kanburi	19.12.43.	34	Canberra, ACT
NX.47809	Pte.	Vidler, G.T.	2/30 Inf	Kanburi	03.01.44.	26	ChilcottsGrass,NSW
VX.45053	Pte.	Vernon, J.S.	2/29 Inf	Kuie	29.06.43.	23	Hamilton, Vic.
TX. 5563	Gnr.	Viney, L.C.	4 A/Tk.	Tanbaya	14.11.43.	32	Cooee, Tas.
TX. 5826	Pte.	Vincent, D.B.	2/29 Inf	Kanburi	09.12.43.	22	Ulverstone, Tas.
QX.10119	Pte.	Williams, K.G.	2/26 Inf	Kanburi	04.12.43.	38	Cal Lal, NSW
QX.11012	Pte.	While, H.E.	2/26 Inf	Lower Sonkurai	23.05.43.	31	Brighton, U.K.
QX.14102	Pte.	Watt, H.	2/26 Inf	Tanbaya	03.09.43.	27	Southport, Qld.
QX.14158	Pte.	Warden, V.S.	2/29 Inf	Upper Sonkurai	21.10.43.	23	West Preston, Vic
QX.15004	Pte.	Way, W.E.	2/26 Inf	Kanburi	01.12.43.	39	
QX.15154	Pte.	Western, W.G.	2/26 Inf	Upper Sonkurai	17.11.43.	30	Grantleigh, Qld.
QX.15197	S/Sgt.	White, A.M.	2/26 Inf	Kanburi	30.11.43.	26	Pawngille, Qld.
QX.15224	W0.2	Wilson, H.N.	2/26 Inf	Lower Sonkurai	08.06.43.	32	Sandy Bay,Tas.
QX.15667	Pte.	Winkel, H.E.	AAOC	Lower Sonkurai	01.06.43.	35	Brisbane, Qld.
QX.15701	Pte.	Westcott, H.W.	74 LAD	Lower Neike	19.05.43.	23	Innisfail, Qld.
QX.16536	Pte.	Ward, W.J.	2/26 Inf	Kanburi	14.12.43.	42	
QX.16684	Gnr.	Wehl, J.R.	2/10 RAA	Kanburi	21.01.44.	23	Roma, Qld.
QX.19997	Pte.	Webb, H.A.	2/26 Inf	Tanbaya	12.10.43.	37	
QX.21455	Pte.	Watson, R.A.	2/30 Inf	Upper Sonkurai	08.11.43.	32	Rockhampton, Qld.
QX.21939	Pte.	Whyatt, L.	2/30 Inf	Kanburi	27.12.43.	33	Booval, Qld.
QX.23446	Pte.	Wright, J.	2/26 Inf	Changi	18.03.44.	22	Allora, Qld.
QX.23588	Pte.	Wilkinson, L.J.	2/29 Inf	Kanburi	08.11.43.	26	Brisbane, Qld.
QX.24253	Pte.	Wright, N.T.	2/29 Inf	Kanburi	25.03.44.	21	Ascot, Qld.
NX. 595	Pte.	Winters, L.	2/30 Inf	Kanburi	04.12.43.	32	Queanbeyan, NSW
NX. 4404	Pte.	Wynn, L.R.	27BdeHQ	Kraw Krie	28.06.43.	28	Yarra Bay, NSW
NX.10735	Cpl.	Weston, F.L.	Provost	Kanburi	08.01.44.	30	Curban, NSW
NX.18235	Gnr.	Windsor, E.A.	2/15 RAA	Changi	27.05.44.	41	Merewether, NSW
NX.26243	Pte.	Wright, M.	2/26 Inf	Tanbaya	20.10.43.	36	Walgett, NSW
NX.26511	Pte.	Wilson, G.B.	Fd.Bkry	Lower Sonkurai	22.06.43.	35	Dunedoo, NSW
NX.26685	Gnr.	Wood, K.	2/15 RAA	Upper Sonkurai	27.09.43.	24	Kogarah, NSW
NX.26860	Pte.	Watts, F.S.	2/30 Inf	Neike	21.11.43.	38	Kadungle, NSW
NX.31067	Cpl.	Webber, A.V.	Provost	Kanburi	13.01.44.	29	Kyogle, NSW

NX.31918	Sgmn.	Williams, R.A.	8DivSigs	Upper Sonkurai	24.08.43.	23	Glen Innes, NSW
NX.36242	Pte.	Weston, J. (See Bright, J.)	2/30 Inf	Lower Sonkurai	07.09.43.	30	Geelong West, Vic.
NX.36267	Pte.	Whitteron, E.S.	2/30 Inf	Kuie	10.06.43.	29	Hay, NSW
NX.36483	Pte.	Weiss, H.B.	2/30 Inf	Upper Sonkurai	30.09.43.	33	Singleton, NSW
NX.36545	Pte.	Williamson, C.	2/30 Inf	Upper Sonkurai	13.10.43.	39	Griffith, NSW
NX.37356	Pte.	Waller, D.A.	2/30 Inf	Kanburi	15.12.43.	37	
NX.37472	Gnr.	Williamson, W.J.	2/15 RAA	Upper Sonkurai	22.08.43.	23	Ivanhoe, NSW
NX.37563	Pte.	Wilson, C.M.	2/30 Inf	Lower Sonkurai	31.05.43.	23	Long Jetty, NSW
NX.37682	Pte.	Wallace, N.R.	H.Q.	Tanbaya	28.09.43.	24	Werris Creek, NSW
NX.37706	Pte.	Walsh, R.L.	2/30 Inf	Changi	25.03.44.	30	Byron Bay, NSW
NX.39157	Sgmn.	Williams, H.V.H.	8DivSigs	Tanbaya	15.09.43.	21	Chatswood, NSW
NX.40257	Pte.	Wilson, W.L.	2/3 MAC	Upper Sonkurai	20.09.43.	39	Glen Innes, NSW
NX.40858	Cpl.	Whackett, A.L.	Provost	Upper Sonkurai	05.06.43.	40	Uralla, NSW
NX.45515	Pte.	Williams, J.D.	2/lOFdAmb	Kanburi	23.09.43.	37	Wauchope, NSW
NX.47835	Pte.	Woods, B.R.	2/30 Inf	Kanburi	03.12.43.	18	Bellingen, NSW
NX.47953	Pte.	Williams, F.E.	2/30 Inf	Upper Sonkurai	26.11.43.	24	Murwillumbah, NSW
NX.48755	Pte.	Whalan, R.	H.Q.	Tanbaya	18.09.43.	40	Sth.Lismore, NSW
NX.49282	Pte.	Waugh, N.S.	2/30 Inf	Kanburi	03.02.44.	35	Bangalow, NSW
NX.54108	Pte.	Welsh, W.J.	2/19 Inf	Kanburi	26.12.43.	33	Kogarah, NSW
NX.58631	Pte.	Watson, H.H.	2/26 Inf	Sonkurai	30.09.43.	42	Leichhardt, NSW
NX.59551	Pte.	Wilson, R.G.	10 AGH	Tanbaya	03.10.43.	22	Redfern, NSW
NX.59579	Pte.	Walsh, J.C.	2/30 Inf	Kanburi	29.11.43.	25	Enmore, NSW
NX.69165	Sgmn.	Watkins, C.E.	8DivSigs	Takanoon	04.06.43.	20	Birmingham, UK
NX.71321	Pte.	Wrightson, D.C.	8DivSigs	Tanbaya	24.10.43.	26	Kendall, NSW
NX.73774	Pte.	Wilson, O.W.G.	2/30 Inf	Lower Sonkurai	10.07.43.	27	Lismore, NSW
NX.79537	Pte.	Winstanley, S.	2/30 Inf	Lower Sonkurai	18.09.43.	39	Wyong, NSW
VX.13286	Pte.	Wren, L.	2/29 Inf	Tanbaya	28.09.43.	31	Brunswick, Vic.
VX.27498	Cpl.	Whitbread, W.H.T.	2/29 Inf	Upper Sonkurai	20.06.43.	42	Dandenong, Vic.
VX.32424	Pte.	Woodhouse, J.C.	8DivSigs	Tarsoa	22.10.43.	42	
VX.34084	Spr.	Whytcross, R.D.	2/10 RAE	Kanburi	03.11.43.	27	Kew, Vic.
VX.35781	Spr.	White, A.J.	2/10 RAE	Takanoon	05.08.43.	27	Essendon, Vic.
VX.38561	Gnr.	Williams, H.E.S.	4 A/Tk.	Kanburi	18.12.43.	34	Dunolly, Vic.
VX.39046	WO.l	Waters, H.H.L.	2/29 Inf	Kanburi	09.11.43.	27	Abbotsford, Vic.
VX.39334	Pte.	Winters, T.A.	13 AGH	Tanbaya	02.09.43.	37	Sandringham, Vic
VX.40782	Pte.	Walsh, M.M.	2/29 Inf	Tanbaya	22.12.43.	30	Ballarat, Vic.
VX.42350	Gnr.	Wake, F.J.	4 A/Tk.	Upper Sonkurai	03.10.43.	30	Narromine, NSW
VX.42674	Cpl.	Williams, T.J.	2/29 Inf	Tanbaya	02.12.43.	37	Warragul, Vic.
VX.43795	Pte.	Whitford, M.	2/29 Inf	Lower Sonkurai	09.06.43.	34	Ballarat, Vic.
VX.45944	Pte.	Webb, R.	2/29 Inf	Upper Sonkurai	06.10.43.	39	Carnegie, Vic.
VX.50027	Pte.	Watson, K.E.	4 RMT	Changi	07.05.44.	24	Elwood, Vic.
VX.51487	Pte.	Webster, L.L.	2/29 Inf	Takanoon	10.07.43.	38	Prahran, Vic.
VX.53067	Pte.	Wallace, L.S.	2/29 Inf	Takanoon	07.08.43.	35	East Brunswick,Vic.
VX.55060	Pte.	Wells, M.J.	2/29 Inf	Kanburi	14.10.43.	20	Prahran, Vic.
VX.55090	Pte.	Wansbrough, W.J.	PayCorps	Tanbaya	06.09.43.	24	Parkdale, Vic.
VX.55628	Pte.	Wookey, E.	13 AGH	Upper Sonkurai	06.10.43.	27	Snake Valley, Vic.
VX.55737	Sgt.	Wilkinson, C.U.	27FPkAAOC	Upper Sonkurai	22.10.43.	23	Maffra, Vic.
VX.60177	Pte.	Waddington, E.	13 AGH	Neike	28.06.43.	38	
SX. 9796	Pte.	West, R.P.	Salvge	Tanbaya	25.01.44.	26	Cleve, SA
SX. 9861	Pte.	Wilson, A.F.	AASC	Lower Sonkurai	30.05.43.	27	Rosewater, SA
SX.10925	Pte.	Wright, R.K.	AASC	Kanburi	04.12.43.	23	Tailem Bend, SA

TX. 4829	Pte.	Walker, J.B.	2/26 Inf	Tanbaya	13.10.43.	22	Hobart, Tas.
TX. 5227	Pte.	Welsh, A.W.	2/29 Inf	Changi	02.01.44.	25	Launceston, Tas.
WX. 6878	Sgmn.	Westcott, C.W.S.	8DivSigs	Kanburi	07.02.44.	31	Shenton Park, WA
WX. 8479	Spr.	Wilson, R.S.	2/6FdPk	Upper Sonkurai	16.10.43.	38	Bassendean, WA
WX.10012	Pte.	Worth, W.G.	2/4 MG	Upper Sonkurai	28.08.43.	31	Bellevue, W.A.
WX.10887	Pte.	White, E.J.	Postal	Tanbaya	11.09.43.	37	Perth, WA
WX.11700	Pte.	Waddell, I.E.	27BdeWks	Lower Sonkurai	03.06.43.	33	Victoria Park,WA
WX.11745	Pte.	Willimott, J.F.	2/4 MG	Kanburi	05.12.43.	39	Swanbourne, WA
WX.14450	Gnr.	Williams, D.J.	lHByRAA	Tanbaya	20.09.43.	26	South Perth, WA
QX.17338	Pte.	Young, A.C.	2/26 Inf	Lower Sonkurai	28.05.43.	43	
NX.37283	Pte.	Yeates, T.M.	2/30 Inf	Lower Sonkurai	14.08.43.	19	Sefton, NSW
VX.40674	Cpl.	Youngclause, J.	2/10 RAE	Tanbaya	22.11.43.	46	Sandwick, Zetland
WX. 7648	Spr.	Yarwood, H.	2/6FdPk	Tamaranpat	31.07.43.	33	Walworth, U.K.

SUPPLEMENTARY ROLL - F FORCE

NUMBER	RANK	NAME	UNIT	PL.OF DEATH	D.O.D.	AGE	ORIGIN
QX.23052	Pte.	Carpenter, A.S.	2/26 Inf	Kranji	18.11.44.	27	Ramco, S.A.
NX.43460	Pte.	Garling, G.R.	12Fd.Coy	Kranji	08.10.44.	24	Mudgee, NSW
NX.24824	Gnr.	Peacock, A.	2/15 RAA	Kranji	03.08.44.	43	
VX.24442	Sgmn.	Rooney, K.	8DivSigs	Kranji	09.09.44.	40	Sandringham, Vic
WX. 7014	L/Cpl.	Sales, W.J.	6FdPkRAE	Kranji	12.11.44.	38	Perth, WA

NOTE

These records have been taken from the original Casuality List compiled at Changi by 2 Echelon up to December 1944. The place of origin and age are taken from the War Graves Registers which give the locality of the Next of Kin. The Unit shown is taken from the original 'F' Force Roll and may not necessarily be a man's regular Unit.
There are many versions of the spelling of place names in Burma -Thailand. I have adopted the most commonly used versions taken from the original Casualty List.

Decorations only up to 1941 shown.

NOTE 1

		Q.9366	HQ AIF
Inf Bde	ADMS		17 Apr. 43.
L of C Bde	ADMS (for AGH)		
Medical Bde	Com F Force		
Camp HQ	File		

'F' FORCE - Train No.l.

IJA advise all times advanced 30 mins. Parade will now be handed over *NOT* later than 0230 hrs.

Ref. Q.3931 para 4: Owing to alterations and reallotment of personnel all future injections (i.e. 18-22 Apr incl) are cancelled. Vaccine will be sent with individual train groups and injection completed at destination.

(sgd) THOMPSON
Lt.Col.
AA & QMG AIF

NOTE 2

The medical situation in this camp is extremely grave and is becoming worse every hour. At the present moment cholera is raging – there have been 37 deaths and there are over 90 patients in hospital – new cases are occurring at the rate of 25 or more daily.

Dysentery is still a very serious problem and many men are so debilitated from prolonged dysentery or diarrhoea that they will be many weeks before they are fit for any form of work – meanwhile their resistance to cholera or any other disease is seriously impaired.

Malaria is rapidly increasing and we anticipate that within a week or two there will be hundreds of sufferers.

Taking the situation as a whole it is our anticipation that within one month there will NOT be 250 in this camp fit to do a day's work.

The reasons for this situation are that the men in this camp have been subjected to treatment which it is wrong for any civilised nation to inflict on its Prisoners of War.

In detail:

i. The men before leaving Changi were weakened by dysentery and deficiency diseases (Beri Beri and Pellagra) and were in no condition to withstand infectious diseases.

ii. An assurance was given by the IJA at Changi to the Commander AIF that food would be better here than in Changi and that troops would NOT have to march from the railway to their destination. Neither of these promises have been kept. Relying on the second promise, many men totally unfit to march were included in the Force – very many of these men are now in hospital – some have died.

iii. The hygiene of the camps on the road was appalling and hundreds of men were successively infected by dysentery, by malaria and finally by cholera – the present tragedy is the result.

iv. The conditions of marching were extremely arduous and in some cases unwarrantably cruel. Still men were driven out on to the road night after night, in some cases with high fever or active dysentery. As a result when men arrived here they were completely exhausted.

v. After arrival men were put in an unhygienic, badly situated camp, roofless and with very bad latrine accommodation; all conditions ideal for the spread of disease were present and disease has, in consequence, rapidly spread – your own report that 63 (53?) positive results for cholera were found in about 600 apparently healthy men shows how rapidly and wildly the spread took place.

vi. No adequate rest was given to the men nor was any assistance given to requests for help. On the contrary men were sent out to work and kept out of camp 12 and 13 hours a day in pouring rain – conditions typical NOT to the honourable treatment of Prisoners of War but of slave labour.

At the present moment there are approximately:

37 men dead of cholera. 95 men in hospital with cholera.

250 men in hospital with other diseases.

140 men excused all duty on account of sickness – many of them would be in hospital if there were enough room or drugs or nurses.

150 men are so weakened by illness that they are only fit for light duty.

120 men being used (or have been used) in the case of the sick – of these 30 have already become so sick as to have been admitted to hospital. Thus about 800 men out of 2,000 have become invalids or have been required to nurse the sick within 14 days of the arrival of the troops in this camp – and the number is likely to increase rapidly.

In view of the above facts we demand:

1) That this document be forwarded to the representative of the International Red Cross in Bangkok or Rangoon;

2) That all work shall cease NOT for 3 days, but indefinitely until the present cholera epidemic has been got fully under control. In this circumstance we draw your attention to the promise given on 27th May 1943 that all work would cease for 3 days. This promise was broken the day after it was given.

The reasons for asking for all work to cease are:

i. To enable hundreds of debilitated men to rest and recover their health.

ii. To enable all necessary constructive work around the camp on latrines, roofing and drainage to be done.

iii. To permit of enough men being allotted to nursing work to give adequate treatment to the hundreds of sick and the (rest of the..?) overworked and exhausted nursing staff.

(3) The supply of adequate drugs, disinfectants, soap, lights and other medical supplies.

(4) The supply of blankets for the sick.

(5) The supply of invalids foods, soups and tea and sugar for the sick.

(6) The improvement of the camp diet by extra vitamin-containing food, for example: Rice polishings, towgay, meat, oil and fats.

(7) The supply of water containers, especially 44 gallon drums to enable water to be used on a large scale; also smaller containers for water boiling to make sterilization possible.

(8) The supply of suppressive atabrin for the whole camp – the present small quinne dosage is quite inadequate and without effect.

(9) The supply of a large number of water-proof tents for the cholera area which is expanding daily. At least 30 large tents are required apart from what is now in the camp.

(10) The supply of oil for dealing with mosquito breeding places in the camp – a visit from Capt. Wilson, Malaria expert at Headquarters Camp is urgently necessary to locate these.

(11) The supply of protective clothing – white coats for nurses handling cholera.

(12) As soon as the health of the camp has been improved, which may NOT be for several months, the evacuation of the area by troops and their subsequent treatment in a manner more befitting the honourable Japanese nation whose reputation must suffer gravely if the present conditions continue.

We demand that this document be laid before Lt.Col. Banno and the senior Japanese medical officer for the area, and also before Lt.Col. Harris at the earliest possible moment, preferably tonight.

(Signed) N.McG. Johnston, Major.
Commander AIF Troops Shimo Sonkurai Camp.

Bruce, Hunt, Major.
Senior Medical Officer.

C. Tracey, Major.
Commander, No.1 Bn.

R.H. Anderson, Major.
Commander, No.2 Bn.

SHIMO SONGKURAI CAMP

30 MAY 43.

AWM.54.554/11/4 Appendix IV

Force Headquarters comprised:

Lt.Col. S Harris, O.B.E., in command

Lt.Col. Hutchinson – G.S.O.I.

Lt.Col. Dillon – A.Q.

Lt.Col. Hingston – A.D.O.S.

Lt.Col. Wilkinson – C.R.E.

Lt.Col. Huston – A.D.0.6.

All of 18 Div Headquarters. The latter was appointed Senior Medical Officer and Major C. Wild was Senior Interpretor.

In the AIF component were included 27 Aust. Inf. Bde. Headquarters, the C.Os of the three Infantry Battalions:

2/26 Bn. Major C.D. Tracey

2/29 Bn. Lt.Col. S.A.F. Pond, O.B.E.

2/30 BN. Major McG. Johnston

and Major J.R. Parry, AASC, who was appointed to command a composite battalion comprised of other than infantry personnel.

EXTRACT – AWM Material

F FORCE

MEDICAL PERSONNEL

British	Australian
Lt.Col. J. Huston, R.A.M.C., S.M.O.	Major R. Stevens, A.A.M.C. S.M.O. AIF
Major J.E. Phillips, R.A.M.C.	Major B.A. Hunt, Medical specialist
Major D.G. Gillies, R.A.M.C.	Major E.A. Rogers, A.A.M.C.
Major D.A. Hanbury, R.A.M.C.	Capt. C. Juttner, A.A.M.C.
Major P.E. Routley, R.A.M.C.	Capt. L. Cahill, A.A.M.C.
Capt. A. Barber, MC R.A.M.C.	Capt. F.J. Cahill, A.A.M.C.
	Surgical Specialist
Capt. E. Sillman, R.A.M.C.	Capt. J.L. Taylor, MC A.A.M.C.
Capt. J.F. Partridge, MC R.A.M.C.	Capt. R. Mills, A.A.M.C.
Capt. J. Wilson, R.A.M.C.	Capt. P.I.A. Hendry, A.A.M.C.
Capt. N.J. Emery	Capt. V. Brand, MC. A.A.M.C.
Lieut. L.H. Turner, FMSVF	

A/S. P. Wolfe, I.M.D. A/S D.A. Planers, I.M.D. A/S. K.Gama, I.M.D.
A/S J. James, I.M.D.

Major J. Reid, R.A.M.C. Entomologist

Capt. R.H. Dix, A.D. Corps	Capt. ... Mannies A.A. Dental Corps.
Lieut. P. Sindon R.A.M.C. (Q.M.)	Lieut. G. Veitch: QM
44 B.O.Rs. (REM. E.G. Childs)	225 A.O.Rs (E.O.l E. McGlynn)

Source Material – Reports on F Force –
AWM.554/6, 554/7/1/3/5/6/7, 54/11/7/4, 554/11/4.

UNITS AS ON 17TH MAY 1943 (At Camp Lower Sonkurai)

UNIT	NO.1 BN.	NO.2 BN.	TOTAL
2/26 Bn.	491	31	522
2/29	151	26	177
2/30		503	503
2/18	30	7	37
2/19	23	8	31
2/20	24	3	27
2/4 MG	22	8	30
RAP	120	-	120
2/10 Fd.Reg.	-	6	6
2/15	-	8	8
4 A/T.	-	2	2
R.A.F.	22	-	22
HQ. RAA	-	1	1
2/6 Fd.Pk.	-	4	4
2/10 Fd.Coy.	-	3	3
AASC	1	97	98
Amn.Sub.Pk.	-	9	9
AAOC	1	37	38
Prov.Corps.	13	5	18
Postal	5	1	6
AAMC	28	-	28
2/9 Fd.Amb.	-	8	8
13 AGH	-	10	10
10 AGH	-	9	9
3 Adv.Med.Sts.	-	1	1
2/5 Fd.Hyg.	-	1	1
2/4 MT	-	2	2
2/3 MAC	-	4	4
Div.Sigs.	12	5	17
GBD	-	1	1
Admin.HQ	-	4	4
HQ.AIF	44	12	56
27 Bde.HQ	7	2	9
Fd.Battery	2	1	3
RAAF	-	1	1
MIR	-	17	17
Totals:	998	857	1855

MEN ESCAPING

May 31, 1943. 0730 hrs.

S/Sgt. A.G. McGregor (HQ); Ptes. J.A. Franklin, C.M. Wilson, M.J. Maudsley, M.L. Landow, R.T. Thomas.

June 3rd

Pte. J.B. Golding.

EXTRACT – AWM Material -
F FORCE

TANBAYA HOSPITAL – STAFF

Administrative Commander – Lt.Col. C.T. Hutchison, MC, RA.

O.C. Hospital – Major B.A. Hunt, AAMC

Administrative Officers

Adjutant – Capt. F.E. Stahl, A.I.F.

Quartermaster – Major G.D. McK. Sutherland, R.E.

Messing Officer – Capt. S.S. Roberts, A.I.F.

R.S.M. – R.S.M. Neild att'd SSVF

Medical Officers

Major W.J.E. Phillips, R.A.M.C.
Major P.B. Hanbury, R.A.M.C.
Capt. F.J. Cahill, A.A.M.C.
Capt. E.J. Emery, R.A.M.C.
Capt. G.H. Lowe, F.M.S.V.F.
Capt. J.F. Pantridge, R.A.M.C.
Capt. H. Silman, R.A.M.C.
Lieut. L.H. Turner, S.S.V.F.
Assistant-Surgeon (WOI) P. Wolfe, I.M.D.

Hospital R.S.M. – R.S.M. Childs, R.A.M.C.